Keep Punchin'
&
Keep the Faith!

Bill Roemer

MOB POWER PLAYS

The Mob Attempts Control Of Congress, Casinos and Baseball

A Novel
by
WILLIAM F. ROEMER, JR.

S.p.i.
BOOKS

A division of Shapolsky Publishers, Inc.

MOB
POWER
PLAYS

S.P.I. BOOKS

A division of Shapolsky Publishers, Inc.

For any additional information, contact:
Shapolsky Publishers, Inc.
136 West 22nd Street
New York, N.Y. 10011
(212) 633-2022
FAX (212) 633-2123

10 9 8 7 6 5 4 3 2 1

ISBN 1-56171-168-3

Many of the characters herein are alive and active in La Cosa Nostra today. Some
of the events herein are factual. Some of the characters and many of the events
have been invented and are fictitious. All, however, are based on the informed
knowledge of the author, a 30 year FBI agent.

To Jeannie:
The standard upon which all wives
and mothers would be judged

AUTHOR'S NOTE

"A man is known by his enemies — and how they consider him."
— Anonymous

On January 9, 1992, the federal government introduced their exhibit 446T as part of the evidence in the real life RICO trial of Rocky Infelice and four of his key lieutenants in the Chicago Family of La Cosa Nostra.

Exhibit 446T was a secret tape recording of a conversation between Infelice and one of his key mob members, "B.J." Jahoda. Unknown to Infelice, Jahoda was carrying a wire, a body mike, and was surreptitiously cooperating with the government in their investigation of the Chicago mob.

As recorded on the tape, Infelice had just read one of my books.

"He's pretty accurate in most of his stuff. He didn't lie. You remember, he was a "G" guy here for more than twenty years. A capable man."

Infelice is one of the characters in this book. I hope he will find "Bill Richards" to be "a capable man."

Also in January of 1992, John "No Nose" DiFronzo was arrested by FBI agents at his home in Long Grove, a Chicago suburb. When agents searched his house in connection with DiFronzo's arrest, they found one book: *Roemer: Man Against The Mob*. I was pleased that the mob boss started his library with my book, but my satisfaction soon ebbed.

The agents joked that, since they had found it on the nightstand beside his bed, it had probably served as his sleeping pill.

ACKNOWLEDGMENTS

I wish to acknowledge my partners in the FBI who are characters herein: John Bassett, George Benigni, Burt Jensen, Pete Wacks, Gino Lazzari, Jim Mansfield, Warren Donovan, Bill Kane, Ray Shryock, Jim Mulroy, Andy Sloan, John Danahy, Tom Tolan, and Frank Gerrity. I will sorely miss Mansfield and Shryock, who died while this book was in preparation. Also, Bob Long, Lee Flosi, and Bob Walsh of the Chicago FBI and "Buck" Revell, former Executive Assistant Director of the FBI, now the Special Agent in Charge in Dallas. Also Joe Yablonsky, former SAC in Las Vegas, and Chuck Thomas, former Las Vegas Bureau agent.

Another character who died while I was working on the novel is Bill Duffy, former deputy superintendent of the Chicago Police Department. My prayers are with him.

My deepest appreciation also to Jack Brickhouse, Kup, Steve Neal, John Drummond, Chuck Goudie, John O'Brien, Matt O'Connor and Rosalind Rossi, all top media people in Chicago.

Thanks to Esther and Mark Schulman, the proprietors at Eli's, and Bill Downey and Ben Stein, the general manager and owner of Harry Carey's. Also Cathy Hamm, concierge at the Sheraton Plaza, Mike Levy, general manager at the Midland and Tony Tontini, the owner/maitre d' at the Dining Room of the Ritz Carlton in Chicago.

I must thank mob characters Tony Accardo, Gus Alex, Joe Ferriola, Pat Marcy, Toots Palermo, Al Tocco, Vince Solano, Butch Blasi and Donald Angelini. I spent thousands of hours conducting investigations of them as an FBI agent.

Thanks to Fred Foreman and Jeff Johnson of the United States Attorneys Office in Chicago for allowing themselves to be characters in this work.

Miles Cooperman, of the Cook County Sheriff's Office, is always there for me. So is Bill Hartnett, of Here's Chicago, an old FBI pal at Quantico and in New York.

Jerry Gladden, Bob Fuesel, Jeanette Callaway and John Conlon, my associates in the Chicago Crime Commission, can't

be forgotten. Likewise, Greg Kowalick of the Division of Gaming
Enforcement of the New Jersey Casino Control Commission, Tom
Carrigan, formerly the Chief of Intelligence and Investigation for
the Nevada Gaming Control Board, and Ron Asher, current Chief
of Enforcement for the GCB.

Another character herein I thank is Herb "Speedy" Newman,
the Las Vegas "sports investor."

I also thank Lou Spalla of the Arizona Department of Public
Safety's Intelligence Unit for his insights into Laughlin, Nevada.

Also to Kristina Rebelo, the free lance writer from San Diego,
who keeps me abreast of so many things.

I extend my appreciation to Jerry Gotsch, former McClellan
Committee investigator and Labor Department official, who
has been so helpful through the years. Also to Jim Bredican of
the Cook County Sheriff's Office and Roy Suzuki of the Chicago
Courtwatchers.

No acknowledgment would be complete without thanks to my
sons, Bill III and Bob. Bill for his special help in depicting events
in Laughlin, Nevada and Bob for the reminisces of his baseball
career. And to Bob's wife, Earlene, and their star student-athlete
sons: Chris, Matt and Tim.

Obviously, I extend my sincere gratitude to my publisher, Ian
Shapolsky and his staff.

Thank you one and all.

INTRODUCTION

This is a novel.

As stated on the copyright page, many of the characters herein are alive and active in La Cosa Nostra today. Many of the events are factual.

However, I want to make it clear that the protagonists and many of the events are fictitious.

I want to make this clear because of my experience with a previous book I wrote, *War of the Godfathers*. On the copyright page and in the introduction I attempted to make it positively clear that it was a novel and that many of the characters and events were fictitious. However, almost immediately upon publication, the book reached the best seller list. *On the non-fiction list.* I presume the reason was that my first book, *Roemer: Man Against The Mob*, my autobiography, had been a non-fiction best seller. Reviewers apparently assumed *War* was a follow up to *Man*. It was not—and neither is this, although many of the characters are the same.

Bill Richards, for instance, continues in this effort. He is the fictitious senior agent on the Organized Crime Squad of the Chicago Office of the FBI, just as I was for decades, and many of his experiences parallel mine. Tony Accardo actually was the consiglieri of the Chicago mob, the former bodyguard of Al Capone and a killer in the St. Valentine's Day Massacre. Gus Alex actually is the head of the "connection guys," the unit of the Chicago Outfit responsible for corruption of public officials. Joe Ferriola was actually the boss of the Chicago mob. Pat Marcy is a functionary of the Regular Democratic Organization of the First Ward in Chicago. John Gotti is the boss of the Gambino family in New York. Jack Brickhouse and Harry Carey have long been Chicago Cub broadcasters. Almost all of the FBI agents who play roles herein have been or are FBI agents. Yet some of the prime characters are fictitious. As are the primary episodes.

I have attempted to use all my experiences as an FBI agent for thirty years, as a consultant for ten years to the Chicago Crime Commission and as an investigative attorney representing news organizations being sued for libel for eight years, as a foundation for this writing.

I have personally confronted almost all of the actual characters in this book in the above capacity, especially as an FBI agent. It has been said by the former governor of Illinois, Dick Ogilvie, also a former federal prosecutor, that I have confronted more mobsters than any lawman in history, including Eliot Ness. I assume that is true. In 1988, Pulitzer Prize winning reporter Denny Walsh from *Life*, called me "the most decorated FBI agent in the history of that organization" after his canvass of FBI agents and former agents. That could be true. Jackie Cerone, when he was the boss of the Chicago mob, swore under oath that I was "the nemesis" of the Chicago mob, "the famous former FBI agent who dogged the footsteps of (mob members) for years, in a tireless effort." I *know* this is true, at least the part about my trying.

I point out the above, not to boast, but to allow the reader to evaluate whether what I write is credible. If the story didn't actually happen—as much of it didn't—it sure could have. Nothing that happens herein is outside the realm of palpability. Much of what happens here happened before—or at least something like it did. Much of it happened on my watch. Much of it happened to me.

This is the story of two families, the mob family and the FBI family who reside in the Chicago suburb of South Holland. That's where I lived and where I coached several teams I write about herein. All of the locales I write about here are places I know well.

I worked in the FBI in Chicago for 24 years and in New York City for two years. I worked in Las Vegas and Lake Tahoe on many occasions. I have visited Lake Titisee in the Black Forest in 1985 and 1988. I was taken to the police station in Donaueschingen after a traffic accident. I worked in San Francisco and Palm Springs a dozen times each. In Miami a couple times. In Philadelphia and Atlantic City a couple times. I worked for the FBI in Tucson for two years. Laughlin, Nevada is the only place where I create a scene herein of which I am not personally familiar. There I rely on my son Bill III, who has visited Laughlin four or five times a year for the past five or six years.

I have watched hundreds of Cubs games in the past 50 years. Many of them I observed from the vantage point of the press box, thanks to my good friend, Jack Brickhouse. I especially thank him for his insights at lunch with him at the Pink Poodle at Wrigley Field, the private press club; in the press box and on many nights on the town, especially at Jim Saine's, the old Rush Street sports hangout, and now at Eli's.

In any event, I have attempted with this story to tell it like it is— like the mob and the FBI really are. I know I have succeeded in that. My humble hope is that I have done it so as to make it enjoyable. Thank you for your consideration of this work.

Again, as I have in the introduction to all my books, I want to congratulate my former colleagues in the FBI on the fine job they are doing in the fight against organized crime. I said in recent introductions that we are seeing the light at the end of the tunnel in this war. I continue to see this progress. Recently I addressed some 200 current law enforcement officers in Chicago. I said then, in the parlance of the fight game, of which I was once a part, that we are currently in the 11th round of a 15 round championship prize fight. We are winning the late rounds. However, we have 4 more rounds to go and in order to win the battle we must continue it, fighting with both hands as aggressively as we can. We can't ease off now as our opponents, tough guys all, have ample time to stage a comeback.

I especially congratulate my former associates in Chicago and in New York. In Chicago, the upper echelon of the current leadership of the mob is on trial in two separate prosecutions. One, "Operation Gambat," as it is officially known in the FBI and "Kaffe Klatch," as the press dubbed it, includes Pat Marcy as a defendent. I testified before the U.S. Senate Permanent Subcommittee on Investigations years ago that Marcy is the mob's man in politics in Chicago. In New York many top leaders, including John Gotti, are either under prosecution or in prison.

My motto in life has been "Keep Punchin' and Keep the Faith!" I urge it on all those involved in the fight. This book, again, is testimony to all those who fight the good fight against the mobs everywhere.

MOB

POWER

PLAYS

CHAPTER ONE

Rocco Robust on the Carpet

Tony "Joe Batters" Accardo was upset. Some disturbing news had come his way.

In his role as *consiglieri*, Accardo had recently elevated one of his proteges into the top spot in the Chicago family of La Cosa Nostra. Now, something very unsettling to Accardo had come to his attention. There were indications that his ward may have a skeleton in the closet—that he might have done something he might not want the mob to be aware of.

Since it was Accardo's job to advise and counsel on the major decisions made by the top leadership of the Chicago mob, he called for one of his famous "sit-downs" at Meo's Norwood House, a restaurant in the western Chicago suburbs. Every day, between noon and three, the Meo family reserved the only table in a alcove for Accardo and his guests, whether Joe appeared or not. Nobody else could enter, unless they were invited. The alcove was a perfect spot, specifically constructed for the purpose of Accardo's clandestine meetings with his associates, unobserved by law enforcement or the press. He could see out, but no one could see in.

"Joe Batters" had been "made" into the Al Capone mob in the mid-1920s. Having demonstrated his ability as a killer for the Circus Cafe Gang, a young band of burglars and thieves on the west side of Chicago, he was given an early assignment as one of Capone's bodyguards. In 1929, he "made his bones" by being one of the triggermen assigned by Big Al to wipe out the Bugs Moran Gang in the infamous St. Valentines Day Massacre. Capone himself gave Accardo the nickname which his associates would use in talking to or about him.

1

"This kid is a real Joe Batters," Capone had informed his subordinates after Accardo had battered two of Capone's foes to death with a baseball bat.

When Capone was imprisoned in 1931 and was succeeded by Frank "The Enforcer" Nitti, Batters had become a "capo." After Nitti killed himself in 1943, Accardo became the "underboss" under Paul "The Waiter" Ricca. When Ricca went to prison for extorting money from Hollywood studios, he selected Batters to be the absolute boss of the Chicago mob. Accardo had held this spot until 1957, when he voluntarily stepped aside and inserted the flamboyant Sam Giancana into his spot. However, the mob insisted that he become *consiglieri*.

Batters had "been there" from Capone into the nineties. He had seen – and made – history.

Accardo was picked up in his Caddy from his home in Barrington Hills by bodyguard-driver, Sam "Wings" Carlisi and protector, John "No Nose" DiFronzo. When they arrived at Meo's, DiFronzo preceded Accardo into the restaurant and checked it out. When he returned to signal that it was "clean," Accardo emerged from the back seat and, with DiFronzo in front and Carlisi behind, entered the restaurant.

Joe's protege had already arrived. Nobody kept Batters waiting! In Chicago, a summons from the mob dinosaur was like a summons from God. Actually, it commanded more respect. Mob members went to church just three times: when they were hatched, hitched and scratched.

Carlisi and DiFronzo took their assigned positions in the main dining room, outside the alcove. The only one who would be privy to this "sit-down" was Rocco "Robust" Robustelli.

Joe Batters didn't waste time on formalities. He didn't even wait for his regular order of minestrone to arrive. He got right down to business.

"Rocco, I hear some things I don't understand. I want you to explain them to me."

"I don't know what you mean, Joe," the startled Robust replied.

"What I hear disturbs me, Rocco. There is one guy who has

been out front for the "G" ever since they started on us guys. I know you know who that is. Now I'm being told he has gone to bat for your kid. Explain all this to me. Why would Richards go out on a limb to do a favor for a member of your family? Does he owe you somethin'?"

Tony Accardo was referring to Bill Richards. There was not a hoodlum in—or outside of—Chicago who was not familiar with the grizzled old FBI agent whom J. Edgar Hoover had assigned to the organized crime squads in Chicago some 33 years after he had formed the FBI. In 1957, Hoover had finally decided that "the Mafia is not a myth" and brought the FBI into the fight against organized crime for the first time. There was no mobster worth his salt in Chicago who Richards had not arrested, surveilled, interviewed or monitored.

Robust's swarthy face turned red. "For Christ's sake, Joe. You gotta understand. If you think I ever snitched to Richards you're mistaken. He and I go way back, you know that, I've told you all that before."

Joe Batters said nothing for a moment. His steely eyes glared into Rocco's and he could see the sweat on Robust's forehead.

"I know you two guys go way back, Rocco. Up until now you've handled it right. But what has been brought to my attention now, I got some questions about. Take your time. Tell me."

It was not an invitation. It was an order.

Robust knew he had to convince "The Man" that there had been no betrayal: that what Richards had done was not a quid pro quo for something Robust had done for him. Or for anyone else in "the G." If he could not convince Joe Batters that afternoon, it would be the end of his reign as an upper echelon leader of the Chicago La Cosa Nostra.

It would mean the end of something even more important to him. His ability to live one more day.

PART ONE

CHAPTER TWO

The Two Families

South Holland is a suburb of Chicago about 20 miles south of the Loop, founded by the Dutch Reformed community, most of whom had migrated from Holland, Michigan.

However, years later, the village was invaded by an influx of Catholics, many of them influenced to buy there by Notre Dame graduate Howard Quinn, the president of Pacesetter Homes.

The Richards family moved into one of Quinn's Pacesetter Homes, on Rose Drive in the old section of South Holland, centered around Van Oostenbrugge Park.

Bill Richards was a young FBI agent, assigned to the Chicago Office. Richards would journey an hour each way to and from the FBI headquarters, driving the entire three miles or so from his home to the Illinois Central Railroad station on Sibley Boulevard, also called 147th Street, in Harvey. He would then catch an express to the Loop emerging at Randolph Street. From there he would walk the ten or twelve blocks to his office.

Once the area around Van O Park was sold, Howard Quinn began building south of 162nd Street. Here, however, he built a much more expensive home in an area which had been almost completely undeveloped, with few, if any, old Hollanders. Whereas Richards had purchased his home for $16,500 with a $900 down payment and a 4.5% mortgage plus interest and taxes payments of $102.46 per month, the Robustelli family purchased their house in the new section of the village for $100,000. The home in the old section consisted of 1100 square feet with no garage whereas the house in the new section was 3500 square feet.

Unlike Richards, Robustelli had a very small commute to his

work. He was a "soldier," the lowest rung on the Chicago ladder of La Cosa Nostra. His territory was headquartered in Chicago Heights where he worked under the aegis of "capo" Frankie LaPorte, who was in charge of the southern suburbs of Chicago from Riverdale on the north to Kankakee on the south and from Calumet City on the east to Joliet on the west. Robustelli's usual commute was about one mile. From his home to Calumet City.

Calumet City at the time was the prime vice den in the mob territory bossed by Tony "Joe Batters" Accardo. Batters' top gun in "the Heights" was LaPorte, who, in turn bossed Dominic "Toots" Palermo, the "street boss" of Cal City. Under Palermo, who also lived south of 162nd Street in South Holland, was his "button man," Robust.

The Richards family consisted of Bill, his wife, Jeannie, and their two sons, Bill III and Bob. Bill III and Bob would both attend St. Jude the Apostle school just east of Cottage Grove on 154th Street in Dolton.

The Robustelli family consisted of Rocco, his daughter, Linda, and son, Richard. Linda and Richard would attend Holy Ghost parochial school located on 170th Street. Rocco's wife, Gina, had died of the complications of pneumonia just several month prior to their move to the Village of Tulips.

In 1957, J. Edgar Hoover initiated what he called The Top Hoodlum Program, to which each FBI Office in the country would assign at least one agent. In New York, twenty-five agents would be assigned. In Chicago, ten. One of the ten was Bill Richards, who had been working on "security matters" for the first seven years of his tenure in the FBI. Now he would be a charter member of the Top Hood Program, assigned to Criminal Squad Number One, C-1, in the Chicago FBI office.

The supervisor of C-1, Ross Spencer, twenty-five year veteran of the Bureau, called the young agent into his office.

"Richards," he said, "we see you live out in the south suburbs. Most of our agents live west and northwest. To facilitate matters, we're going to assign you to work the mob out south. We're assigning you two hoods to investigate as your special targets. One will be Gus Alex, the boss of the Loop for the mob, and the other will be Frank LaPorte, boss in Chicago Heights and the rest of the southern suburbs. It will be your job to learn all you can about these two guys and to identify their subordinates. Learn who they associate with, what they do, how they do it, where they hang out and, hopefully, you determine what federal law they are violating, if any, and produce proof which will send them to federal prison. For all the years the FBI has been in existence, since 1924, Mr. Hoover has maintained these guys are violating only local laws. Now he has mandated that we determine which federal laws they are breaking and develop the evidence to send them up for such violations. Go get 'em."

With these general instructions, Bill Richards was cut loose, given his head. Since Gussie Alex seemed to be the more important of the two targets he had been assigned, he started on him. He soon found that not only was Gussie, or "Slim" as he was code-named by his associates, the boss of the Loop, he was also a key member of what the mob called "the connection guys." The FBI would call Gussie's function "the corruption squad." Richards found that Alex was working directly under Murray "The Camel" Humphreys, the elder statesman of the mob and another guy who would soon be assigned to Richards, to develop and maintain a large stable of public officials, politicians, judges, law enforcement officials, labor leaders, legitimate businessmen and almost anybody in position to extend favorable treatment to the mob. Only after several months of working almost full time on Gussie did Richards turn his investigative attention to Frankie LaPorte.

Richards found that LaPorte lived in Flossmoor, an affluent suburb located some seven or eight miles south of South Holland, and that he headquartered in Chicago Heights. It wasn't long before Richards identified Palermo as LaPorte's street boss in Calumet City.

At first, during those early years of the Top Hoodlum Program, Richards had little time to worry about small fry like Rocky Robust. His usual routine during the day was to work in the Loop on Alex—

and then spend his evenings working in the southern suburbs on LaPorte and his crew.

The name Robustelli meant almost nothing to Richards in the fledgling years of the Top Hoodlum Program. When the name did come to his attention, it wasn't because of the father—it was because of the son.

Richards was invited to manage a baseball team in the minor leagues of the South Holland Little League. His son Bob, was on the team and Richards noticed the name Richard Robustelli among the other players. Although Richards may have heard of the father at that time, he hadn't made the connection. It wouldn't have made any difference if it had.

It wasn't long, however, before Richards become aware of the heritage of his young player. Rocky Robust showed up to root for his son at the first game. Richards began to put two and two together.

Isn't there a Robustelli in the outfit? Working out here under Toots Palmero, he thought to himself.

The next day he checked his file on Palermo. There was the name. Richards checked it out. He found an old photo, a mug shot, of Robustelli when he had been arrested and convicted for auto theft in the Maxwell police district on the near southwest side of Chicago, in what is called "The Patch."

Rocco had been eighteen at the time. He was now much older, but the photo showed that Rocco and Richard's father had the same features.

It made no difference to Richards. He would not visit the sins of the father on the son. If Richard Robustelli could play ball, he would get the same opportunity from Bill Richards as the other members of the team. In fact, since Richards considered such parentage a handicap, his visceral feeling was to extend to Richard every possible advantage he could. He encouraged his son, Bob, to be very friendly with young Robustelli. It soon become obvious that young Bob, a pudgy youngster without great foot-speed but with a fine arm, would best be suited to catch. When it become apparent that Ricky, as his teammates began to call him, also had a fine young arm, Bill Richards began to develop him as a pitcher. Soon the top battery for the minor league Wausau Lumber team was Robustelli and Richards. The friendship between the two blossomed.

Mid-season, Bill Richards devised a plan. Perhaps he could use the coincidence that he was managing the son of Rocco Robust to get close to the father. At this stage of the Top Hood Program, the FBI had no hard-core, "made" members of the Chicago Outfit who were informants for them and against their fellow mobsters. Robust was a low level mobster, but he was a "made guy." If he could be "turned," it would be a real coup.

Richards put his plan into effect. At the next game, Richards made it a point to approach Rocco.

"Ricky is really developing into a fine pitcher, Mr. Robustelli," Richards said, with a big, friendly smile on his face. "And he's a great kid, a real joy to have on the team. All his teammates get along with him really well, especially my son, Bob. You and your wife have done a fine job in raising him."

Robust was on guard. It had become well known among team members and their parents that Richards was an FBI agent.

"He ain't got no mother," Rocco grunted.

Richards hadn't known that. He was surprised.

"She died a couple years ago," Robust stated, softly.

"I'm sorry to hear that," Richards responded.

That was the end of the first conversation between the two who would eventually become adversaries.

CHAPTER THREE

The Two Assignments

It wasn't long before Bill Richards was brought to the attention of Rocky Robust. Emphatically.

Frankie LaPorte called a sit-down of his crew, the Chicago Heights faction of the mob. Included were top men and soldiers—the entire bunch. Al Pilotto, Al "Caesar" Tocco, "Dago Tony" Berrotoni, Richie Guzzino, Chris Messino, Billy Dauber, Clarence Crockett, Frank D'Andrea, Tony Pelligrino, Jerry Scalise, Toots Palermo, Jerry Scarpelli, Al Trojani, and Rocco Robustelli. All were "made" guys, except for Crockett and Dauber, who, not being Italian, couldn't be "made," but were important "money makers." The sit-down took place in LaPorte's vending machine company offices in the Heights.

"Fellas," LaPorte announced, "we got a real problem on our hands. I just got back from a meet with Giancana and the other capos in Chicago. The FBI has really focused onto us. They got a crew of guys, ten of them, who got nothin' to do now but spy on us. Murray Humphreys just got back from Washington where he met with the congressmen who are on our pad. They told him they call this the Top Hoodlum Program and they have 'targets' all over the country. The top guys in 'our thing.' And I'm fuckin' one of them! They got ten guys in Chicago, ten FBI guys, workin' on this program. One of them is assigned to me. And in workin' on me, he'll be workin' on all of youse. Hump says this guy's name is Bill Richards. He's a young FBI guy, Hump says. He was able to get a lot of good info from the congressman we got on the Judiciary Committee, Libby—Roland Libonati. That committee got a full report on just what the Justice Department and the FBI are up to.

It's a good example of what we can get when we spend the time and money to make these politicians. Libby was able to get all the info from his spot on that Judiciary Committee of Congress. So we get a leg up on what the G is doing. Now Hump tells all of us, all us capos, who the FBI guy is who is assigned to each of us. So we can do some checkin' of our own, see what makes the guy tick, where he lives, how we might be able to put him on the pad. Al Tocco, I'm gonna assign you to that job.".

With this, Rocco Robust stirred. "Frankie, I know this guy."

"*You* know this guy? How the fuck do *you* know this guy?" Frankie LaPorte was obviously perplexed. He knew nothing about Richards, how does this piss-ant soldier know the FBI agent assigned to investigate him and his crew?

"Hold on," Robust responded. He obviously didn't like the way this was starting out. "This kid, Richards, he lives where I do. In South Holland. It just so happens he is a Little League coach there. And my kid is his star pitcher."

Nobody said a word. They all held their breath until LaPorte could let this information sink in. Was this good or bad? The crew seemed to lean away from Rocky Robust.

After a few moments, LaPorte began to think out loud. "This G guy, he's your kid's Little League coach?"

Robust just nodded.

LaPorte carried his thoughts further. "You ever talk to this guy?" he asked.

"Yeah, once. He likes my kid. Told me I done a good job raising him."

"He does, huh," LaPorte came back. The rest of the crew leaned even further from Robust. Silence prevailed.

"You know where in South Holland this guy lives?" LaPorte queried.

"No, but I can find out easy. My kid has been to his house a couple times for team meetings. I know it's over on the other side of town, in the old section, not where Toots and I live."

"I'll tell you what," LaPorte said. "This could be a good break for us. I'm gonna have you work with Al Tocco on this. You two guys put together on this Richards. Find out all you can about him. But let me warn ya. Don't get too fuckin' close to this guy. Hump tells us that one of the things the G wants to do is turn some of us to their side. Make fuckin' stool pigeons out of us, get us to snitch. Remember your oath of omerta. The oath you took when you was made. No snitchin'! Any guy suspected of stoolin' will be clipped. Giancana made that very fuckin' clear at our meet in Chicago. Fuck around even a little bit and you get whacked! Now I'm gonna assign Al and Robust to this guy, but watch yourselves."

When the sit-down ended, Al "Caesar" Tocco met with Rocky Robust. Tocco was an experienced guy. He had done some "heavy work" for the LaPorte crew and ranked #3 in the group, directly under LaPorte's top kick, Al Pilotto.

"I want you to find out everything you can about this Richards," Tocco told Robust. "Get his street address, find out about his family. You say he has a kid on this Little League team. Any other kids? His wife. Anything. It would be nice we could get a picture of this guy. Who does he pal around with out there? What neighbor is he close to? What does he look like, how does he dress? What's his routine? Maybe we can tap his phone. Get his phone number. Who does his wife buddy with? Where does she shop, River Oaks? What kind of car does he drive? Do his pals from the FBI come around? What do they look like? Where do his kids go to school? Now be fuckin' careful, don't let your kid know what you're doin', but pump him. Have him buddy up with Richards' kid. Find out what he can, but don't let him know why you're interested. Be careful."

Then Tocco had another thought. "Does Richards know what you do?"

Robust thought for a minute. "I don't think so. He's never cracked to me as if he knows. The only time I talked to him he was very friendly. If he knew I was "made," I don't think he'd be so friendly."

"You heard what Frankie said, tho. The G is lookin' to make snitches. He might have a line on you. You got to watch your fuckin' step with this. If Sam Giancana thinks you are too close on this, you know that fuckin' guy, he'd clip you in one fuckin' minute." Tocco left no doubt in Robust's mind about that.

At about the same time, Bill Richards was making a move of his own. He knew who Rocco Robustelli was. Not a very important figure in the affairs of the La Cosa Nostra, but a "made" guy—a soldier, a button man, what they call in New York a wise guy. A good fella. And from what Richards could see, a young sharp guy. Probably with a pretty good future in his line of work. He had come out of "The Patch," like Giancana, Alderisio, Battaglia, De Stefano and so many of the top guys in the Chicago mob. Most had moved into the western suburbs. Rocky, much younger, had moved south. But he had solid connections, seemed to have native intelligence and was obviously a guy Richards should keep his eye on.

There was no file on Robust in the Chicago FBI office—or anywhere else. So Richards wrote a memo requesting that one be opened and assigned to him. Spencer, his supervisor, agreed. The file number 92-1042 was opened entitled: "Rocco Robustelli, aka Robust. Anti-Racketeering." A-R for short. Actually, it was a nice deal for Richards. Occasionally, usually on days when he had a Little League game, he could head for home at about three in the afternoon and, at five, have a good reason to call Spencer and request that he be "signed out" without returning to the office. It was a privilege he could not abuse, but, on the other hand, a reason to spend much more time working on Robust than he ordinarily would.

And so it came to pass that Rocky Robust was assigned by his boss to investigate Bill Richards while at the same precise time Richards was assigned by his boss to investigate Rocco Robust.

CHAPTER FOUR

Robust Does a Job; Gets a Job.

The Chicago Heights sit-down brought Rocky Robust to the attention of his capo, Frankie LaPorte. LaPorte instructed Al Pilotto to keep his eye on the young soldier while he worked with Al Tocco on the "investigation" of Bill Richards.

Learning Richards' routine and habits was easy for Rocco. He lived at 15608 Rose Drive, his wife's name was Jeannie and he was 6'1" tall. His phone number was EDison 3-9185 and his two sons, Bill and Bob, attended St. Jude The Apostle School. Richards was a devout Catholic; his wife was a volunteer at St. Jude and a boy scout den mother.

Tocco and Robust set up a very loose surveillance of Richards. Using Toots Palermo and Jerry Scarpelli, a mob hit man, in another tail car, they found that Richards usually left his home in South Holland around 6:40 every morning, drove to the I.C. station in Harvey and took the train into the Loop where he walked to his office. They found that his return varied. On some days he arrived very early. Many times, he would not return home until ten or eleven at night and sometimes he didn't come home at all.

Al Pilotto credited his young soldier with the results of Richards' investigation. He found Robust was doing a good piece of work in Calumet City under Toots and decided it was time to move Rocco up. The mob lieutenant who had been in command of bookmaking and loan sharking had not been producing what he should and Pilotto influenced LaPorte to move Robust into that spot, putting him in charge of what was a pretty nice piece of the mob's territory in the area just south of the Chicago city limits.

LaPorte called Rocky into his headquarters in the vending company in Chicago Heights.

"Rock," he said, "you done a nice job on this G guy and Toots tells me you work well with him in Cal City. We're moving you up. We're giving you Joe Ippolitti's district. Everything south of the city line to and including Dolton. You'll work next to Toots. He keeps Cal City, Burnhan, Lansing and that area and Jimmy The Bomber will be on the west side of you. Blue Island, Calumet Park and that area. Midlothian. How does that suit you?"

Robust was excited. "Great. Thanks a lot, Frank. I'll do a good job for you."

"Yeah, I think you will. Now you sit down with Joe Ip and he will turn over all his spots to you. He's got about 20 offices in those towns and bookies in each. Set up a headquarters for yourself, a main office. Some restaurant or something. If Ip don't cooperate by cutting you into everything, let me know. He won't like it when I talk to him, but I'll make it plain that it's a done deal. Now, one more thing. You're gonna be makin' a lot more dough than you have in the past. We got to find a spot for you, in some legit business where we can launder enough for you to show IRS you can live like you do. Otherwise, they'll come in with a net worth and expenditures case against you. You got any spot where you think you can move into?"

Robust shook his head.

Al Pilotto, also present, had obviously given this some thought. "OK, here's what you do. I'll talk to my people here in Local 5 of the Laborer's Union. I'm the president. We'll move some people around a little and make you a B.A., Business Agent. You'll have to show up at the hall once and awhile, maybe go out and help one of the real B.A's. once and awhile to get yourself what they call a profile. So when the G comes around we can shove some people who can say they seen you doin' some work. We'll put you on the payroll for a couple thousand a week. Then you kick that back to me out what you're making in your district. You'll have plenty left over. Then on your income tax you show that $25,000 or so as your income. We'll give you W-2 forms and show you on our payroll.

Just don't go wild with a couple Caddys, trips to Europe, when you eat out pay cash so it don't show up on any credit cards, buy your wife a fur coat, pay cash. Don't send your kids to some big fancy school. Got a dish on the side, pay cash. And keep it quiet. You show $25,000, IRS got to show you made three times that to make a net worth case stick. Capish?"

Rocky nodded. He was quite happy. He was moving up. And a lot of it was due to the fortunate chance that his son was being coached by one of the FBI agents who was assigned to the Top Hoodlum Program investigating the Chicago Mob. Not that he wasn't sharp enough to take advantage of it.

The next two years were good ones for Rocky Robust. He worked hard and his district in the near south suburbs flourished. It wasn't long before it was much more productive than it had been under Joe Ip.

It also wasn't long before Al Pilotto took over as the capo in the southern suburbs. Frankie LaPorte, who had been ailing with heart problems, had been spending much of his time in northern California where he owned some gold mines. More and more Pilotto was running the show. When LaPorte died, Sam Giancana called Pilotto to a sit-down at his headquarters in the Armory Lounge. The sit-down was attended by the top men, including the other capos, in the Chicago family of the La Cosa Nostra.

Giancana got right to it. "Al, you've done good work out south. I've talked to J.B. and to the rest of the boys here today. We all agreed you are the guy to take over Frankie's spot out there. He always gave us good reports on you when he was alive and he also recommended you before he passed. So we're here today, all of us, to welcome you as a capo. Congratulations."

It wasn't much of a speech but it got right to the essence of the matter at hand.

Giancana went on. "Now, Al, we got to move up somebody to work under you, to take charge out there when you're away or not available for some reason. Who do you suggest?"

Pilotto didn't hesitate a second. "Caesar Tocco. He's a good man, done some heavy work, and he's in charge of our best territory, the Heights itself and Park Forest. He's done a good job."

Giancana looked around. Most of the top guys assembled at the Armory were familiar with Tocco. Ralph Pierce, who had the south side of Chicago, adjacent to the southern suburbs, spoke up. "I work with Tocco a lot. His wire room and mine lay off each other. He's a good man. I think Al has made a good choice."

It was settled.

Pilotto went back to the Heights and sat down with his brother, the chief of police in Chicago Heights. It didn't hurt that the new capo in the southern suburbs had a brother who was the top local law enforcement officer in its principal town.

"I'm the new boss out here, Tocco is my right hand." He need not say more to his brother.

Then Pilotto called Tocco in. "I feel I want to make some changes in our organization, put my own people in better spots. Some of Frankie's guys, like The Bomber, that Catuara, in Blue Island, are gettin' lazy. I want to shake some people up. Here's what I been thinking. This kid we got in Dolton-Riverdale. Robust. He's been doin' some good work. Let's give him a test. If he does good, let's move him into Blue Island to go with the rest of the district. Give him Blue Island, Calumet Park, Islip, Midlothian. I think he could make somethin' much better there. What do you think?"

Tocco liked Rocky Robust. He had worked closely with the youngster on the Bill Richards thing.

"Good idea. What do you have in mind for a test?"

"The Bomber ain't gonna give up this district easy. I'll call him in. Give him the word. I expect he'll fight it. Then we have Robust talk to him. Give him the idea if he don't move aside, he gets clipped. See how Rocky handles that. If he chickens, don't put muscle on The Bomber, then he ain't the right man for the job. Or for anything better than that what's he already got. But he moves Jimmy out, handles it, then he deserves this move up. In any event, it will shake Catuara up. If Robust moves him out, okey we got a tough young guy taking over that district for us. If The Bomber fights him and wins, then we see he is still tough enough to beef up that district for us. We win either way."

Tocco thought it was a great idea. Pit the young, up and coming Robust against the aging Jimmy "The Bomber" Catuara. If the old man proved he still could win such a fight, all well and good. If Robust showed he was the young bull who could displace the old bull, so much the better for the organization. First, Pilotto had to clear it with Giancana who, in turn, would have to clear it with the *consiglieri*, Joe Batters, since it might come to a hit on Catuara or Rocky Robust. Any such major developments like such had to be cleared by the capo involved with the boss and by the boss with the consiglieri. At least in Chicago where the *consiglieri* was Tony "Joe Batters" Accardo.

When Al Pilotto journeyed back to the Armory Lounge, he found it was to Giancana's liking. A little blood on the streets of Chicago from time to time fit the Giancana mentality. Giancana, though, had more trouble convincing Accardo. Accardo understood that gangland killings are counter productive for the mob. It aroused the public. People such as Virgil Peterson of the Chicago Crime Commission held press conferences. The media made each gangland slaying in the Chicago area front page news and the lead item on the TV nightly news. John "Bulldog" Drummond of Channel Two, Art Petacque of the *Sun-Times*, John O'Brien of the *Tribune*, Chuck Goudy of Channel Seven and the other top media folks in Chicago helped frame their fine reputations covering mob murders. And when they raised the issue to the forefront it caused law enforcement to learn some answers to the loud and constant questions.

Nevertheless, it was Joe Batters' policy to give his boss and his capos their heads. If Pilotto and Giancana wanted this, OK. It might not be wise, but on balance it would be bad policy to turn down the first request made by a new capo, especially when he wanted to reorganize what he considered a poor situation and move new blood into position.

Accardo sanctioned it.

The next move was for Pilotto to call in Rocky Robust. The meet took place in the vending machine office. Al Tocco was also present.

"Rocky, we got a move up for you. You done a good job on the Richards thing, now you've done a good job in Riverdale-Dolton. Now we want to move you into Blue Island. Midlothian, Islip, that district," Pilotto offered.

Rocky immediately grasped the implications. "How about the Bomber? How does he feel about that?"

"He don't know yet. We want to talk to you before we talk to him," Pilotto explained.

"Knowing that guy, he ain't gonna take this lightly," Robust quietly murmured.

Pilotto and Tocco nodded in unison. They waited.

Rocky grasped the idea. He was no dummy. "You mean if I want the territory it's OK with you guys, but I got to move Jimmy out myself."

"That's what it amounts to. Of course, we'll give you backup. You tell us who you want from our outfit and you got it. But you're out front. Jimmy fights back, he comes after you. You understand that?"

Robust understood. He realized he was at the crossroads of his career. If he backed off now, he could languish in Dolton-Riverdale-Harvey-Phoenix. A nice living, very comfortable. Brought him in just under $100,000 a year or so. He could do the things in life with that. Support his family nicely. On the other hand he would show weakness if he didn't take Pilotto and Tocco up on this offer. He would lose face. Someday they might send somebody after him. He made his mind up. Quickly.

"OK. Fine. I'm for it."

"Good," Pilotto responded. "OK, we'll call The Bomber in and let you know." The "sit-down" was over.

That afternoon Catuara was summoned to the vending company. It was put to him. He didn't like it. Not one bit. "No fucking way!" was his response. He immediately got up from the table and stalked out.

Robust got a phone call in his office, one that he had established himself in Riverdale at The Little Bit of Italy restaurant. "We talked to Jimmy. He said no. Now you go talk to him." The message from Pilotto was right to the point.

This was it. Back off now and it was a one-way street. To eventual oblivion. But Rocco Robustelli had never done something like this before. Actions in Cal City, on Bill Richards and for gambling and juice in his district had all been more or less benign. There had been no need for heavy stuff. Could he handle it? Could he prove himself? Not only to Pilotto and Tocco but to himself? Rocky took his piece, a snub-nose .38, from the desk in the Little Bit. He knew where he could find Catuara. After all, he had been laying-off with Jimmy The Bomber, in his adjoining district, ever since he had been taking it over. He drove to Jimmy's main office, the rear end of a realty office on Burr Oak at California in Blue Island. He walked in. There was Jimmy with three of his guys. One was his top guy, "Babe" Tuffanelli.

"Talk to you alone a minute, Jim?" Rocky asked.

Catuara knew what it was Robust wanted to talk to him about. "Stay where you are," he said to his men. "I want you to hear this, it concerns all of us."

Robust didn't like this. He had no choice, however.

"Jim," he said, looking The Bomber right in the eye, "you've been told you're out and I'm in. How do you want to handle it?"

"Fuck you, fuck them. Stick your big finger up your culo!"

That was pretty clear. Robust took one last shot. He looked from Catuara to the three men with him. "It's gonna happen, one way or another. It's orders from the top. You guys throw in with me, you stay. Throw in with him and you go with him. That goes for all of you. Spread the word." With that he turned on his heels and walked out.

"Fuckin' guy's got his nerve," Catuara sputtered.

The battle was joined.

The first thing Robust did was to journey south from Blue Island to Chicago Heights to recontact Pilotto at the vending company. He told Pilotto of the results of his talk with Catuara.

"What I need now, Al, are two or three guys to work with me, guys who have done some heavy stuff in their time," he told Pilotto.

"OK, that's what I promised you," Pilotto replied. "You've

worked with Jerry Scarpelli before, on the thing with the G guy. You can have him. And he knows Jimmy. I'll give you two more guys. Patsy Padrone and Gino Martini. All three of those guys have banged up some guys."

So it was that Rocco Robustelli started a caper which would be his making or breaking.

CHAPTER FIVE

The Hit

Jimmy "The Bomber" Catuara was in his seventies. Like Rocco Robust, he had grown up in the Patch. He still spent a great deal of time in his old neighborhood.

Rocco was able to get a line on all of this through his old pal, Dino Valente. Valente also lived in the new neighborhood of South Holland and operated a music company and a jukebox and billiard business. He did a lot of business in Blue Island and had gotten to know Jimmy Catuara. Well.

Rocco sat down with Dino at Barthel's Supper Club in Dolton.

"Dino, I got to get a line on Jimmy Catuara. Just between you and me. You tell me he lives on Kilbourne in Oak Lawn. What's his pattern? What does he drive? When does he usually leave his house?"

"Whoa, Pal," Valente replied. "Sounds to me like you're planning something I want no part of."

"Whatever I'm plannin', don't worry about it. Let's just say I've got the backing of Al in the Heights. If you want me to tell him you clammed up on me, OK. See how much business you keep from our joints. You want to keep out of this, you better move from South Holland, take your business elsewhere."

Rocky was as forceful as he could get. He was beginning to get the hang of being a tough guy.

"OK, OK, calm down," Valente hissed. "I don't know nothing about his pattern. But he drives a red Caddy and he does a lot of business in his old neighborhood and on the near north side. He usually spends the mornings in Chicago and the afternoons and nights in Blue Island."

Rocco then convened with his hit crew: Scarpelli, Padrone and Martini.

"Scarpelli, you and Patsy work together in one car. Martini and I will work the other. First thing we got to do is set up on Catuara's house in Oak Lawn. Let's set up at five. So we don't miss him. And we play it by ear from then on. When we get our chance, we take him out. Now we got to get some pieces. I'm sure you guys got pistols, but we need a shotgun or two. One for each car."

Scarpelli, a guy who had already hit four victims, had the answer to that. He could get them.

"Next thing, we gotta get a van. Can't sit in a residential neighborhood in a couple of cars."

Padrone accomplished that. He stole one that had a good pickup. They could park it in Catuara's neighborhood early in the morning, a half block from his residence facing away from it. They could observe out the rear windows of the van.

The foursome set out the next day. About six, The Bomber exited his garage in his red Cadillac, heading east to California and north to 95th Street. As he turned east again, Robust and Martini lost him. They had not been in contact with Scarpelli and Padrone, not having the ability to communicate by car radio or by walkie-talkie, and were fearful of being made. They had hung back too far and had gotten tangled up on a red light as Catuara turned onto 95th Street.

"We got to get better organized," Robust told his crew. "Let's meet again tomorrow morning and try it again. We got an idea now he goes east on Kilbourne. Jerry, you and Padrone set up a couple blocks east of his house. We'll sit west a half block again. Nobody seemed to have any unusual interest in us there. If he goes west, we'll do our best to take him alone. If he goes east, like today, we'll tail along and you can back us up as we pass you."

The next day it went much better. Just after six, The Bomber left his garage in his red Caddy. East he went to California. The old man was careless. One thing mobsters learn early—or at least are taught early—is to vary their patterns. Not to use the same route twice in a row. But Catuara did. When he passed Scarpelli and

Padrone, followed loosely by Robust and Martini, they were in position to follow from a block and a half away. When they got to 95th Street, they were ready. They speeded up and were with Catuara when he turned onto 95th. The van was caught by the stop light once more, just as it was the day before, but Scarpelli and Padrone were with their prey. Robust and Martini speeded up, breaking all speed limits. Soon they saw the black souped-up Chevy driven by Scarpelli. Ahead was Catuara in the red Caddy. As he got to the Dan Ryan Expressway, the world's busiest freeway, he entered it, heading north. Now the foursome was in good position, following closely but shielded by the heavy traffic, just looking for the right time and the right spot.

Catuara proceeded past the Loop. At the Ohio Street exit, he pulled off the expressway. He was heading east. When he got to La Salle Street, he headed north.

"Don't lose him now," Robust yelled to Martini, who was driving.

Robust had his shotgun ready. He wanted to do this himself. If he allowed any of the other three to do it, he would only get credit for masterminding the deal. But, if he fired the fatal shots himself, he would get much more credit.

Catuara headed into a fairly remote industrial area on the near northwest side. When he got to the intersection of Hubbard and Ogden, Robust seized the opportunity.

"Pull up right beside him," he cried to Martini. When Martini did, Robust opened up. Both barrels of his shotgun with double O buck. Catuara slumped.

"Stop," Robust shouted, jumping out of the van and, with his .38 pumping a shot point blank into The Bomber's head. He may have been dead already, but Rocky was taking no chances. One more, into the neck. And then one more, into Catuara's back as he slumped sideways onto the passenger seat. It was Friday, July 28. Rocco Robustelli had "made his bones."

"Take off," he shouted to Martini as he jumped back into the van. He waved at Scarpelli and Padrone.

"Go" he yelled. Off they went. They got away clean. No

witnesses. The body would not be discovered for several minutes. By then, both vehicles were heading south, back the way they had come on the Dan Ryan.

Robust was new at this. He reported personally and directly to his capo, Al Pilotto.

"You hit him right now? Son of a bitch, get out of here. Quick!"

Pilotto was street-wise enough to grasp the implication that if Robust been followed from the killing field to himself, he would be implicated in murder. It was a blot on Robust's victory, but when nothing transpired to link him to his capo, it would be all but forgotten.

Pilotto kept his promise. Within hours, the word was on the street in Blue Island. Hadn't Rocky Robust threatened Catuara? Right in front of three witnesses? And he told them he would be taking over? This is what reputations are made of. Walk into a mob boss's office, in front of three of his top guys, and tell him if he didn't get out, he'd be taken out. And then, within a matter of days, doing it.

Robust needed little to expedite his takeover of Blue Island. Everyone fell right in line. After all, this guy had the ability to enforce his edicts. And he had the sanction of the head capo, Al Pilotto.

In thanks to Scarpelli, Padrone and Martini, Robust put them to work. Scarpelli was at his side, his number one man and his driver-bodyguard. Padrone and Martini were given choice books, one in Dolton and one in Midlothian. Robust immediately called a sit-down with Catuara's workers.

"Shape up, work hard, be loyal to me, recognize what has happened, and why, and you'll be treated good. Fuck up, fuck around, and you'll join Catuara. It's your choice."

What choice? The Blue Island crew had little. They fell in line.

Rocco Robust was only in his mid-thirties. But his district, once two good districts, was a productive as any held by any other Chicago mobster.

When Al Pilotto and Al Tocco reported the next week to Sam Giancana, they were greeted warmly. Things had gone very well.

An old mob guy had outlived his usefulness, had slipped in his dotage, had been disposed of and new blood installed. Sure, the Chicago media made it a big story. Sure, there were those like Marlin Johnson, the special agent in charge of the FBI, who promised results in solving yet another Chicago gangland slaying. But this was just one more which would go unsolved. Rocco Robust was home free. Sitting pretty. A mobster on the rise.

CHAPTER SIX

Not the Time or Place.

The Little League season was nearing its countdown. Bill Richards was now coaching the major league team under manager Earl Gossett. Young Bill was the pitcher-shortstop, alternating those positions with the star of the team, Steve Mikulic. Bob Richards, just nine, had become the starting catcher in this 9-12 year old league. A rookie with great promise. Another rookie with at least equal promise was Richard Robustelli, now called Ricky by his teammates.

The team mother was Jeannie Richards and the official scorer for the team was eleven-year old Linda Robustelli.

Wausau Lumber was nearing the championship. Earl Gossett was a fine manager who got the most out of his young players. In addition, he drafted keenly. He had a great eye for young talent. Furthermore, he had had the keen insight to recruit coach Bill Richards, in spite of his inability to accept mental errors by the kids. He sometimes forgot that they were not quite grown up.

The reason Earl Gossett was acute in recruiting Bill Richards as a coach was because he also got Bill's sons. Young Bill was as good an eleven-year old as there was in the league. And Bob Richards was an outstanding nine-year old. The only other nine-year old in the league as good was Ricky Robustelli.

For Jeannie Richards, the two Robustelli kids had become a special project. She knew that their father was a mobster. When Bill learned that Robust had taken over the lucrative Blue Island territory, he suspected who the killer of The Bomber had been. There was no way he could prove it, but one of the first chunks of a modus operandi in investigating a crime is to find a motive.

Who would gain by this killing? In this case the only beneficiary had been Robust.

But that didn't deter Jeannie Richards. All she knew was the Robustellis were good kids. Motherless. In need of some motherly compassion, devotion, guidance, and love. Jeannie extended her affection to Linda and Ricky and made it a point to sit next to Linda in the bleachers at the game. Linda was never accompanied to the games by her father. She regularly bicycled to the games with her kid brother and sat near the bench so that she could determine from Gossett and Richards whether it was a hit or an error, an earned run, a wild pitch or a passed ball.

Linda soon became aware of Bill Richards. And visa versa. Young Bill had some idea there was something unusual about Linda's father, but his father never spoke adversely about Robust in front of the kids. Some of the other fathers who followed the team at Veteran's Park voiced their suspicions of Robust more than his father ever did. There was no reason for young Bill not to take a shine to the pretty brunette who hung around his mother. No reason at all. Not only was Linda a pretty young thing, but a very nice person, a real young lady–and attractive.

Since young Bill was also a sharp young guy, it was natural for Linda to be attracted. They soon became good friends.

At the same time, Bob Richards and Ricky Robustelli were getting to know each other. When Gossett made Rick a starting pitcher for Wausau, he made it a Robustelli to Richards battery. "The R and R Boys," Gossett dubbed them.

The situation presented problems for the FBI agent.

"Honey, do you think its good for you and Linda, and for Bill and Linda to be close? And for Bob and Ricky? I mean we come from opposite ends of the social spectrum. I can foresee where someday Robust and I are going to square off, one way or another, against each other. I'm really giving this relationship between you and Linda, Linda and Bill, Bob and Ricky, a lot of thought."

Jeannie had thought about it too. "Let it happen naturally. Whatever develops between the kids will happen. There's not much we can do about it. And it may be a transitional thing. When the Little League season is over, the Robustellis will be at Holy Ghost and our kids at St. Jude. They won't see each other until next summer. It's nothing to be concerned with."

Bill accepted that. As always, Jeannie had things in perspective.

However, the "square-off" would come sooner than Bill Richards expected.

A few days after he had dusted The Bomber, Rocco Robust showed up at the family picnic celebrating the end of the Little League season.

Robust and Bill Richards, Sr. came into contact once again. They had seen each other regularly at the games, two or three times a week. But, with Bill in the dugout or on the coaching lines and Robust well back in the stands, they had had no reason to converse.

Rocco, flush from his triumph, was more than a little cocky. Bill didn't appreciate Robust's attitude at all. The picnic was no occasion for Robust to throw his weight around and or try to make a big man of himself in front of the kids and their families.

Bill Richards accepted it. For awhile. But, when Robust spilled his drink on the mother of one of the players, Bill moved forward. He had had enough.

"I suggest you apologize to the lady, Mr. Robustelli," he said with a stern look on his face. He suspected that many of the fathers, hearing the gossip about the activity of Mr. Robustelli and knowing that Richards was an FBI agent, were watching closely. Richards felt if he let this pass it would undermine his respect.

Robust looked at Richards. "I expect you think you're man enough to make me, Mister Richards."

"Yeah, I think I'm man enough to make you, Mr. Robustelli. But I don't think this is the place. This is a Little League picnic. If we spill drinks on women, we express our apologies. We expect we are all gentlemen here."

Robustelli looked around. It was obvious he was outnumbered. Not that any of the parents would join Richards if it came to a fight, but they were obviously on Richards' side in this disagreement.

At this point Earl Gossett, as the team manager and the organizer of the picnic, stepped in.

"OK, this isn't the time or place. You do what you want, Mr. Robustelli, you are our guest here."

Robust glared at Richards. "This may not be the time or place, Richards, but there may be one someday. You watch yourself." With that, he motioned to his two kids, both badly embarrassed, and hustled them from the park.

Richards watched him go.

Yes, he thought to himself, someday there may be a time and a place. He smiled and turned his attention back to the picnic.

Jeannie Richards figured she knew what her husband was thinking. She knew him well.

CHAPTER SEVEN

The Richards Family Extends.

Young Bill Richards' baseball career came to an end playing in a neighbor's yard. His fall on an aluminum divider needed 70 stitches to repair.

But Bob's career flourished. As did Ricky Robustelli's. The next years of the "R and R Boys" were starring ones as they finished their seasons in Little League, American Legion and Connie Mack.

The battery of Robustelli to Richards, both now eighteen, attracted the score of major league scouts who followed the players. Both also starred on the gridiron, Bob as a quarterback and Rick as the star running back.

Bob Richards received some sixty five offers for football and baseball scholarships to colleges. He made it clear to each school that only those colleges allowing him to skip spring football practice to play baseball would be considered. The list narrowed considerably, especially since Bob was a quarterback which necessitated extra practice time and work on the play-book.

After visits to Stanford, Michigan, North Carolina State and Pennsylvania, Bob settled on a full scholarship at Notre Dame, where his brother, Bill, was already a distance runner on the track team.

Ricky Robustelli, though every bit as good an athlete as Bob, was not as fortunate. His football offers were few and far between. The University of Arizona, however, wanted him. Not only did the football coach want him, but Jerry Kindall, the head baseball coach. Kindall had been a star major leaguer, with Minnesota and the Cubs, and was now establishing a great baseball power at the

University of Arizona. Ricky quickly accepted the offer.

Bob Richards was drafted by the Atlanta Braves even though he had committed to Notre Dame. But Rick, the other half of the "R and R Boys," was not drafted by any major league team. Doubts about the system were beginning to get to Bill Richards.

Richards had become very close to Ricky as the years went by. Rick had played on every team Bill coached in the summer leagues and, as Rick and Bob became the closest of pals, Rick and Linda had increasingly spent more and more time at the Richards household. Rick had become like a third son—not only to Bill but to Jeannie.

Most of what was happening went right over Rocco Robust's head. He wasn't home enough to grasp what was happening. Whenever Robust would return home to find the kids gone, he was told by the housekeeper that they were "at one of Rick's ball games." Like many mob fathers, Rocco loved his kids, but left their upbringing to the feminine side of the family.

Ricky and Linda Robustelli came to be closer to Bill and Jeannie Richards—and to young Bill and Bob—than they were to their father.

Bill thought it was a situation which might have ramifications down the line somewhere and, for that reason, brought it to the attention of his boss, Ross Spencer. He was told to put it into a memo for the file and to be very circumspect. He was not ordered to cut off the relationship, but to take special care that it did not interfere in any way with his assignment to put the father in prison.

It was a unique situation. It would take special care. And then some.

CHAPTER EIGHT

Well on the Way.

Rocky Robust had things going so smoothly in the district assigned to him that he was given more territory, amounting, more or less, to about one-third of the southern suburbs of Chicago. He soon became one of the more powerful guys in the Chicago mob and began to spend more time in Chicago itself, making it a point to stop into the Armory Lounge on a regular basis. In a society where it was a sign of power to pick up checks, Robust was able to have Tony the bartender put a few on his tab. He was soon friendly with all the top mob guys in Chicago.

But the Chicago outfit was running out of top guys—capable guys. Bill Richards and the FBI was having great success against the Chicago mob. First they put Giancana away. When he come out, he abdicated his position as boss and fled to Mexico where he would remain for eight years before being deported. His position was taken by Sam "Teets" Battaglia, then Felix "Milwaukee Phil" Alderisio, then Jackie Cerone. But the FBI got them all.

Adding to the problem was attrition attributed to death from natural causes. Murray Humphreys, Frank Ferraro, Ralph Pierce and Les Kruse were all wiped out in a space of a couple years. Except for Gussie Alex, this was the entire "the connection guys." "The connection guys" made sure that a cadre of corrupt officials were developed and maintained so that favorable treatment could be afforded the mob. Without crooked cops, judges, politicians, labor leaders and public officials, no mob can operate efficiently. For decades, the connection guys had insured that there were scores of such public officials available to the mob in their time of need, especially in the southern suburbs where first Frankie LaPorte and now Al Pilotto had been most successful in developing local and state police officers and putting them "on the pad," corrupting them.

Due to the attrition, Gussie Alex was on the prowl for capable mob members who might have the ability to succeed Humphreys, Pierce, Ferraro and Kruse.

At Meo's, Alex made this very clear to Tony Accardo.

"Joe," he started, "I'm looking for a good man to step in and help me with the connection guys. I can't do it all myself. About all I'm doing now is maintaining what we got. I can't get out, I don't have the resources to get out and look for new guys. I've got Pat Marcy in the First Ward and his crew helping me more now than they used to, but I can't do it all just with what I got. I got to get a good new guy."

Joe Batters took it under advisement. That same afternoon he called Butch Blasi and made an appointment to see him the next day in the alcove at Meo's.

When Blasi arrived, Accardo explained the problem to him. For years Blasi had been Accardo's driver, bodyguard and appointment secretary when Accardo had been the boss. Then he had assumed the same capacity with Giancana. And then with Battaglia, Alderisio and Cerone. There wasn't a more savvy or experienced guy in Chicago than Blasi.

"Joe," Butch started, "I think I know just the guy. He's done some nice things out south under Frankie and now Al. They've given him a lot of territory out there and I understand he's handling it well for them. Now, more than that though, the reason I think he might fit in as a connection guy is because he's already gotten his feet wet in that area. Frankie and Al put him with Tocco to find out what they can about this guy the G has out front for them, this Richards. As I understand it, he done a good job. Got us a lot of good info on Richards. Another thing, he's been coming in and getting together with us here in Chicago. None of the other guys out south have ever done that. And he gets along well. Doesn't throw his weight around but moves around pretty good. All the guys like him. I've gotten a good look at him and I think he'd be good. He's a good lookin' guy, dresses well, talks good. He also made his bones. Took out The Bomber after Al gave him the OK to do it if Jimmy resisted his move into his district about three, four years ago. You remember that, you OK'd it."

Yes, Joe Batters remembered that. Although it wasn't necessary that a member of the connection guys be a killer, it was a real mark of distinction in any mob to have excelled in the heavy work. No mob anywhere can flourish if it can't enforce its edicts. Like a prize fighter who can't hit, can only box, any mobster who can't kill is eventually going to be limited in his progression inside the mob. So what Blasi was telling Accardo was the Rocky Robust had the tools—all the tools. He was already accomplished in that area of the mob's business which is its lifeblood—gambling. He had done some minor connection guy work—on Richards. And he had accomplished some heavy work—the hit on Catuara. In totality, that is the 1,2,3 of the job description of a mobster, although not necessarily in that order.

The following day, Joe Batters went downtown, something he seldom did. He met Gussie Alex at Gussie's favorite hangout, Chez Paul, a uppity French restaurant, and told him that he may have a solution for Gussie's problem.

"Slim," Accardo said, calling Alex by his mob code name, "Butch tells me there is a guy in Pilotto's crew out south who might be the guy you've been looking for to fill that spot. Guy's name is Rocco Robustelli. They call him Robust out there."

Robust had obviously come to Alex' attention before. "Yeah, I've heard of him. He's got the district where my mom lives, in Evergreen Park. He went over and paid his respects to her when he moved into Evergreen. Told her if there is anything she needs, garbage, street cleaning, stop sign on the corner, snow removal, sidewalk repair, problems with the neighbors, all the stuff a guy can get done in his district, just to let him know. And I hear he's made some moves with the pols out there and with the coppers. Yeah, I know who you're talking about."

"Well, why don't you go see Al out south and see if he would OK it. Tell him you talked to me and I'll go for it," Accardo said.

Gussie had one other thought. "Al might not go for it. That's a lot of work, to run a district and then work with us. I know. I had the Loop for several years and worked under Hump with the connection guys at the same time. It takes a lot of time and you got to be a top guy to get it all done."

"Well, go see Al and if he OK's go see Robust. See what they both think."

The next day Alex called Al Pilotto and asked him to came into the mob headquarters on the second floor custom tailor shop at 620 North Michigan.

When Pilotto arrived, Alex put it to him.

Pilotto went for it. At first, he felt a twinge of jealousy that he hadn't been invited himself. It had never happened before; no south suburbanite had ever been asked to be a connection guy. But then he realized that Robust, as a member of his organization who had been elevated by him, was an extension of the Pilotto street crew. Any recognition one of his men got was credit to him personally. He told Gussie that he had his sanction.

The next day, Rocco Robustelli was invited to the tailor shop. Pilotto told him how to get inside. "Park your car three, four blocks away, on State Street. Then walk to the corner of Rush and Ontario. Clean yourself, make sure nobody's followin' you. Enter the building on Ontario. As you get inside, you'll see a corridor going east, to your left. That corridor will take you about a block, into another building. This building is on Michigan. When you get to the front of the building, on Michigan, walk up the stairs to the second floor. As you get to the second floor, right in front of you is this first class tailor shop, Celano's. Want to make an impression, get yourself one of Jimmy's custom suits. You'll pay top dollar, but you'll have yourself the best suit money can buy. And all the outfit guys will be impressed. None but the top guys in the outfit buy their suits from Celano. Nobody else can afford them. But when you get inside, ask for Jimmy. Tell him Slim sent for you. They got a private office there, to the south side of the tailor shop where all the top guys meet. Jimmy will show you."

Robust did as instructed. The next morning at ten sharp he presented himself at the tailor shop.

Gussie got quickly to his point. As he talked he sized Robust up. What Butch Blasi had told Joe Batters seemed to be true. Nice appearance, especially for a mobster, a hoodlum. Nicely dressed, although Gus could see that Jimmy Celano could do nice things for this young guy.

Rocco was intrigued. He knew about the connection guys and what they did. It was an honor to be a member of such a group. In fact, it was rare that an Italian was invited to join. In the mob it was not rare for an Italian to be highly placed—except in the connection guys.

In any event, it was an honor. And Rocco Robustelli recognized it as such. He readily accepted. The first thing Slim did was take him to Nick, one of the tailors. He ordered him three suits, the obligatory mob fedora, three pairs of slacks, six custom shirts and six ties. "Put it on my tab," Gussie told Nick. He knew it was a good investment. A suit from Celano's was the touch of class recognized in both worlds. An aura of wealth and power was necessary for a connection guy when he approached a target for corruption. In the underworld if a hoodlum could say, "this suit comes from Jimmy Celano," that signified he was "in."

Rocky Robust had made another significant move upward in the organization. As a street boss and a member of the connection guys, Robust was now one of Chicago's more prominent made guys.

Unless he stepped on his dick now, he was well on his way.

CHAPTER NINE

The Labor Racketeer.

The Chicago family of La Cosa Nostra was undergoing a major change in leadership. The G had put the four absolute bosses in prison, all in the space of six years. The Giancana Family was in serious trouble. Attrition was setting in. No one had been groomed to take over as boss.

Fortunately, Tony Accardo was still available. The mob forced him to return from his townhouse along the fairways of the Indian Wells Country Club in the Palm Springs area and take over the reigns. He named Joey Aiuppa as the day-to-day boss to complement his leadership. Joe Batters continued to call the major shots, just as he had been doing when he suggested to Gussie Alex that Gus bring Rocky Robust into the connection guys, but he would spend more time on the Chicago turf. However, it would be Aiuppa who would run the minute by minute operations.

They added one more "A" to the leadership, Accardo, Aiuppa –and Alex. Accardo had been impressed with Gussie through the years as he observed what Alex had been doing as the boss of the connection guys. Joe Batters recognized how vital it was to the operations of the mob to have the boss of those corrupters in a position of authority. As one of the Triple A's running the Outfit, he could make any move necessary immediately. Alex became the first top boss without a vowel ending his name anywhere in the country. It was unprecedented.

When Alex was elevated, it enhanced the prestige inside the Outfit of Rocky Robust. Now he could walk into the Armory and pick up checks without question.

Robust was soon given an important assignment by his new mentor.

"Rocco, I got a job for you," Alex told Robust. "It's an easy one for you to start, to break your cherry on, but it's important to us. We can't afford to screw this up. It's a labor job. Let me give you a little background. When Jake Guzik was the boss of us guys, he got us started into labor. Then when Hump took over after Guzik died, he really got us going in labor. He handled most of it himself. With the help of Joe Glimco and Paul Dorfman, Red Dorfman, Allen's pa. We got all kinds of guys in labor. Glimco in Local 777 of the Teamsters, for instance. Some guys we control, some we have a lot of influence over, like Hoffa, but he tells us to shove it once and a while, we really should do better there, but he's good for us. There's a couple of our own guys, like your boss, Pilotto, in Local 5, and Vince Solano, in Local 1. Our own guys, made, capos, in fact. Then there's Dominic Senese in Local 703, Tony Spano in the Bartenders, Local 450, Clarence Jalas in Local 110 of the Moving Pictures operators Union and Gus Zapas in Local 46. We got guys all over Ed Hanley's Hotel, Restaurant and Bartender's Union. They call that the Culinary Workers out in Las Vegas and we need them there. And in Atlantic City. There's local 14, the Amalgamated Industrial Union. There's Local 705 and 710 of the Teamsters, Eco Coli in Local 727, Joe Springola in Local 1001, Local 714 of the Teamsters, Local 136 of the Machinery Movers. Lots of them. As I say some we control, some we got influence. Some we can give orders to, some we ask for favors and expect to get them. Some we keep in line, some we got to give what our lawyers call a quid pro quo. Some tell us they can't do anything and they don't unless we use what we call Chicago methods—money or muscle or both. You get the picture?"

Robust nodded. He was keying himself to the personality of Alex. Whereas Guzik and Humphreys, the former head connection guys had been long winded and bombastic, Gussie was very low key, very soft spoken, a reserved personality.

"Now there is one local here where we have had good influence in the past but we're not asking, we're telling. That's Local 593, the

Hotel, Motel Service Workers, the Drug Store, Sports Events and Industrial Catering Employees. They're located in the Loop, on Wells Street. Now, for years we had Kurt Hilgendorf in there. He was our man. But he passed on and we thought we put a guy in there we could trust. But he's a wishy-washy guy, got no guts, always worrying about what will it look like if I put that guy in, if I pull those guys out, if I picket that place. You with me so far?"

Robust nodded again. So far he could understand all of this. He had a concept of what the mob's influence was in Chicago and with what locals, but here it was—from the horse's mouth. He had even met a couple of the union leaders like Senese and Zapas. And, of course, Pilotto.

Slim took up the story. It was long-winded for him. "Now this local, 593, is important to us. They unionize the sports arenas. Like Soldier Field, even though the Park District runs it. Like the Stadium, the Coliseum, the Ampitheatre. Wrigley Field and Comiskey Park. They'll organize this new place in the planning stages, the Horizon in Rosemont. So that's important to us. Besides, we get an in with Arthur Wirtz thru this local. He owns the Stadium and the Black Hawks. We had something going with him when him and Jim Norris had the IBC, the International Boxing Club. It gave us an "in" in the fight game. Me and Ralph Pierce handled that when Ralph was alive. OK?"

Again all Robust could do was nod. "OK," Gussie responded. "Now here's what you do. I'm gonna call this guy, his name is Bill Terry. T E R R Y. Tell him I'm sending you to see him, that you will be in his office on Wells Street at 11 tomorrow morning. And that he is to pay you the respect that he would pay Hump or me. That you are one of us now. OK?"

This time Robust said "yeah."

"But be very careful, Rocco. This guy is crafty. I wouldn't put it past him to have the place bugged. That's one thing you have to worry about when you go into somebody new or somebody who you can't trust. That they carry a wire. Bug you. So meet him there. But tell him you want to take him to lunch. That's why I say 11 o'clock. Bull shit with him a while, try to butter him up for half an hour or so, feel him out. Now see if he's trying to pull something on you, he'll have the place bugged, thinking you are gonna talk there. But now you pull a switch on him, you're taking him out of there. He ain't got time to get himself wired up, the G would have to do that on him. Takes about 10 minutes to do it. So stay with him, if he goes to the can, go with him. He says I got to take a piss, you say I do too. If I know Terry, he won't say I got to take a leak, he'll say I got to wash my hands. A little swishy kind of guy, OK?"

Robust went back to his nod.

"Now, Rocco, when you get him to lunch. Lean on him. Let him know that you and I are not happy with the way things are going in 593. Don't threaten him, but be strong. Let him know that we put you on him because you don't fuck around. Let him believe that now he's got some muscle on him. But don't say that. By your attitude, let him know that you mean business. Don't get specific, just let him know that from now on it will be you who touches bases with him and that when you touch you expect he is going to jump. The next time around, we'll test him out. We'll ask him to pull his workers out of the Stadium just to shake Arthur Wirtz up, just let Wirtz know we're still here, still in business. We got to shake guys up now and then, make them see us. Al Capone may not be here any more, but Tony Accardo is. Get into their mentality. You understand everything I'm saying to you?"

Robust did. "Yeah, sure. I'll handle it. What do I do after I'm finished, check with you?"

This time it was Gussie's turn to nod. "Call me here after ten any morning. If none of us are here, Jimmy or Nick will answer. Just ask for Slim. Tell them to call, let's see, we haven't given you a name yet. What do we call you?"

"Out in the Heights they call me Burly. Like in Robust."

Slim smiled. He liked that. "OK, that's easy to remember. Burly."

The next day Robust called on Bill Terry pursuant to the arrangements Gussie Alex had made with Terry. The conversation in the union offices was desultory and then they moved to Gene and Georgetti's, a restaurant on the northwest side of Chicago.

Soon conversation got down to the nitty-gritty.

"Listen, Bill Terry," Robust said in a low voice as he leaned across the table toward him, "Gussie tells me you don't play ball like you ought to. He wants to let you know that I'm the guy who will be touching base with you when there is something to our mutual interest if you know what I mean. I understand you been put where you are with our help. We don't do things like that if we don't expect something out of it. You and we wash each other's hands, you know what I mean?"

Robust had leaned far across the table. His eyes lined up directly into Terry's. But Terry had gotten away with playing it coy with the Outfit for the several months or so he had been in office. Gussie had been too busy to "educate" him and had not had the manpower otherwise to do so. So Terry returned Robust's gaze without flinching. By his attitude, without saying a word, he indicated that he continued to feel he was his own man. Robust got the drift. The minestrone had been served. With one swoop it was served again—right onto Terry's lap. Robust continued to fix his eyes on Terry's as if nothing had happened. To Terry's credit, he hardly moved. No one in the restaurant noticed what had taken place. Rocco arose, flipped a fifty dollar bill on the table and walked out.

An hour later, Bill Terry got a phone call back at his office on Wells Street. "I hope you got my meaning, Terry. The next time it might not be minestrone. Now change your pants and meet me tonight at seven at the same place." It wasn't a request, it was an order.

At seven sharp, Terry reappeared at Gene and Georgetti's. This time the pair enjoyed one of the specials of the house, the veal scallopini. Towards the end of the meal, Robust idly mentioned that "it would be appreciated" if there was a work stoppage Saturday night, "just for an hour, at the Stadium." Just to send a message to Arthur Wirtz during the warmups of the Blackhawk-Red Wings game. The "request" was made during the desert. Terry just nodded. He didn't want his cannoli in his lap. Or anything else. He understood that one piece of the "Chicago methods" was being applied to him. The muscle. He would rather it had been the money. The other part.

Saturday night the members of Local 593 walked off. Just for an hour. But Arthur Wirtz, the owner of the Stadium and the Blackhawks, got the message. Just as Bill Terry had.

When Gussie Alex got the report that night at his condo on Lake Shore Drive, he smiled. Maybe this new kid on the connection guys had the stuff.

CHAPTER TEN

Two Fine Careers—And A Mystery.

At the same time that Rocco Robustelli became a connection guy, Ricky Robustelli became a Wildcat at the University of Arizona.

The 105° Arizona weather was his first problem. Ricky wished he had played less baseball during the summer and spent more time getting into football shape. He began to pine for January when he could throw off his football uniform and don the Wildcat baseball togs.

The reason for his inability to be drafted to any major baseball league organization remained a mystery, but his natural ability was obvious to all his Arizona coaches.

When the season opened, Rick dressed and found himself fourth string at tailback on the depth chart. He got in for the last two minutes as the Wildcats romped, 44-13. It was not a great season for Rick. He did not log enough playing time to earn a letter. When he watched the baseball team playing their fall schedule in the warm autumn weather in Tucson, he wondered whether he should be on the diamond instead of on the gridiron.

At Notre Dame, Bob Richards ran into the same problem. When he reported to Notre Dame for football practice, he found himself in precisely the same situation as Ricky Robustelli found himself at Arizona—out of football shape. Just as Ricky found it hard to wait for spring baseball, Bob Richards found himself in the same position.

Both, however, got lucky. The baseball coaches from both colleges recognized the innate abilities of the two boys and the situation changed. Far apart, both pals were playing baseball in the spring, not football.

Ricky had a great season. He soon moved into the Wildcat starting rotation and wound up the season with a fine 3.50 ERA and with six wins under his belt. At the end of the season he was the team's third starter. Bob Richards also had a good season.

The next seasons would be even better for the two. Bob would win the starting catching job in his sophomore year and retain it in his junior year. At the end of the season he was the captain-elect of the Irish.

Ricky would be every bit as good—in tougher competition. Arizona would win the World Series of College Baseball in Omaha in Rick's sophomore year. At the end of his junior year he was elected Most Valuable Player in the Pac-10.

Both Linda and Bill Richards had also transferred to the University of Arizona and Bill and Rick became even better friends as they spent time together on the campus. Rick became even closer to his sister. The kids were bonding together, tighter and tighter as the years went by.

At the end of their junior years, Bob and Ricky again became eligible for the major league draft. Bob was drafted again, this time in the ninth round by the Chicago Cubs.

Ricky Robustelli again went undrafted. No one outside the major league organization could understand it. It defied reason. Ricky was perhaps the finest pitcher outside the professional ranks.

The public had yet to become aware of the parentage of Ricky Robustelli, but the inner sanctum of baseball was well aware of it.

CHAPTER ELEVEN

The Killer And His Dilemma

Robust was becoming the mob's favorite hit man.

"Robust, you been spending too much of your time in Chicago. We need you out here for awhile. I've talked to Gussie about it and he says it's OK." Al Pilotto seemed very earnest as he confronted Robust in the mob headquarters.

"What's up?" Robust replied. "My district has been runnin' good. Our profits go up every month."

"I know, I know. That's why we need you, Burly. You've proven to be probably the best man we have out here. With your district and with the heavy work we gave you, when you chopped The Bomber. Now we got some more heavy stuff and we want you to ramrod it for us."

Robust was perplexed. He had been spending the bulk of his time in Chicago. The Heights had slipped away from his attention.

Pilotto continued. "You know this Billy Dauber. He's been around for some time and been a good worker. But, now we find he's a snitch for the G. We suspected it when some of our chop-shop guys were indicted out here, and now we confirmed it. There's no doubt."

Although Robust was not involved in chop-shopping, the practice of chopping up stolen cars for their parts and then reselling those parts to private car repairmen so that no trace could be found of the stolen car itself, he knew what Pilotto was talking about.

Pilotto continued. "So what we want, Rock, is for you to get those guys who helped you on the hit on Jimmy. Martini, Scarpelli,

Patsy. Track Dauber down and clip that stoolie. Do it quick and do it final."

Robust put his old crew together. On July 2, Patsy Padrone stole a blue Ford van. Dauber was living with his new wife, Charlotte, on Monee Road in Crete, just south of Chicago Heights. As he and Charlotte drove home in his late model Caddy, he was ambushed by the foursome. The only difference in the hit was that this time a rifle was used to complement the shotgun. Robust applied the coup d' grace to Dauber with a .30-30. Unfortunately, Charlotte had to go too. She was in the wrong place at the wrong time. Robust made sure she could not testify with a .30-.30 bullet to the head.

Nick D'Andrea was the next guy on Pilotto's list. The foursome got him on September 13. Lured to the killing by Jerry Scarpelli, his buddy, who told him that he had some work for him, D'Andrea was taken at gun point in the same blue Ford van to an area near Crete, where Robust stuck a knife into his stomach—six times. When D'Andrea's car was discovered at 9:30 in the evening, it had burned to ashes. So had D'Andrea's body.

The next subject on Pilotto's hit list was another old pal, Sam Guzzino. Sam, then 51, had been with Pilotto for years. But he had worn out his usefulness; he was losing his marbles. He had become a danger. Guzzino's body was found in a ditch near Beecher, another south suburban village. Robust slit his throat to signify that he had been silenced because he talked too much and then shot him with his trusty .38.

Pilotto had one more victim before Robust's mission was done. In Chicago, it was a no-no to get involved with drug dealing, at least as long as Tony Accardo was "The Man." If Tony Accardo found out that a man working for the Outfit in the southern suburbs was using and dealing there would be hell to pay. And it would be Al Pilotto, the capo in charge there, who would pay it.

So Bobby Subatich had to go—not only was he a user, he was a dealer. Subatich's mother reported him missing and his body was discovered in the trunk of his car in the parking garage at O'Hare.

Chalk up another score for Robust.

But the shooting wasn't over yet.

Al Tocco was ambitious. He was tired of being number two man. He wanted to be the capo. He felt Robust out. How did he feel about working for Pilotto? Would he rather that his old pal, Tocco, the guy he had worked for when they put together all that info on that G guy, Bill Richards, be the man out south?

Robust looked him right in the eye. "Keep me out of anything like that, Al. I'm not getting mixed up in any revolt. I've been brought up to believe in the organization. If Joe Batters and Joey O'Brien want Pilotto out, they'll say so. Give me an order from them and you've got your man. But, unless you're speaking for them, I'm out of it."

Robust was in a precarious spot. He knew that Al Caesar Tocco was plotting to do away with his boss, his capo. Should he sit on this info or should he take it to Pilotto so that he could be warned.? Or should he take it into Aiuppa, the overall boss of the Chicago Mob?

Before he could decide, the deed was done. Al Pilotto was golfing one day at the Cherry Hills Country Club. While on the 12th hole, he was ambushed. Four guys rushed at him and his foursome. Al and his golfing buddies were unarmed, except for their golf clubs. They were no match for the ambushers. But the ambushers were sloppy. They shot Pilotto several times, but not fatally. He was rushed to St. James Hospital in Chicago Heights. After several touch and go days, he recovered.

Not that he was out of the woods. Soon after, the FBI came down on him. He was indicted in Florida, along with Tony Accardo, for defrauding a union pension fund; that of the Laborers Union. Although Joe Batters would skate—he has never spent a night in jail in his lifetime—Al Pilotto would not. He was convicted.

Pilotto was succeeded by Al Tocco. What Tocco couldn't accomplish by the ambush on the golf course, the FBI did for him.

The first thing Al Tocco did was call in Rocky Robust.

"Rock, I want you to be my number one guy out here. We've worked well together in the past and you've done good things."

Robust had anticipated this. He had taken a dislike to his old mentor. It didn't sit well with Rocky that Tocco had tried to take his capo out. He wondered how the FBI had been so fortuitous to zero in on Pilotto. He wanted no part of Tocco. But he would not put himself in the trick bag by refusing the offer. It was one he couldn't refuse. Not unless he wanted to be watching over his shoulder forever after. Tocco had proved his lack of loyalty. He would have no restraint in coming after Robust. So Rocco pretended he was honored; he accepted.

However, Robust had an ace up his sleeve. He figured his spot on the connection guys would eventually be his lever for elevation in the mob. However, he had things running so well, more or less by remote control, in his district that he sure didn't want to give that up. He had Scarpelli, Martini and Padrone running things for him so smoothly that he hardly had to supervise them at this point. Now he had to figure out a way to keep all that, but to divorce himself from Al Tocco. That would be no easy matter. Tocco was now the top man in the Heights, the man to whom he reported. How could he break away from him and yet keep the lucrative territory he commanded? He got an extra stipend for his work with the connection guys, but it was the income from his district that provided the bulk of his income.

It was a dilemma.

CHAPTER TWELVE

Luck

Bill Richards hoped to magnify Robust's dilemma. Richards had been on the Top Hoodlum Squad of the Chicago FBI for years now. In fact, there were no other early Top Hood agents in Chicago who remained a street agent. He had had his opportunities for promotions, but he enjoyed the challenge on the street. He loved the confrontation of the mobster, the chance to face him down, destroy his income, thwart his plans, put him away. He would never be anything but a street agent – of his own choosing.

Bill was mapping out a new line of attack. Bill had been working primarily on Murray "The Camel" Humphreys and on Gussie Alex, his two assigned "targets." But Hump had died and Bill had time to switch his attention to other targets. Living in the southern suburbs, he was aware of what was happening in the area, including the killings, the succession of Tocco to Pilotto's old spot and the succession of his old adversary, Rocco Robustelli, to be the number one man to Tocco.

But Robust had not commanded his full investigative attention when Hump and Gussie were around. Hump's death left a void. So Richards set his investigative sights on Rocco Robustelli.

Bill instituted a very loose "fisur," physical surveillance, of Robust and found that Robustelli left his home in South Holland about ten each morning, driving his late model Caddy west to South Park Ave, north on South Park to Sibley Boulevard, 147th Street, and then out 147th Street to Halsted and then north again on Halsted to 127th Street and then west on 127th into Blue Island. In Blue Island, on Burr Oak, just east of Sacramento Avenue,

Richards discovered Rocky's headquarters in a back room of the Sunset Lounge.

While working with the idea of obtaining a search warrent at the Sunset, Richards cultivated the bartender there. Gus Nazos was a trusted Robust associate, not a member of the mob, not made, but trusted. He had been to Joliet twice on burglary charges and was used by Robust as his appointment secretary. Any mob guy or bookmaker who wanted to meet with Robust had to go through Gus Nazos.

Bill intercepted him one evening after he got off work. "Gus," he told Nazos, "my name is Bill Richards. I'm with the FBI." He exhibited his FBI credentials to Nazos. "I'd like to talk to you. Would you join me in my car?"

Gus Nazos was not anxious to repeat his experiences "inside." Two stretches in Joliet were enough for Gus. When Bill Richards made his request, it was like a command. He did as requested. One meet led to another and soon Gus was opening up to Bill about what Robust and his men were doing in the district. Bill Richards soon became aware that Robust not only kept his bookmaking records in the back room of the Sunset, but also lists of the payouts he was disbursing to the police officers, politicians, magistrates and sheriff's deputies "on his pad."

Richards spent three days in his office, crafting an affidavit showing probable cause for a search warrant on the Sunset Lounge, specifically the back room. In the ten days it took to grant the affidavit, Rocco got lucky.

Although he was unaware of what his adversary was up to, Rocco had been making moves to get out from under Al Tocco. He had gone to Joey Aiuppa and made the request that he be given something a step up from where he was now. Things were going great in Blue Island and the rest of his territory, but he felt he was ready for something better.

Robust's request came at the right time.

"Here's where we're at, right now, kid," Aiuppa had informed Rocky. "I think you're cleared for this. Joe Batters is stepping out. Out as boss, although he'll be consiglieri again. Gussie has never wanted his spot as a boss. He's too fuckin' nervous for that. So he's wanted out. Now, I like it right where I am and Jackie Cerone is out of the can and Joe wants him to share with me. That's fine with me. So Jackie and I are going to be runnin' things. But we need an underboss. A number two guy. Somebody to take the load off us. I been talkin' to Joe Batters and he likes you. So I talked to Gussie. He likes you. But he don't want to lose you. You'd have to give up Blue Island and the district out there but you'd have to stay as a connection guy. You'd more than make up what you got coming in from your cut as the underboss but you'd lose your cut from your district. Would you be willing to do that?"

Robust sure as hell would be willing to do that. He wanted out from under Tocco. He enjoyed his work as a connection guy. And the additional authority as underboss to the big boss of the whole Chicago mob would be right up his alley.

"OK, Rock, let me take it up with Jackie and Joe. If they OK it, I'll give it to you."

When Aiuppa took it up with his cohorts, Accardo, Cerone and Alex, he found that Alex endorsed Robust without reservation. Accardo and Cerone had not worked closely with Rocco, but knew him enough to recognize ability when they saw it. They were particularly swayed by the endorsement of Gussie Alex, who knew him best. They sanctioned the appointment.

Almost as soon as Robust moved out of the Sunset Lounge, taking his records with him, Bill Richards moved in to find it empty.

The bird had flown the nest.

CHAPTER THIRTEEN

Robust Throws Fear.

It was Jerry Scarpelli who provided the link.

When Rocky departed from Blue Island and the other suburbs, he turned things over to Scarpelli. Since Scarpelli had performed so well for him, not only in the district but on the several hits which had been accomplished, Robust rewarded him. He also made sure that Gino Martini and Patsy Padrone were taken care of. He brought Gino along with him as his driver and bodyguard and made Patsy his appointment secretary. Anybody who wanted to meet with Rock had to go through Patsy.

But it was Scarpelli who brought out the role of Gus Nazos in the raid of the FBI on the Sunset Lounge. Suspicious of a leak, Scarpelli questioned Nazos repeatedly about the circumstances. How did the G know what was in the back room? That search warrant was pretty damn specific about what the G was looking for!

Eventually Gus Nazos broke down. He didn't admit that he had been Richards' source for the affidavit, but he did admit that Richards had interviewed him. He denied he furnished any information. But Scarpelli had his suspicions. He journeyed into Chicago and sat down with Robust at Giannotti's.

"Burly," Scarpelli said, "I think I found the jigger in your woodpile in Blue Island. Maybe not. You remember Gus, the bartender at your joint?"

"Sure, Robust replied."

"Well, he admits meeting your friend, that G guy, Richards. He don't admit telling him anything but he admits Richards zeroed in on him. He don't seem to me to be tough guy. I doubt he stood up to Richards very long. What do you think?"

Robust thought about it. "Yeah, you might be right Jerry. We probably made a mistake leaving him there when we started meeting there. We should have brought in one of our own guys in that spot."

Rocky gave it some more thought. "You know, Jerry, I've been thinkin' about something. The rules are we don't hit cops or people like newspaper guys, or judges or such. But if I could get the OK from Joe and from O'Brien, I'd like to throw a little fear into that asshole, Richards. Back him off a little. We might be able to set up him through this Gus."

Scarpelli was surprised. Never had he thrown fear at a cop, nonetheless a G guy. Nor had he known of such a thing in the years he had been a made guy.

Robust dismissed Scarpelli by saying, "Let me think about it. Stay in touch. And keep that Gus in sight. Don't let him disappear. Not yet."

When Robust left Giannotti's, he walked east a couple blocks to the Armory Lounge. He walked up to Butch Blasi and asked, "O'Brien busy? I'd like a few minutes with him." When Blasi determined that Aiuppa was free to meet with his underboss, Robust put the situation to him. "Now I don't want to chop Richards. I know you guys have made it clear that stuff is counterproductive. J.B. would never go for it. But I want to back him down. Throw some fear at him. What do you think? I think I can lure him into a trap and wait for him. Do it easy. I think I know a guy he's trying to make into a stool pigeon. Wait for him to show up and throw some shit at him. He's getting too fuckin' close, coming into my joint in Blue Island. Lucky I was just out of there or I might have had it. Let's put some second thoughts into this guy."

Aiuppa thought about it. He knew he didn't have the power, even as the boss, to authorize his underboss to do this thing. But he would pass it on to Accardo and discuss it with his co-boss, Cerone. What should he recommend? Eventually he decided Robust had a good idea. And Robust had demonstrated in the past that he could handle something like this. Not when the G guy was the intended victim, but in various other situations when work was demanded – heavy work.

So Aiuppa took it to Cerone and to Joe Batters. Cerone liked it. He was disposed towards the tough stuff. He had been involved in a lot of it. So had Accardo, of course. But Batters didn't like it. Counterproductive. Hit a G guy and the whole fuckin' FBI and the press and the Chicago Crime Commission and everybody else makes it the crime of the century. But Aiuppa persisted. Like every other hood of any stature whatsoever in Chicago, Aiuppa had been confronted by Richards. And Aiuppa had a particular hard-on for Richards. Years before, the FBI had been shadowing Aiuppa when he was travelling in Kansas. On this occasion Aiuppa and two of his cohorts had pulled off a highway and blasted away with their shotguns. Blasted scores of doves sitting on telephone lines in the Sunflower state. The FBI had immediately made themselves known. Arrested Aiuppa and his pals. And charged them with violation of the Migratory Bird Act! The what? What kind of a bull shit charge was that against a major mob boss? But the arrest held up and Joey had done time at Leavenworth as a result. Hard time. Hence his hard-on for Richards and his FBI mates.

Joey persisted in his argument to Cerone and Accardo. Finally, Tony agreed. "But just throw some fear. You don't kill him."

Aiuppa took the glad tidings back to Robust. "Set it up. Do it."

Robust sent for Scarpelli. "We got the OK on the hit on Richards. But just to throw fear. Now here's what I want. Get this bastard, Gus, and have him set up a meet with Richards. Have him call Richards and tell him he's got some good stuff for him. Let's see, have him meet Richards, where? Find out where he's met Richards before. Then we'll be waiting for him. Here's what I want. We can't kill him. But we can cripple him. Get some plastic explosive. You can do that from your cousin who works in that quarry in Thornton, for Material Service. Then we have Gus meet with Richards inside a bar or restaurant or some place. Then while he's inside, we plant the stuff in his car. Gino can open any car. We put a detonator in the stuff. When Richards comes out and gets ready to drive away, we detonate it. Put it under the floor mat. Blow his fucking feet off. J.B. says we can't chop him, but this will slow him down some, huh?" Robust obviously was happy with his thought. He laughed. And then again.

So they set it up.

When Richards got a call from Gus, he was unsuspicious. He thought his attempts to make an informant out of Gus seemed to be going well. He drove out to Poor Richards restaurant in Glenwood and parked in the lot, locked the Bureau car and entered the restaurant. Richards thought Gus was unusually nervous, but he did have a couple of nice pieces of information for him.

Pleased with the evening, Bill even had a stinger as an after-dinner drink. He watched Gus as he left the restaurant and waited ten minutes. He put on his galoshes and overcoat and walked out to the Bureau car. He turned on the ignition and backed it out.

He had almost made it to the road when Robust detonated the explosive under his feet!

The maitre d' at Poor Richards jumped when he heard the explosion. He ran out into the parking lot to the smoking car. The inside was charred. The driver, whom he recognized as having just left the road-house, was slumped over. There was blood, a lot of it. He rushed back into the restaurant and dialed the emergency number.

CHAPTER FOURTEEN

More Luck

The emergency room nurse found his FBI credentials. And his gun. She immediately called the FBI office. Burt Jensen was the supervisor on duty. The complaint agent who took the call, Bill Dougherty, gave it to him fast. "St. Francis Hospital in Blue Island. Ambulance just brought Bill Richards in. Tough shape. Seems there was a car bomb. I know he's working tonight because he and I have a handball game tomorrow and he hoped he wouldn't be out too late."

Jensen called Vince Inserra, Bill's supervisor. Inserra instructed Burt to call Richards' wife.

"You know Jeannie. Just tell her Bill is in the emergency ward. Then tell her you're calling Jack McDonough and Gerry Flemming, they live in South Holland. Tell her they'll pick her up as soon as possible and take her to the hospital. Then call them. If one of them isn't available call R.O. Murphy, he lives there too. Quick. And then have them call you with a report on his condition. Then if we get any leads, call out some other guys out south and get them right on it."

When Jeannie got to the hospital, the doctor gave it to her. Straight.

"He's a lucky guy. How many of us wear galoshes these days? Especially ones with steel plates in the soles? They saved his feet. Otherwise they'd have been blown right off. We've got him up in the operating room right now. He won't be playing any golf soon, but I think he might this summer."

Bill was taken to a recovery room where she could see him. He gave her a hug.

"I guess I got cocky, careless."

Jeannie smiled in her tears.

"It could have been a lot worse," Bill added. She nodded.

McDonough and Fleming spoke to Bill briefly before taking Jeannie home and heading for Poor Richards to do a crime-scene search.

Jeannie called Bill, her son, in Arizona and Bob at Notre Dame. She informed them that the mob had gotten dad, but that he seemed to be ok, at least as far as any permanent damage was concerned.

Bill III put two and two together. As close as he was to Linda and Ricky, he could not keep secret his suspicions that their father had done this to his father.

Linda placed a call home.

"Dad, did you have anything to do with this?"

"I think that's a fuckin' rotten thing to say, Linda! Why would you think I had any fuckin' thing to do like this? Is that what you think your father is. A fuckin' killer?"

Linda backed down. Maybe she had over-reacted. But she was not completely satisfied. She realized that this was the real world in which she lived. But reality was striking close to home. Maybe, in her shock, she had misjudged her father.

Both Linda and Ricky realized that there was a wide gulf between their two fathers. Although their father might not have personally exploded the bomb, or whatever it was, it must have been his associates. Since there was obviously bad blood between the two, even if he didn't have a part in it, Linda didn't think her father would be very sympathetic to Bill Richards.

Bill's doctor gave him the good news. In spite of many stitches in the foot, the shin and the calf, Bill would walk—and run—again, with a lot of therapy and hard work. He would require crutches and a cane, but, if he worked at it, he would be walking by August.

CHAPTER FIFTEEN

Old Cape Cod

Bill Richards would have more than pain to fight that summer.

Finishing their junior years in college, Bob and Ricky were both recruited to play in the Cape Cod League. When Bob got the call, he accepted to play for Cotuit immediately. The Cape Cod League is one of the fastest summer leagues in the country. Could he influence Ricky to sign as well, the team wondered? He not only could, he did.

With that, the two pals were reunited. Now twenty one, they had played on the same team each summer since they were nine. The R and R battery.

Cotuit, a small village, is located between Hyannisport and Falmouth. Beside a plentitude of girls, the downtown Cotuit Inn has a friendly bar called the "Swamp Fox."

Bill and Linda soon arrived on the Cape as well, recently graduated from Arizona. Bill was soon announcing the Kettleer games on the local Cotuit radio station, while Linda worked as a hostess in Hyannis, less then a half hour from Cotuit.

It wasn't long before the rest of the two families arrived on the Cape. Bill and Jeannie took a great "meadow" cabin near a cranberry bog. Bill was recovering nicely from his injury and could now walk without a limp. He played golf every other morning, walking the first nine holes. The frequent golf did wonders for his feet and legs.

Rocco Robust arrived unannounced on the Cape. His kids were not that happy to see him after all that had happened. He checked into the Cotuit Inn and walked the couple blocks to the ball yard. Sighting the Richards family in the middle of the stands on the home side of the field, he plunked himself down on the visitors side.

Things went smoothly for the first few nights. Rick and Linda dutifully spent some time with their father during the day, but evenings were spent at the Swamp Fox, where they would be joined by Bill and Linda and, occasionally, by Bill and Jeannie.

It was inevitable that the two forces would eventually meet. Robust eventually become bored after ten days. There wasn't much for a mobster to do in Cotuit. The Swamp Fox, the lounge in the Cotuit Inn, was the only game in town, more or less. He had stayed out of the lounge even though he was staying in the best room at the Inn. Robust finally stuck his nose into the Swamp Fox. It was a mistake.

Bill's legs had now recovered almost to their full strength. Rick had pitched his third shut-out of the Cape Cod season, striking out 10 and walking just one and Cotuit was now tied for the league lead with Falmouth, the perennial league champion. In addition, Bob had three hits and three RBI's that evening. All in all, it was a good night to celebrate.

As soon as Robust got a look at the celebration in the lounge, and took notice of the participants, he exited, but not before Bill Richards caught sight of him. Bill hurried to the front door and out onto the street in front of the inn.

"Robust!" Richards shouted. "Hold on, I want a word with you!"

Rocco hesitated. This wouldn't exactly be his style—to be accosted by an FBI agent in this fashion, alone. Even when it was obvious the FBI was not on official duty.

Richards hurried to Robust. The street was deserted.

"I think I've got a score to settle with you, Robustelli!"

"Fuck you, Richards," Robust snarled back.

"Yeah, that's about what I thought you'd have to say, Robustelli." Richards had his dander up. "You want to deny you had anything to do with my injury?"

Robust looked around. There were no witnesses.

"I only wish there had been more explosive that night, Richards!"

Although it was not exactly an admission, it was also not a denial. Rocco certainly wasn't the least remorseful.

Richards pushed against Robust. He had his suspicions before, but now he knew exactly who had been responsible for the worst injury of his life—one that could very well have killed him and which obviously had been meant to cripple him for life. He pushed his chest against Robust.

Robust recoiled. "You cocksucker, think you're a fucking tough guy, don't you Richards!" No one had ever pushed Robust around and gotten away with it. He had been in dozens of street fights in The Patch. Many a foe had gone down under a barrage of blows from Rocky Robust.

Robust threw a roundhouse right hand at his foe. It caught Bill high on the head, enough to stagger him but not enough to stun him.

Richards had been a Marine Corps and Notre Dame boxing champion—four times. He jabbed his right hand into Robust's teeth, knocking out the two front ones. He then stepped in with his back hand, the left, and exploded it into the solar plexus of Robust. With blood gushing from his mouth, Robust collapsed, the wind completely knocked out of him. He landed with a thud on the street. He was conscious, but grasping for breath.

Richards stepped back. He looked down on Robust. And waited. In a minute or so, Robust recovered. Enough to regain his feet. But not enough to carry on the fight.

"Richards, you'll regret this night! We'll get you if it's the last thing we do!"

Richards and Robust had battled before—verbally. But now the war was full fledged. The two enemies were now deadly. What had been professional was now personal.

Jeannie, Bill and Bob Richards and Linda and Ricky Robustelli were completely unaware of what had transpired outside the Swamp Fox. Robust put his handkerchief to his mouth and hurried to the front of the Cotuit Inn and up the stairs to his room. Bill waited a minute or two to fully compose himself and then reentered the Swamp Fox. He picked up the half empty bottle of Schaefer's beer, poured it into a glass, and gulped it down. The conversation went on as if nothing had happened.

The next day, without saying a word to anybody, Rocky Robust checked out of the Cotuit Inn, drove his rental car into Boston and went to a dentist, who repaired the damage and put in two false front teeth. Robust drove into the heart of the shopping district in Boston, checked into the Four Seasons Hotel on Boylston Street, and slept for 14 hours. When he awoke he called the concierge at the Four Seasons and arranged for a reservation on the next plane from Boston Logan Airport to O'Hare. When he arrived, his anger had not cooled.

"That fucking cocksucker thinks he's tough. He'll have another think coming before I get through with him!"

Back in Cotuit, Ricky Robustelli struck out the final batter, his 13th.

The Kettleers were Cape Cod League champs!

It had been one hell of a summer. Bill had battled back to health, had taken on his arch-enemy and Cotuit had won the pennant!

Now it was back to the war in Chicago!

CHAPTER SIXTEEN

The Lady Lawyer.

She was a sharp lady. Connie Constable had been around for awhile, but she was still in her twenties. A graduate of Mundelein and DePaul Law School, she had grown up in Oak Park and attended Oak Park-River Forest High School, as did many of the upper echelon of the mob. None lived on the 900 block of Columbian Avenue where Connie was raised, but there were many within a ten mile radius.

So, it wasn't out of the ordinary for Connie Constable to meet Rocco Robustelli.

Rocky returned home from his ill-fated trip to Cape Cod. He had made an appointment to check his dental work, specifically his two front teeth and wasn't in a particularly good frame of mine when he entered the office. His frame of mind got worse when he found the dentist had an emergency and was backed up anywhere from a half hour to an hour.

Rocco couldn't help but notice the lady sitting next to him. A little younger than him but that was the way Rocky liked them now that he was in his forties. Rock fingered his tie, pushed back his hair and smoothed out the crease in his Celano slacks.

"Lousy way these doctors waste people's time, isn't it?" he asked, turning towards the object of his attention.

"Yes," was the only response he got. The lady was reading a condensation of *Worldly Goods* by Michael Korda in an old *Cosmopolitan* Magazine. She didn't look up.

Rocco Robustelli had been rebuffed before.

Connie Constable, however, had not even glanced at Rocco. If she had, she wouldn't have recognized him, even though his photo had been in the *Tribune* and the *Sun-Times*. Although she was familiar with Sam Giancana and Tony Accardo and had seen Chuckie English, Sam Battaglia, Paul Ricca and Jackie Cerone in the neighborhood, she had no reason to associate Rocco with them.

Several weeks before, Rocco had had dinner with Pat Tuite, one of the most intelligent people he knew and a prominent defense attorney. Pat had been talking about something to do with Helen Gurley Brown, the publisher of *Cosmo*.

"That Helen Gurley Brown, she knows how to publish a magazine, doesn't she?" He asked.

Now he had Connie's attention. For the first time she looked at the man in the adjacent chair.

"Yes," she said. Again. But this time she added a bit, giving Rock some hope. "I'm surprised you know this magazine, though; it's mostly for women. Or at least I thought women would be its readership."

Robust was out on a limb. He had never even leafed through a *Cosmopolitan*. He changed the subject.

"Have you been Dr. Harkensee's patient long?"

"No, not very long," Connie replied. She turned back to *Cosmo* and the condensation of the Korda book.

"The reason I ask, you sure don't look like your teeth need any attention. They're beautiful." Rocco figured he could get away with that. Had he admired her figure, face or legs, she would have been turned off. But teeth are a different area. No lady gets offended if you come on by telling her she has nice teeth.

Connie laughed. "Well, thank you." Then she made Rocco happy. She indicated she might be interested in carrying on the conversation. She asked, "how about you, your first visit?"

Now the conversation began to flow. Connie even laid down her *Cosmo*. She shifted her body in order to look straight at him. He was well groomed, had a nice smile and seemed to be very sure of himself, but he had not made a pest of himself. There seemed to be something about him which was unusual. Maybe he was worth knowing. Anything to take her mind off what lay ahead, a root canal.

Rock finally reached into his card case and produced his business card. Business Agent of the Laborer's Union, Local #5. Not the most prestigious card to hand to a young lady, but, oddly enough, Connie smiled and seemed impressed.

"My, isn't this a coincidence," she said. She handed Rocco her card. Attorney At Law.

"I interned while I was in law school with McCarthy, Duffy, Neidhard and Snakard. One of the founding partners is John Duffy. He's the brother of Bill Duffy, the Deputy Superintendent of the Chicago Police Department. I used to have lunch with John and Bill. Bill used to talk about the Laborer's Union. I don't remember much about what he said, though."

Anything Bill Duffy would have said about the Laborer's Union would have been bad. Bill Duffy was, until he died in 1991, the most knowledgeable expert on organized crime in the history of the Chicago Police Department.

"How about dinner?" Rocco asked. "I like the Dining Room at the Ritz-Carlton. Do you?"

Connie had never been there, but she knew its reputation. She'd like to try it. But with this guy? On the other hand, he showed good taste. Connie was not a loose girl. Not in the least. But she was an attorney, she could handle herself. And, like any good lawyer, she had a spirit of adventure.

The date was made. Rocco Robustelli, the hood, had a date with Connie Constable, a nice girl. Connie kept a little bit back by telling Rocco that she'd like an early date because she had an early court date the next morning. She let Rocco know that the date was for dinner, not for anything else.

Rocco was a bachelor. His kids didn't look to him for much, if anything. His business was no longer in the southern suburbs. Although he was a Business Agent with Local 5, the position was a sham. He didn't need a place in South Holland. He had graduated from that. He had come a long way from working the State-Line strip joints and banging the head of a bookmaker.

Rocco decided to dump the hayseeds and move out of the

town where you couldn't even buy a drink on Sunday.

The more Rocco thought about it, the more he liked the idea of shedding South Holland and the staid life it represented. He needed something a lot closer to the things that occupied him now. Working for Gussie meant he had to attend Gussie's conferences every morning at ten. Trouble shooting as the underboss to Aiuppa meant he had to meet with Joey out west most every evening. Most of his day was spent all over Chicago.

Rocco Robust put his home on the south side of South Holland up for sale and began to look for something more suitable.

CHAPTER SEVENTEEN

An Exciting Year!

Their senior seasons continued great for Rick and Bob. Ricky led the Wildcats to their third consecutive PAC-10 championship and both were again eligible as the annual major league draft approached.

Ricky Robustelli had not been drafted on his two previous occasions. Now that he was again eligible, Richards questioned several major league scouts about his possibilities. Many of them shrugged their shoulders. Some winked, some smiled. Finally, Bill's relationship with Bob Prince, the veteran Chicago Cub scout, paid off.

"Bill," Prince said, "I'm not supposed to know. But, every time I hand in a report on Robustelli, it's clear that the Cubs aren't interested. I understand his dad is a mobster of some kind. You'd know more about that then I would. What I found out, Bill, is that Peter Ueberroth, the Commissioner of baseball, has blackballed Robustelli. Because of his father. He doesn't want any taint on "the game." He figures Rick would be influenced by his father and his father's friends. If anything ever happened where Rick made an error or threw a wild pitch in the clutch, suspicion would attach to him that he was dumping a game, that the gamblers had gotten to him through his dad. Ueberroth has issued a decree: Robustelli doesn't get drafted. He doesn't play pro ball."

Richards had suspected that Rick's parentage had something to do with it. He hated to learn that his suspicions were true, that the moguls of baseball were so prejudiced that they would prevent Rick from earning a living in a profession for which he was well equipped. He decided to try to do something about it.

Ten days before the draft, Bill called his pal, Jack Danahy in New York. A former FBI agent, Danahy was director of security for the National Football League and close to the director of security for the Major Leagues of Baseball. Danahy got him an appointment with Peter Ueberroth in New York.

Bill got right to the point.

"Mr. Commissioner, I'm here today as an FBI agent, but not in any official capacity. For years, I've been the coach of amateur ball clubs in Chicago. Among my players are four who have been drafted. One is my own son."

Peter Ueberroth broke in. "Yes, I know."

Bill knew Ueberroth ruled baseball with an iron hand. He took advise from his colleagues, especially from Joe Reichler, his director of public relations, and from the league presidents, and from most of the club owners, but, when push comes to shove, it was Ueberroth who made the final decision, sometimes against the consensus.

"Mr. Ueberroth, there is another young man, a fine young man, who I have coached since he was nine years old. I'm sure you've heard of him. Ricky Robustelli."

Ueberroth raised his eyebrows. He said nothing.

"I won't try to tell you what I think of his baseball abilities. I'm sure you know what the scouts have been telling you for years. Now I wouldn't be here to tell you he is a great young prospect. I'm here because I am the senior FBI agent on the organized crime squad of the FBI in Chicago, assigned to the investigation of Rick's father, Rocco Robustelli. I'm sure your director of security has been giving you reports on the father for years. I'm sure everything he says about Robust is accurate. He is the underboss of the Chicago mob. A bad guy. One of the worst. Right in the tradition of Al Capone. It's even possible that one day soon he will be the boss of the Chicago mob. I'm not trying to sugar-coat Ricky's father. I know him well. I've encountered him dozens of times. I've even traded punches with him. We are not friends and, when I say that, I'm understating the case. He's a killer. The very worst kind of human being. As I say, I'm not carrying any brief for Rocco Robust. But, I am here to argue for his son."

Bill paused, in an attempt to gauge the attitude of Ueberroth."

Ueberroth remained impassive, however. He said nothing. He was waiting for the next shoe to drop.

"Ricky Robustelli is as fine a young man as I have ever met or expect to meet. I have known him, as I say, since he was nine. He's been in my house a hundred times since then. My wife is like his mother since Rick's mother died when he was six or seven. I'm as close to him, and closer to him, then his father. His older sister is like our daughter. My son, Bill is very close to her. They both attend Arizona with Rick. Rick's closest friend is my son, Bob. Even though they attend different colleges, they grew up together and have played on the same team each summer since Little League, right through last summer when they were on the same team in the Cape Cod League. What I'm trying to say, Mr. Ueberroth, is that Ricky Robustelli is much closer to me and my family than he is to his father. I could go on and on with instances of the many good times we've shared together."

Ueberroth spoke, briefly, "I get the picture."

"Then I'll get to the bottom line. I will guarantee to you, with all the sincerity I possess as an FBI agent, as an old Marine, as a Notre Dame graduate, as a God-fearing man, that if Rocco Robustelli ever came to his son and suggested he dump a game or do anything inimical to the best interests of his team or "the game," baseball, that Ricky would spit in his face. The old man, Mr Ueberroth, has no hold on the boy. I'm not trying to be immodest, but in the interests of this situation, let me say, that I have much more influence over Ricky than his dad does, much more. Even without that, the boy is a man. He knows right from wrong. He's a practicing Catholic, unlike his father, attended parochial school, and I'm sure he's much more moral than 95% of the players who will be drafted next week."

Ueberroth remained silent.

Bill couldn't be sure whether he was having any influence on him.

"Let me say one more thing. The Cubs have the first choice in the draft next week. I understand they consider Rick the number one prospect in the draft. Let them pick Rick and I guarantee I'll stay close to him. I'll be in position to know if anybody in the Chicago mob tries to influence him—including his father. I'll work closely on this with your security staff. As I say, I'm the senior FBI agent on the organized crime squad in Chicago, have been there for years, and have no intention of taking any promotion which would take me off that squad. Listen, Mr. Commissioner, I know this kid and this situation better then anybody in the world. I think what you've got here is a unique opportunity. You've never had a mobster's son with so much baseball talent before. No mobster's son has ever been worthy of being drafted by baseball before. And when it happens, you've got the FBI agent, who knows him and his father like no one else in the world, going to bat for him and guaranteeing to you that the boy will be a credit to everybody in "the game."

Ueberroth stood up. "I'll take everything you say under advisement."

As Bill stood up, he threw one last shot. "You might talk to Jerry Kendall also, Mr. Ueberroth. There's another unique opportunity for you. Jerry Kendall is one of the all time great people in major league baseball. A real credit to the game. He's had Ricky for four years at the U.A. I know he's told your scouts that Rick is a great prospect. And a great person. Follow up what I've said about Ricky as a person who could resist anybody from the wrong side of the tracks. Ask him if he's ever seen Joe Bonanno or Bats Battaglia or Pete Licavoli or Pete Notaro or any of those hoods out there in Arizona hanging around Rick."

Bill left the offices of Ueberroth to taxi back to La Guardia. He had no way of knowing whether his presentation to Ueberroth had had any effect. He had gone out on a limb. The Bureau had not cleared his meeting with Ueberroth. Bill had done what he thought was right.

As he returned to Chicago, he hoped he would see the result of his trip to the Big Apple in the baseball draft the next week.

The *Chicago Sun Times* headline confirmed it. Ricky was the number one choice in the player draft, selected by the hometown Chicago Cubs. Bob joined him on the same team as a third round selection. Both were assigned to Geneva of the New York-Pennsylvania League, a Class A league located in the Finger Lakes area of New York.

Just as they had the previous summer on Cape Cod, Bill and Jeannie spent four weeks in the Finger Lakes cheering for the two kids. Ricky quickly established himself as the top pitching prospect in the league.

Once again, Robust arrived virtually unannounced, appearing in the stands during a game with Newark. Bill didn't spot him at first until Jeannie pointed him out.

Bill had wondered how he would react if Robust showed to watch his son play ball. He doubted he would react as he had in Cotuit. He had decided that if Rocco showed up in New York, he would put a tail on him to find out if he was attending to mob business. Bill had made arrangements in Chicago, before he left, to "fisur" Robust, physically surveill him, if he showed up.

The first few days produced nothing, but, on the third day, Bill hit paydirt. Tailing Robust, he was amazed to see a road sign announcing the town of Apalachin. My God, he thought to himself, this is where it all began!

Bill didn't recognize the two men who greeted Robust, but they were straight out of hoodlum central casting. When the trio entered a large mansion, Bill turned back to the small village and hustled to a pay phone. Dan Hogan, one of Bill's old handball partners, was now working in the Buffalo office of the FBI. Although Hogan couldn't get to Apalachin, he alerted the New York State Police at Vestal and asked them to rendezvous with Bill. Almost as soon as Bill returned to the estate, there were two cars of New York State Police. Bill thought one of them, a lieutenant, looked very familiar. He was. It was Edgar Croswell, the same trooper who had intercepted the first famous sit-down.

Croswell was the old hand at this. He identified the house as the home of Joe Barbara, the same house where the Apalachin meeting had taken place in 1957 and caused J. Edgar Hoover to initiate the Top Hoodlum Program.

"Let's just do what I did before, Richards. Let's just walk right in and break them up."

The local police actually have much more authority in situations like this than the federals. There certainly was no federal crime being committed here. In fact, there was no violation of any state law, but state law does gives peace officers the right to investigate situations of this nature. Not to arrest, but to make inquiry—to force their citizens to identify themselves and to explain the nature of their business.

Croswell sent two of his men around the back. Then he and Richards knocked on the front door. There was no response. Then they heard a shot from the back. And then another. They heard shouting. They rushed to the back. They found the two troopers had made a catch. Three swarthy looking guys had run out the back door. When they were ordered to stop, they had not heeded the command. Hence the shouts and the warning shots, fired into the air. The threesome had then come to a stop.

Richards and the troopers approached the men. Bill heard Robust hiss under his breath when he recognized his old foe, a long way from his beat in Chicago. "Fucking son of a bitch!"

Croswell recognized the other two men immediately.

"This guy here," he said, stabbing his finger into the chest of one, "is Stefano Magaddino, the boss of the LCN in Buffalo."

Then Croswell turned to the other figure. "And this guy here, this is Russell Bufalino, the LCN boss in Scranton." Robust was in some pretty august company.

Croswell ordered his men to keep an eye on the trio and gestured to Bill.

"What do you want to do? We don't have much authority to do anything here. These guys were peacefully meeting, committing no crimes."

"Nothing you can do, at all?" Bill asked.

"Well, we could probably bring them in for investigation. They did fail to follow the orders of a police officer when they ran after being ordered to stop. That's what we did last time. Then we convened a grand jury and put questions to them about the nature of their meeting. When they took the Fifth, refused to answer, they were held in contempt of the grand jury. But their convictions were overthrown on appeal. I'm afraid we can't do that again."

Bill bowed to Croswell's judgement. He had no jurisdiction here.

"Well, I would appreciate it if you would do what you can. If you feel you have enough authority here to at least take them to your headquarters, even if that's all, that's fine with me. It's your deal."

Croswell nodded. He stepped forward. "OK, we're taking you mugs to the slammer."

All three detainees set up a loud protest. Robust carried it the furthest. He was by far the youngest of the group, with the others being in their seventies. "Fuck that!" he shouted. "No fucking way! You got no right! We're minding our own business. Sitting in a house, having a cordial drink of wine together. What law have we violated?"

He had a good point. But Bill had little patience with this self-acclaimed tough guy. It didn't take Bill long to lose his cool when confronting Rocco Robustelli. "Rocco, you better do what the man says. And do it fast! You're a convicted felon. You better obey orders if you know what's good for you!"

Bill didn't know what being a convicted felon might have to do with it, but he had made to do with what he had—he had thrown the best shot he had. Which wasn't much.

"Fuck you, Richards! You're harassing me! You always do! You're lucky you're standing! You think you're such a fucking hot shot. Think because you used to be a half ass fighter you can push people around! Fuck you, Richards! Fuck you!"

Bill, realizing what weak ground he was on, had the good sense not to respond to the taunts. Very quietly, he pushed up to Robust. "You're not in Chicago now, Rocco, not with fifteen henchmen around to help you. You threw a punch at me once before. We've got witnesses here. You want to throw another one, right now? I'm sure everybody here would allow you. Step back, troopers, let this man have some room. Let's see how tough he is."

The troopers gave Rocco room. For a moment it looked like he would throw a punch as he had on Cape Cod a summer before. Robust stood his ground for a few moments. Then he uttered what now seemed to be his motto: "Fuck you, Richards!" He turned his back.

With that, Croswell stepped forward.

"OK, men, lets take them in."

Robust, Magaddino and Bufalino were marched into the state police cars and driven to Vestal.

The New York State Police couldn't keep Rocco detained for long. When Geneva played Oneonta that evening, Bill saw Robust in the stands. He laughed. Robust was actually thumbing his nose at him.

Richards knew that the antagonism between Rocco Robustelli and himself was becoming more and more dangerous. Robust wasn't the most stable guy in the world. Push him too much and his instability would lead to an explosion more powerful than plastic explosive under a car's floor mat. Discretion might be the better part of valor as this "relationship" went on!

When the best prospects in the Cub organization were brought to the instructional league in the fall, both Ricky and Bob were invited.

It had been an exciting year—for everyone.

CHAPTER EIGHTEEN

To The Top

When Rocky Robust returned to Chicago from his experience at Apalachin, he found a changing guard there. The FBI had convicted Allen Dorfman, and Joey Aiuppa and Jackie Cerone had also gone down.

Obviously, the income to the Chicago Outfit was diminished. When Rocco got the call to meet with Tony Accardo, he had a good idea of what it might entail.

"Rocco," Batters began, "we're in a hell of a shape. Some of the guys want me to come back one more time and run things. I say to hell with that. I've done it twice, that's enough for anybody. Besides I'm in my late seventies, I don't have the energy anymore to get involved every day. So I'm going to stay just like I am. The consiglieri."

Robust waited for the other shoe to drop. If Accardo was not coming back, Robust knew who might be tabbed to take the top spot.

Accardo continued. "So I've talked it over with Gussie. He don't want back up top again either. He'll continue as the boss of the connection guys. He's got Pat Marcy and John D'Arco working with him now and Joey Glimco to handle labor. You have been handling a lot of that, but we're gonna divorce you from that now."

Rocky felt he knew why.

He was right.

"So, Rocco, congratulations. You're the new boss."

Accardo smiled and reached out his right hand to Robust. He grabbed Rocco by the shoulder with his left. It was as simple as that. Rocco Robustelli was now a successor to Al Capone! It was a nice feeling.

Now he would have to line up a crew. He picked Joe Ferriola as his underboss and kept Vince Solano as the capo of the north side. He didn't want a fight with Al Tocco, so he left him in the southern suburbs. He let Ferriola keep the west side, the Loop and what was left on the south side. Rocco kept Jerry Scarpelli, Gino Martini and Patsy Padrone close. They were his palace guard. Whenever he needed something in particular he could call on them. They were proven.

Rocky decided to establish a headquarters downtown. In the Loop—where all the action was. His first inclination was to find a good spot on La Salle Street. But he immediately realized the implications. Too busy, too many people who would not only recognize him but anybody who he might call in. No good.

Then it became obvious. State Street. What had been for decades "that great street." It no longer was. If Robust were to establish his headquarters on State Street, in the Loop, he would be well located. It seemed the ideal location.

Rocco reconnoitered State Street. He found his location across the street from two of the most famous landmarks in Chicago: the clocks of Marshall Field's.

Probably be a good spot for a haberdashery, he thought. Robust had to have a "beard." He couldn't put up a sign: Headquarters of the Chicago Mob.

Robust reached out for Benson Duglash. Benson had been a first class clothing store owner on the north shore, with a chain of stores in several of the best suburbs up there. However, Benson Duglash had over expanded. In need of money, he had to eventually go to the mob. Now, the mob owned his stores—and him. Benson Duglash lost everything.

Robust put it to Duglash. Open up a Benson Duglash across from Marshall Field's on State Street. Put in a line of top clothing. Duglash protested. State Street was no place for a Benson Duglash store. Who would venture there in search of top men's fashion? Rocky Robustelli gave Benson Duglash his best look. "Mr. Duglash. What position do you think you're in today? Maybe thirty years ago, but not today. I'm giving you a proposition. Open up and operate a Benson Duglash store on State and I give you $750 a week. No matter what you sell, what profit you make. You in position to turn that down?"

Rock had his new headquarters. The sign read "Benson Duglash's Gentlemen's Attire." Suits started at $1,000 and went up from there.

Robust spent almost as much money on the back of the store as he did on the rest. An expensive cherrywood bar ran along one side of the room. A large cherrywood desk stood on the other side. The long Thomasville sofa on another wall was big enough for six large bodies. Large Henredon easy chairs filled the room covered with inch deep Karastan carpeting. The office was sound proofed and Rocco installed a buzzer and security system. Rock would be warned of any suspicious entrants and would inspect them through a peep-hole in his "office" door. He stocked the bar with the best: Chivas Regal, Absolut, Heiniken and Beck's. But also with Old Style. There would be some of his guests who would still be mired in the old tradition.

Now Rocco looked for a new home. His real estate agent out in South Holland had gotten a nice bid and Rocco would make a nice profit.

Rocco settled on Outer Drive East, a nicely located condo building overlooking Lake Michigan. Since walking was part of Rock's exercise regimen, he could walk from Gentlemen's Attire to Outer Drive East. And Outer Drive East has the Riviera Club, a fitness center with a pool under a bubble along Lake Shore Drive.

Rocco Robustelli was flying high. It was all his. Occasionally he had thoughts of Bill Richards and the loss of his son and daughter's respect, but those were only occasional low spots.

Rocco Robustelli was king of the Al Capone domain. Pretty heady stuff for a young Italian boy from The Patch.

And he had only just begun!

CHAPTER NINETEEN

Accardo Learns!

It was through Jack Brickhouse, one of the most respected men in Chicago, that Tony Accardo learned that Bill Richards had done a favor for the son of Rocky Robust.

Jack Brickhouse had been the voice of the Chicago White Sox and then the Chicago Cubs for more than forty years. When Peter Ueberroth was opportuned by Bill Richards to take away the restriction which blackballed the drafting of Ricky Robustelli, he counseled not only with the ownership of the major league team, but with those involved in media relations. It was natural that he should turn to Jack Brickhouse. Brickhouse knew Chicago. He didn't know Rocco Robust, of course, but he was familiar with the territory and the players.

Brickhouse had always had problems with a baseball blacklist. Major league baseball was not the gaming industry. Nevada might have its "black book" of excluded persons from casinos, but not major league baseball. It seemed a dangerous precedent. Brickhouse advised that Bill Richards had given "the game" its perfect out.

"Anything ever goes wrong, now or whenever, all we're got to do is let it out that the top FBI agent in Chicago came to us and was a character witness for the kid—endorsed him and strongly urged us not to blacklist him. I've checked into this Richards. He's very reputable here in Chicago. He's our perfect buffer, not a scapegoat really, but our out. How can we not recognize what he's recommending to us? Something goes wrong down the line, Richards is the guy we can throw up to cushion us."

It seemed like good advice. Ueberroth took it. Ricky

Robustelli was deemed to be as eligible as any other young prospect. His playing ability was the only criteria and Ricky was drafted – on the first pick.

And the information began to funnel down.

Alderman Ed Burke is a former seminarian, a former police-man, and highly respected. One evening Ed Burke was at a party thrown by Tom Carey, of the race-track Carey family. Stopping in for a short time was Jack Brickhouse. In idle chatter, Brickhouse mentioned the Robustelli situation to Burke. After all, it was not a secret that Robustelli had been drafted. It was the talk of Chicago, good chatter for cocktail parties. What Brickhouse had to add was that Robustelli had been blacklisted, but that Peter Ueberroth had taken down the barrier because a senior FBI agent, Bill Richards, had recommended that he do so. Brickhouse didn't consider the information confidential and it seemed a good idea to get it out for the good of "the game".

In the same spirit, Alderman Burke mentioned it to his fel-low council member, Fred Roti, alderman of the First Ward. Roti passed it on to the mob's man in the Regular Democratic Organi-zation of the First Ward, Pat Marcy. Pat Marcy immediately sped to his mentor, Gussie Alex, with the inside information. Alex in turn took it to his boss, Tony Accardo.

It was at this point that Tony Accardo, perplexed as to why Bill Richards, of all people, would want to do something for Rocco Robust, called Robust to the sit-down in the alcove at Meo's.

Accardo sat alone in the alcove, perplexed.

What an unusual situation!

"The FBI agent who is out front for the G in the fight against us guys is like a second father to the son of our boss? When has anything like this ever happened before?" Accardo has been around since Al Capone. Nothing close to this had ever cropped up before. This was one situation Joe Batters had not had an answer for. He thought he was too old to hear new stories.

What had finally assured him that the incident was not serious enough to cut down his protege, was the hatred Robust expressed

for Richards. It was obvious that Richard's act on his son's behalf
had infuriated Robust, who was himself powerless. Ricky Robustelli
wanted only one thing in the world—to play professional baseball.
His father not only could not give it to him, but was an obstacle.
Not only couldn't Robust help his son, he was the reason Rick had
been outlawed. Through no fault whatsoever of the boy.

Richards had managed to influence the commissioner of
baseball to drop the ban. And Robust had been the one to cripple
Richards?

Accardo had been unaware of Robust's actual physical en-
counters with Richards until Robust informed him during the
meeting. However, it solidified Accardo's opinion that this unique
situation did not require that he ease Robust from his position on
top the Chicago mob.

He had left the matter status quo. He had selected Robust to
succeed himself; he had to continue to show confidence in him.

But Joe Batters had not survived for forty years for nothing. He
would keep an eye on Robustelli, to see what might develop.

And whether the mob could profit by it.

PART TWO

CHAPTER TWENTY

Corny But Nice.

Connie Constable had been courted before. After all she was a most attractive Oak Park girl. Sharp, personable, intelligent, and an attorney.

This courtship, however, was unusual. The man she had met in the dentist's office in Oak Park was different. The morning after their meeting a large basket of flowers had arrived in her office. The card read "Hope those beautiful teeth are feeling better today." A few days later, an hour or so before she was to leave to keep their date in the Dining Room of the Ritz-Carlton, a beautiful orchid corsage had arrived.

I didn't know some gentlemen were so old fashioned, she thought.

When she arrived at the Dining Room, located on the upper floor of the hotel, Tony Tontini, the maitre d', left his podium and greeted her.

"Miss Constable, welcome to the Dining Room! We are so happy to have you with us tonight! Mr. Robustelli is anxiously awaiting your arrival."

It was all quite nice. The table was obviously the best one in the house, tucked away close to a waterfall. She was swept towards the table. Jackie O'Shea, the pianist for the evening, broke off from the piece she had been playing and played, very loudly, "Miss America," and then, as she was being seated, "A Pretty Girl Is Like a Melody." O'Shea had been retained by Robust just for the evening.

It was a little too much. But also quite nice.

The meal was outstanding. Tony Tontini employed the top

chefs in Chicago and her host had outdone himself preparing for the evening. He was as gracious a gentlemen as she had even dated. She was used to elegance. Nobody from Oak Park would be so corny as this man, but it was nice to be treated so graciously.

Rocco Robustelli was nice. He was, of course, on his best behavior.

I've been with a lot of broads in my life, he thought to himself. This girl is a real lady. I'm going to treat her like I think a lady should be treated.

Rocco's concept of how a lady should be treated was a little old fashioned, but it had the right effect.

Connie Constable was impressed. Probably more than she should have been. She had had a tough day in court and the prospects were that she would have another the next day. She was defending a negligence case, a personal injury action where her client had obviously been at fault, had had a few drinks and had run his car through a stop sign and hit another car, slightly injuring the elderly lady who was driving. Connie had wanted to settle, but her client had refused. A wealthy young man from Highland Park, he had the idea that he was above the law—at least a little. He was, therefore, hard to deal with. She had a loser on her hands and she knew it. The respite at the Ritz Carlton had come precisely at the right time. She should be back in the office, preparing the testimony for the next day, but she had little evidence to present. Besides, this client didn't deserve any better. He was wrong and she knew it. So did he. She would do her best to charm the jury the next day. Since she was good at that, the client would get more than he deserved.

The interlude at the Ritz came just at the right moment in Connie's life. She had been courted by several nice young men in her life time and was now 27. Virginal, but not a virgin, she had learned by this stage in her life how nice it was to be with a man. But she was selective. Her choices hadn't been many and had been top of the line, first class. Rocco Robustelli was not what she had heretofore considered "top of the line."

He has his good points. He was good looking, well dressed and had a presence about himself. He had gone way out of his way to demonstrate to her that she was something special. He was a good conversationalist, although not the most articulate man she had ever dated. He had a certain rough way about him, but he had a nice sense of humor and the evening was a very pleasant one.

Connie Constable had had a very pleasant time. As they left the Dining Room, Jackie O'Shea swung once more into her entry song. "There She Goes, Miss America." Again, corny, but again, quite nice. The other patrons looked up from their meal, paused in their conversations and smiled in her direction. They didn't recognize her, but figured she was someone special. And perhaps she was a Miss America; she was certainly being treated like one.

All in all she was impressed. However, the evening wasn't over yet. As Connie and Rocco exited from the elevator from the lobby at the Ritz to the ground floor, they were greeted by a sharp looking young man, not in uniform but very nicely dressed. He tipped his hat to the couple, was greeted by Rocco as "Gino" and escorted them to the street outside to a beautiful grey stretch limousine. Inside was a television screen and bar.

"One last nightcap, Connie," Rocco intoned. He then spoke to "Gino."

"The lady would like to go home." He looked at her, not knowing where that was, but keeping to their bargain that this evening was not to be elongated.

"Sandburg Village," Connie said. When they arrived, Rocco jumped out of the car and held the door for Connie.

"This was truly a nice night," he told her. "I'd like to call you tomorrow to see if you enjoyed it and to see if we can have another." He had quickly indicated that he intended to make no move on her that evening and that he looked forward to another time.

"I'll be in court most of the day. But I'll be back in my office around four," she said as she hurried into her building, smiling at the doorman and hustling up to her twelfth floor apartment.

Later, as she passed a mirror while readying herself for sleep, Connie Constable caught herself smiling.

Connie had known that evening that when Rocco called the

next afternoon she would respond favorably. That evening was the first of several. During none of them had Rocco "gotten fresh," as they say in his neighborhood. He was taking his time for the first time of his life. This was not just a piece of fluff; this was a lady—a lady who might be out of his league. But Rocco Robust had never felt that anything was really "out of his league."

Connie Constable soon realized that Rocco was serious. And that she enjoyed his attentions. He was acting the gentleman, taking her to the best places in Chicago: the Consort Room, Eli's, Morton's, Arnie's, the Empire Room and The French Quarter. They even went to the boisterous places on occasion, like Harry Carey's and Ditka's.

Finally, during an evening at the Moulin Rouge, Rocco had taken her into his arms. She found she liked being there. She found that she was stirred. That night, as they left the elegant lobby of the Fairmount, and, as the ever-present "Gino" escorted them to Rocco's stretch limo, Rocco said something different.

"My home, Gino."

Connie was suitably impressed. The penthouse at Outer Drive East was done very, very nicely. Rocco has employed Jane Molson of Lake Shore Refinements as a decorator and it had overwhelmed most of the "broads" Rocco had brought home. It didn't overwhelm Connie—but she was impressed.

Rocco went to the stereo. "A little Caruso?" he asked. Connie smiled. A little corny, but in keeping with Rocco's manner.

Rocco motioned her to sit on the sofa and took her in his arms. A hug. And then a kiss. First a short one. Then a longer one. Then his hand was on her knee. Stirring, she responded. Not exactly in kind, but enough to let him know she wasn't resisting. Then the corniest trick in the book. He actually picked her up and carried her into the bedroom—to the most enormous bed Connie had ever seen. Cornier yet, it was a four poster. He laid her down and lay down beside her. He was sweet and gentle. It was slow. And measured. And cautious. It went on for a long time. Until Rocco was sure she was satisfied. Not until then did the real Rocco Robustelli come forth. And then it was hard. And sure. And big.

When it was over, Connie Constable lay back. Exhausted. Although she had not been overanxious, she had waited a long time for this. It had been well worth waiting for. Rocco Robust was something else!

After a while, Connie got up.

Rocco opened his eyes, "Want to spend the night here?"

"No, I better not. What would 'Gino' think?"

Rocco smiled at that. He knew what "Gino" would think.

Connie seemed determined to go and Rocco wondered how she had taken it. She seemed to be pleased, but, of course, he couldn't be sure. One thing he knew. She hadn't faked it. He could feel that. He dressed and escorted her down the elevator, out to the lobby where "Gino" was waiting to take her back to her apartment.

When she arrived home, Connie went to her full length mirror. She looked at herself.

"Well, young lady, you're something else. Where do you think you're heading?" It was a good question.

CHAPTER TWENTY ONE

The Commission Sit-Down

When Rocco became the boss of the Chicago family, he soon journeyed to Fort Lee, New Jersey, as an automatic member of the Commission, the ruling nationwide body of La Cosa Nostra.

Accompanying him on this first venture to a meeting of the Commission was a man who was no stranger to such sit-downs. Tony Accardo had been to a dozen Commission meetings since he first represented Chicago in 1945.

The nature of the sit-down was to plot La Cosa Nostra's plans for a major casino at Lake Tahoe. It was a major move. In 1977, after New Jersey voters had approved the referendum authorizing gambling in Atlantic City, the members of the Commission had granted the eastern mobs the rights to make what they could on an exclusive basis in Atlantic City. The Boardwalk was theirs. In return, Chicago was granted exclusive access to Las Vegas, except for those casinos "grandfathered in." The five New York families, the Philadelphia family, the Patriarca family of Boston, and the DeCalvacante family of New Jersey were given Atlantic City to make what they could of it.

Because of the strict regulation of the Casinos, however, the eastern mobs had been unable to make a nice thing for themselves along the Boardwalk. They were disillusioned with their pact with Chicago. They were offering a compromise proposal. Chicago would keep Las Vegas. But, since Nevada had toughened up in recent years, and had become a tough place for the mobs to infiltrate, the Commission wanted to make an end-run around Las Vegas.

In preliminary caucuses, the Commission had decided to invade Lake Tahoe, a beautiful spot located beneath the Sierra Nevada mountains. John Gotti, the boss of the powerful Gambino family in New York, had made the proposal.

Robust and Joe Batters arrived at LaGuardia and taxied to the Plaza Hotel. It was Accardo's favorite New York hostelry. Joe thought it might be his last trip to New York and he intended to enjoy it.

Accardo found a message waiting in his suite: Meet me down the street in the Jockey Club at six. The message was unsigned, but Accardo and Robust knew that John Gotti was requesting that they meet him before the sit-down. John Gotti had risen to power after his predecessor, Paulie Castellano, had been ambushed outside a Manhattan restaurant, Sparks Steak House.

The Chicago duo walked the block and a quarter to the Jockey Club and found Gotti, surrounded by bodyguards. In Chicago there was no real need for bodyguards. Drivers, but not really bodyguards. Chicago was a one-mob town. There has never been a gangland slaying in Chicago not sanctioned by the top. Chicago mob bosses walk their streets with impunity—unlike their New York brethren.

Gotti wanted a caucus before the Commission meeting the next day. If he could reach an understanding with Accardo and Robust before the sit-down then it would go much smoother when all the dons met.

Gotti welcomed the visitors from the Windy City to the Big Apple and inquired about their flight and accommodations.

"Got some snatch lined up here or do you want me to fix you up?" he asked Rocco.

In the society of the Gambino's, it was the polite thing to ask. Knowing how his mentor, Accardo, felt about such activity, especially when there was business to be done, Rocco declined the offer.

"What do I call you, Rocco or Robust or what?"

Robust shrugged. It didn't matter much to him; this guy was never going to be a major actor in his life.

"Anything. Joe calls me Rocco or Rock. That's good."

"OK, Joe and Rock. Here's what I want to talk to you about. How do you guys feel about our proposal? Let me make it clear." Gotti leaned forward, very seriously. This was major for his interests. Skim from a casino was all-important. After their agreement with Chicago in 1977, the Gambinos and the others had gotten the short end of the stick. Now they wanted to recoup.

"Here's what we are proposing," Gotti resumed. "The Nevada gaming authority is zeroed in on you guys in Las Vegas. There's where 70% of the action out there in Nevada is and so that's where they're focusing. Fuck Las Vegas. You guys got what you want there, keep it. But let us into Tahoe. We done a reality study there, a feasibility study as our lawyers call it, and it looks like we could sneak in there. There is room for one more big hotel there. They got those four big ones on the south shore and a couple like the Hyatt in Incline Village and the Cal-Neva on Crystal Bay on the north shore. But there is room for another. Let us have it."

Joe and Rocky knew this was Gotti's opening gambit. They knew he was not serious that Chicago, having gotten the whole state of Nevada in the 1977 accord, would now give it up without consideration. They merely smiled at Gotti. Neither responded.

After almost a minute had gone by, Gotti opened up again. "Why not? You guys got nothing at the Lake. You dogs in the mangers or something? You don't go in there, but you won't let anybody else either?"

Joe Batters spoke up for the first time. "John, we have done our own study at Lake Tahoe. Don Angelini, our capo in charge of the west, has been encouraging us to go in. We're just waiting for the right spot at the right time. You go in there and it shuts us out. There ain't room for more than one more big joint there. You take it and that's it. No way."

Gotti had expected this response. He knew he wasn't going to get Lake Tahoe for the Gambinos without some concessions. But he had thrown his best shot. Now he would get serious.

"OK, I can understand that. I'll make a big compromise for you. Show you I ain't no pig. Let's make it a joint venture. You put up whatever share you want in the joint and we'll put up what we want. Up to fifty percent each. We go 50-50 if you want or, if you want less, that's fine too. But not more than 50%. How about it?"

Accardo and Robust had already come to a meeting of the minds with each other. A "joint venture" was just what they wanted. They had decided, in discussions before they had journeyed to New York, that a perfect solution would be to diminish the extent of their jeopardy in building yet another major hotel at The Lake. Now Gotti was proposing the eastern mobs put up at least half the cash needed. The spider had fallen into the web. Accardo and Robust didn't even glance at each other.

Finally Accardo spoke up. "John, we'd like to help you guys out. We know things haven't gone well for you in Atlantic City and you got nothing anywhere else to skim. Tell you what. Rocco and I will talk about it tonight and tomorrow we'll let you know. You put it on the table tomorrow. Rocco and I will see if we can't accommodate you."

They left it at that. Gotti remained behind to pick up the tab and worry about whether his three bodyguards were alert. Joe Batters and Robust walked back, unescorted, to the Plaza. They really had nothing to discuss. Gotti has proposed just what they wanted. All they had to do was be a little condescending tomorrow and pretend they were being nice guys by letting the east into their west.

The Commission sit down, held in an old roadhouse near Fort Lee in New Jersey, didn't last long. As long as it did, however, agreement was reached.

John Gotti, the most powerful of the New York mobsters, spoke to his conferees.

"I met with Mr. Accardo and Rocco here, his new boss, last night on Central Park South. I put it to them what we agreed on. That they can have whatever percentage of our joint at Lake Tahoe they want, up to 50% if they give us the right to come into Nevada."

"Whoa, John!" Robust spoke up. It was time to show his fellow commissioners that he was running Chicago—with Joe Batters permission, of course.

"Back up there, just a minute. First of all, we have no agreement on that. You presented it to us. We have taken it under advisement. And second, come into Nevada? We're talking strictly
Lake Tahoe. Not the rest of Nevada. That is reserved for us, all of
it. If we let you into Lake Tahoe, that's the limit. And we are a long
way from giving you the Lake."

Gotti leaned forward. "You mean you ain't gonna go along with
what I put to you last night?"

"No, we're not." Rocco stated.

Accardo was surprised. But he let his protege do the talking;
he wanted to see what he had up his sleeve.

Robust continued, "Here's what we will go for. Nothin' else.
We put up 35% of the cash. For that we get 51% of the hotel."

The eastern mob leaders screamed, "No fuckin' way!"

Later, Accardo was proud of his younger successor. The final
deal had not been his idea; he had not thought of it. But it was a
good one. Chicago would put up 51% of the cash, for which they
got 51% of the control. Enough to give Chicago the final say so.
They allowed New York to name the hotel manager, usually the top
spot. But Chicago, very knowledgeable about how the skim works,
would name the casino manager. Then they would alternate the
pick of the shift bosses, the pit bosses, the head of security, the
floormen, the stickmen, the slot managers and the rest of the casino
employees.

Robust started to recommend a location for the hotel, on the
south shore, in accordance with a feasibility study by Don Angelini,
but one of Gotti's thugs interrupted.

"Boss, there's a couple suspicious cars out there. I think it's
the G!"

God damn! thought Robust. These assholes screw everything up! Seems like every time we meet in their territory we get
busted up!

The mobsters scrambled and into their cars before the Bureau
agents were quite in place. Unfamiliar with the territory, however,
Joe Batters and Rocky Robust got lost in Harlem.

Robust was driving. As he got to the corner of Amsterdam

Avenue and 125th Street he had no idea where he was. He turned north when he should have turned south, back toward Manhattan. He soon realized that they were not near the Plaza on Central Park South. They finally spotted one of New York's finest who jerked his thumb in the right direction.

Two dumb fuckin' ginzos, the cop thought.

Joe Batters and Rocky Robust had won their day with the eastern mobs. But the mob venture in Lake Tahoe was off to a bumbling start.

CHAPTER TWENTY TWO

The Tahoe Summit.

Rocky Robust shifted his base of operations —on a part time basis—to Lake Tahoe. Countering John Gotti and his involvement in the planning, construction and casting of the key employees at the new hotel-casino, Robust decided to protect his interests. He himself spent a great deal of time at the Lake. He had his capo in charge of the Chicago mob's interests in the west, Donald Angelini, with him at all times, but he himself was the major player.

The hotel, rising above any other structure at the Lake, was called The Tahoe Summit. It was in a prime location, looking out over the lake itself and over the Sierra Nevada Mountains. It was ideal.

Although busy, Robust found he was lonely. He had developed a real attachment for Connie Constable and found that he missed her. He had never before let a woman intrude into his thoughts. He banged them, one "broad" after another, for years, but he had never had one get under his skin like Connie had. He cajoled Connie to come to Tahoe and spend weekends with him in his condo in the Tahoe Seasons Resort at Heavenly Valley, just a mile or so from the construction of the Summit. His suite on the top floor included a spa, wet bar, fireplace and a great view of the lake.

He insisted that Connie visit often and she did. Both enjoyed life at the Lake. Robust guessed that "this must be love." Connie loved to hike around the Lake, smelling the fresh scent of the pine trees and the fresh air. She found the ambiance an aphrodisiac. Love making which she had found so enjoyable in Chicago was now much more enjoyable under the pines in Rocky's condo.

But the visits to Tahoe perked Connie's curiosity about Rocco's background. She began to wonder just who he was. Supposedly a business agent for the Laborer's Union, what was he doing in Nevada overseeing the construction of a hotel and casino? From what she could tell from the papers and blueprints scattered around the condo, he seemed to be highly involved.

On her return to Chicago, Connie called John Duffy, the partner at her old law firm, and asked him if he could have lunch with her. She laid her affair with Rocco Robustelli on the line and asked him for information. It wasn't long before she received a call from his brother, Bill Duffy, deputy superintendent of the Chicago Police Department.

When Bill Duffy arrived at her law offices, he questioned her about Robust. He indicated a great interest in her lover. At first, she was quite forthcoming, but, finally, it was her turn to ask some questions. Why was Duffy so interested in Rocco Robustelli, the union man? Bill Duffy leveled with her. Rocco Robustelli was not a union man. Rocco Robustelli was the boss of the Chicago mob.

After Bill Duffy left, Connie berated herself. How stupid could she be? She was supposed to be an intelligent lawyer. She should have put two and two together long before this!

Did she love the guy? She knew she would miss him terribly if she ended the affair. She thought about him much of her time. She knew she enjoyed being with him. She already missed him when he was at Lake Tahoe. When she added it all together, Connie knew that she did love Rocco Robustelli.

She decided to put it to him. That Friday, when she arrived at the airport in Reno, Rocco hugged her and kissed her.

"Want to go down to the Pub-In-The-Pines?"

"No," Connie replied. "I've got something serious I want to discuss with you. We can do it better at home."

At the suite, Rocco threw his coat on the sofa, "What's up?"

"I understand you are the Al Capone of Chicago these days."

Robust froze. He had known that one day she would learn. He had contemplated telling her in his own way, on his own terms, at an appropriate time. Now he wished he had.

"Tell me what you're talking about," he asked, turning towards her.

She leveled with him. "Rocco, I began to question all this. That you are a labor leader. So I went to my old senior partner, John Duffy. Then I got a visit from his brother, Bill Duffy. He told me. All of it."

"Fucking son of a bitch, no good cop!" It was the first time Robust had ever used profane language in front of Connie. She began to realize that there was another side of Rocco she hadn't seen.

"It doesn't matter what *he* is," Connie stated, very quietly. "It's what *you* are."

"Sit down, Connie," Robust said, also quietly. "Calm down. It's time, I guess."

"You admit it?" Connie asked.

"Admit it? Admit what? You'd think it's a crime. Have they ever convicted me of 'being the Al Capone' of Chicago?"

"Rocco, I'm an attorney. Don't try that on me. I'm told you are the boss of the Chicago Crime Syndicate. Now, without any equivocation, is that true or is it not true?"

"Connie, in Chicago there are a bunch of us gamblers who have joined together, loosely, to form an association. Recently they made me the head. That's all there is to it." Rocco hoped this would pacify his lover.

It didn't. "A group of gamblers? Rocco, I didn't just get off the boat. Have you forgotten that I practice law in Chicago. What do you take me for? I'd hope you'd give me more credit for intelligence than that!"

Rocco decided he had better put it on the line.

"OK, Connie. Let's say that what your new friend, the great Bill Duffy, says is true. What difference does this make to our relationship?"

"I don't know," Connie replied. "But if it were true, I'd have to give it a lot of thought."

"I accept you for what you are, Connie. Why can't you accept me for whatever I might be. We've known each other for some time now. We get along just fine. We're right for each other. Why change anything now because some cop tells you something about me. You're a big girl. Can't you evaluate people for yourself? You've got to have somebody you hardly know decide what's right for you? And what is not right? I'm my own man, Connie. And yours. What difference does it make if I'm a member of some club? I'm the same guy you've grown to know for months?"

It was a long speech for Robust. He was arguing for something he really wanted. His experience as a connection guy was holding him in good stead.

Connie was born and raised in the Chicago area. She practiced law on La Salle Street. She wasn't a novice when it came to the facts of life in Chicago. She knew that it was probably true. Rocco hadn't denied it. Rocco knew enough not to let her know anything about himself or his business which might be incriminating. He hadn't admitted it because he wasn't stupid. He didn't want to put Connie in jeopardy from the law—or the mob.

Connie, being an attorney, understood that. She had not, therefore, expected Rocco to "cop out" to her. She had thought all that out when she planned to confront Rocco. She had decided to judge him by his demeanor, by his reaction. If he behaved like a kid caught with his fingers in the cookie jar, she could add two and two and come up with four. She had. She was sleeping with the mob! With its boss yet!

Connie walked into the bedroom and closed the door. This was the biggest crisis of her young life.

Robust left her alone. He had expected this moment. It was inevitable that Connie would eventually learn of the business of her lover. Actually, it was a long time coming. If she hadn't been so busy with her work or was the type to gossip with her friends, it would have come out a long time ago. He was surprised she hadn't noticed anything in the Chicago papers, but he had been lucky.

After a half hour, Connie opened the bedroom door.

"Rocco, I'm not going to stay here this weekend. I'm going back to Chicago. I've got to think this out."

"OK, Babe. But give it a chance. Think it out. Remember

how good it's been. Give us a chance."

Two weeks went by before Connie received a call from Rocco.

"I'm coming into Chicago tomorrow. How about meeting me for dinner at The Dining Room?" Connie had expected the call. She didn't play it coy. She agreed.

This time there was no fuss. Jackie O'Shea was not there to play "Miss America." There were no flowers or corsage. Only the same table by the waterfall. Rocco was already there. He stood as she approached and smiled. Hesitantly.

She smiled back. Faintly. He didn't offer to hug or kiss her. He had already ordered a vodka gimlet and now signaled to the captain to bring Connie an Absolut gimlet.

The conversation was desultory.

"How have you been?"

"How's it going?"

"You look great."

"You look good too."

After dinner, Rocco leaned forward as he did when things got serious and asked, "Well, have you made any decisions about us?"

It was direct and to the point.

Up until that moment, Connie had been unsure. She had leaned one way and then the other. The phrase, "sleeping with the mob" had taunted her. It was a crude way of phrasing it, but it seemed to fit her situation.

Connie looked into Rocco's eyes. They had never looked so sorrowful. They were like puppy eyes, big and brown, and slightly incongruous on a mob boss.

"Rocco, I don't know if I truly love you or not. But I must. I despise what you do for a living. But I find I can't give you up."

She had said it. She cast her eyes down. She didn't want him to see the tears.

Rocco took her hand in his. He tilted her head up. "Baby," he said, "I'm glad. I don't know what I would have done if you had said no."

That was it. The rest of the evening in the Dining Room was two friends, two lovers really, catching up on lost time. The Tahoe

Summit was proceeding nicely, he told her. There were no labor problems. She caught the joke.

That night, in Rocco's condo, the loving was as good as the first night. A little better perhaps, since both had discovered things the other liked best.

Perhaps the tough time was over for both of them.

The Tahoe Summit was completed.

For the opening, Rocco insured that only the best high-rollers were invited and the best entertainment retained. Frank Sinatra opened the main showroom, The Blue Room, named after the Lake itself. The casino was as large as three football fields. In the smaller showroom, called The Deep, a great girl-extravaganza was presented. Rocco, after consultation with Sinatra, employed Donn Arden from Las Vegas as a consultant and retained the most beautiful girls available.

Most important of all, Rocco was able to implement a great potential for the skim. With John Gotti and the eastern partners, he hired a former Metro lieutenant from Las Vegas as the chief of security. George Strickland knew exactly where his bread was buttered and would insure that his men kept strangers out when the skim was going down. Billy Cardwell and Tom Sheldon, masters of the art of skim in Las Vegas, were hired to practice their art at the Summit. The cameras, the eyes in the sky, were set so there was one hole in their coverage – one spot in the casino where drop boxes from under the tables could be waylaid and milked enroute to the counting room.

A practice run was made to initiate the skim. The first night the skim amounted to almost $100,000, portending nice rewards to come.

The opening of The Tahoe Summit was a great success, topping anything that had been seen before in the area. It promised to be a real money maker for the mobs. Rocco Robust would claim most of the glory from the operation – and many of the rewards.

One of the first rewards was Rocco's penthouse in The Tahoe Summit. He turned the job of decorating it over to Connie.

"I don't care what it costs, just don't make it feminine."
She didn't.

But Rocco's business was primarily in Chicago. He had a fine bunch of underlings, but some things needed the attention of the boss. He didn't want Tony Accardo to think he was "doing a Giancana." Rocco had had a successful interlude and a lot of pleasure, but it was now time to get back to the grindstone.

Rocco Robust returned to Chicago. Back to his headquarters at Gentleman's Attire.

CHAPTER TWENTY THREE

Tough Baseball Times

Following their fine seasons at Geneva and Peoria, Ricky Robustelli and Bob Richards were promoted to Midland, the Cubs' farm club in Texas. Almost every player who makes it to the major league Cubs comes through Midland at one time or another.

Rick and Bob rented an apartment together in a middle income area of Midland. At the age of 23, Bob could reach the fences in the power alleys. As a result, going into July, he was hovering near the .300 mark, with 30 RBI's and 7 home runs.

If Bob was having success, Ricky was more than matching it. When the season reached the half way point in June and was about to turn into July, Rick was leading the league in just about everything: wins, ERA, percentage of wins over losses and strikeouts. The radar guns were clocking his fast ball at 95 miles per hour.

Then disaster struck.

Midland was playing a night game in Little Rock, against Arkansas. Bob was catching and the score was tied in the eighth. The hitter hit a medium deep fly to left and the throw came to the plate as the runner came in, head first. As the ball arrived, Bob had the plate completely blocked off. With all his might, the runner drove into Bob. Right into his knee. Bob hung onto the ball and applied the tag.

"Out!" yelled the plate umpire.

But Bob's knee was completely twisted. The next day, the doctor approached an anxious Bill and Jeannie.

"Good news. He's going to be all right. He'll be walking again in a month or so. And one day he'll run again."

Jeannie smiled. That was good news. Bill thought so too. But his thoughts were on something else. "That's fine, Doctor. Thank you for your fine work. But let me ask you, when can he catch again, play ball again?"

The doctor wasn't smiling now. "That's another side of the coin. I'll give it to you straight. I doubt he ever will again."

Jeannie knew that, with his degree from Notre Dame, Bob could make it as well as any other graduate of a prestige college in the real world. But Bill didn't take it as easily. He had groomed Bob to be an athlete almost from the day he was born. Now it was over. He could no longer be a professional athlete. His great attribute had been his catching ability, his great arm and his grasp of the game, the ability to "call" the game. Now he would no longer be flexible enough to assume the catcher's crouch, to be mobile enough to move to block down the pitch in the dirt, or snap up to fire to second base. It was over.

Bill and Jeannie waited with Bob in the hospital until he could be fitted with a cast. It was a sad time for the Richards family.

Rocco Robustelli soon heard about the accident during one of his infrequent phone conversations with his son. Rocco and Ricky were not close, but they communicated. Rocco liked to brag about his son to his associates. He stayed in touch so he was aware of Rick's progress. There was not much more to the relationship than that. Still Robust took pride in his son.

His reaction to the accident was in character.

"Fine, serves that fucking father right. Couldn't happen to a nicer guy."

Ricky not only lost his buddy; he lost his verve. Not anything physical, but his enthusiasm. The loss of his childhood friend took something out of him. He was brooding, down-cast. He had lost his zip.

Bill Richards spent the days with Bob at the hospital, but he was also concerned about Rick. He could see that Rick was unable to deal with the death of a dream—the dream of two buddies that they would continue to be the "R and R Boys" all the way into

Wrigley Field. Rick had been with Bob from Little League. Now he would have to make his way without him and his family. Rick could no longer expect to have his substitute family follow him around the country. Not when Bob would not be with him.

Rick was twenty three now, but still a kid. It had been Bob who made the decisions. It was Bob who was the leader of the two. With Bob around, Rick had not gone out of his way to develop close friendships with the rest of his teammates.

The Cubs were about ready to move Rick up. It was decided that, all things taken into consideration, now might be the right time.

Al Spangler called Ricky into his office in the first week of July. "Rick, I got good news for you. You're going up. To Des Moines. Congratulations!"

It would be a new start for the youngster. Midland was a nice town. Rick had enjoyed Texas, but he was glad to leave. It had not been the best summer of his life. He was looking forward to Des Moines.

Iowa's manager, Jim Essian, welcomed Rick with open arms. He had a fine young ball club, but it was mired in last place in the eastern division because of a lack of Triple A pitching. His instructions from the parent cubs were to insert Rick right into the starting rotation.

Rick gave up five runs in four innings in his first effort, against Indianapolis. The Indians were able to sit on his fast ball and Rick had trouble getting his two and three pitches over, the curve and slider. In his next outing against Evansville it got no better.

The fans in Des Moines were tolerant, but, on his next time out, there were rumblings in the stands when Rick was announced as the starting pitcher. They proved to be right. Essian pulled Rick in the eighth inning.

The Richards family decided to take a long weekend in Des Moines.

Rick received them as what they were—the best friends he had in the world. The Richards, father and son, had seen Rick's progress—or lack thereof—from Chicago. They knew that Rick was having troubles coping at this level. They were surprised. They hadn't expected him to tear up the league, but they had expected that he would have at least a modicum of success.

When Rick greeted them at his apartment, Bill and Bob could see the problem. This was a different Rick than the one they had known. He just didn't have enthusiasm for his craft. He didn't have the verve he had had.

The next day, Bill took Rick aside for a little bit of fatherly advice.

"Rick, you've got a great opportunity here. And you're blowing it. You're dogging it. You've got all the potential in the work and you're letting it go to waste. What's the matter with you? You've worked so hard all your 23 years to get here and now you're letting yourself down. Be a man, Rick! Think of those who love you. Linda. Jeannie. Bill. Bob. Me. I'm sure your dad too. I think it's about time you did a little growing up and worked your ass off at your trade. Seeing you here, moping around, I could kick your butt! You're got to snap out of it, kid."

Sunday, Bill and Bob stayed to watch Rick pitch against Oklahoma City. It was better. Most important, the radar gun clocked him at 93 MPH on ten of his pitches. All in all, he was just about what the Cubs had expected when they moved him up to Iowa.

Before Bill left, he had a chance for a short chat with Rick.

"Kid, you looked like the guy I've known all your life today. I'm pleased with you. You fought today. You didn't make it, but if you keep this up, you will. We'll be seeing you in Chicago."

Rick's face had a smile. One of the very first anybody in Des Moines had seen. He was sorry to see them go. They had come just at the right time to give him the shot in the arm he needed.

The rest of the season went about as the Cub front office had expected when they ordered Rick elevated from Midland to Iowa. He was just a bit over his head in this company. But he showed it wouldn't be long before he would be right in step—nothing sensational, but nothing to be ashamed of, either.

The Cub organization looked forward to next year.

CHAPTER TWENTY FOUR

Gentlemen's and Bum's

When Connie Constable told John Duffy that Rocky Robust lived at Outer Drive East, she accidentally thwarted Rocco's intentions to keep Bill Richards from learning his new address. John informed his brother, Bill, who, in turn, notified Richards.

As part of Bill's investigation, he again set up a "fisur," a physical surveillance of Rocco. FBI agents picked up Rocco as he exited his new building, eager to learn of his daily activity. They found Rocco a tough act to follow.

Rocco walked west on Randolph down the slight incline past the old Standard Oil Building, past the Prudential Building and to the corner of Randolph and Michigan, the location of the Chicago Public Library. There it got a little tricky.

At this point, Robust dashed into the Library and gauged his situation, carefully observing anyone who followed him. Then he walked the entire length of the library to the Washington Street exit. He hurried across Washington into the Pittsfield Building and down into the empty basement. Anyone following him would be spotted immediately. After pausing for another minute or so and finding nobody had come down with him, Rocco returned to the ground floor and exited the way he had come in. He then turned back east until he turned south into the alley between Wabash and Michigan.

When he got to the rear of the building at 15 North Wabash, he ducked inside and traversed half way through the building, where he again paused and waited for a minute. He then proceeded through the building to its entrance on Wabash, darting across the street into the Stevens Building at 16 North Wabash. Again, he paused inside the corridor for over a minute. He then exited alongside Chas A. Stevens and Co.

When Rocky exited, he looked up and down the State Street Mall. Then, he quickly crossed the street and hustled north back across Washington. One half block later he ducked into his destination – Gentlemen's Attire.

The FBI crew finally set up fixed vantage points. Instead of following Rocco into the corridors, they covered both entrances. When he existed on Wabash and then on State, they had him in sight. By the use of car radios and portable walkie-talkies, they kept him under observation. When Rocco exited State Street at Chas. A. Stevens, two agents were nearby to pick him up. They watched as he bounded south and into Gentlemen's Attire across the street from Marshall Field's. Then, they waited.

Jerry Scarpelli was the first to arrive. He had approached from Randolph onto State. Soon after Scarpelli arrived, Gussie Alex appeared from Madison. Fifteen minutes later, Joe Ferriola entered from the north. Either Gentlemen's Attire sold a hell of a lot of suits to hoods or the FBI had discovered the new mob meeting place. Or both.

For several days, Bill Richards and his crew watched Gentlemen's Attire. They were given the use of an office on the third floor of Marshall Field's. Every day, around ten o'clock, they watched as mobsters they recognized – and some they didn't – entered Gentlemen's Attire. Robust was always among them. The FBI had obviously discovered the mob's new headquarters.

Richards' partner, Johnny Bassett, "cased" the place. It was an easy task for a pro like Bassett. After acting as a potential customer, he reported that there appeared to be a large office in the rear of the store, taking about a third of the floor space. He also noted that, although the FBI surveillance team on the third floor at Marshall Field's had noted the arrival of Robust, Scarpelli, "No Nose" DiFronzo and Sam Carlisi that morning, he had not seen them in the store. It seemed obvious they were in the rear office.

Thanks to Bassett, Richards now knew exactly where the mob was meeting in Gentlemen's Attire.

The next step was penetration. Not an easy task by any means. Nor a safe task. Surreptitious entry entailed considerable risk. If the mob kept a "thug" inside during closing hours, he would have every excuse to shoot first and then argue that the persons breaking in were burglars. Since the agents would not be in any kind of uniform and would have no chance to identify themselves as law enforcement personnel, the claim would smack of validity. It would be highly unlikely that a "security guard" of a prominent retailer like Duglash would be convicted by any jury in these circumstances.

Rocco had also used his political pull. He had Pat Marcy, the mob's man in the First Ward, contact Captain Fred Pope in the Central District of the Chicago Police Department. Marcy instructed Pope, who held his command with the approval of the First Ward, that he wanted extra protection, especially at night, of Gentlemen's Attire. A police squad car was parked outside the store on a permanent basis. Unaware that they were guarding the mob's headquarters, the police simply knew their commander was inordinately interested in securing that particular location. It became perhaps the safest place in Chicago.

Against these odds, Bill Richards and his crew planned their entry.

Robust had a security system installed. Not only was the front protected, but the rear window in the office.

Johnny Bassett developed the informant who supplied the probable cause necessary for an electronic surveillance, a bug. Bassett's informant had been called to account at Gentlemen's Attire to explain why his bookmaking establishment was not keeping pace with the expectations of the mob. Judge Abe Marovitz approved Richards' affidavit and authorized the penetration. Any information obtained by the "bug" could thereafter be used as evidence against the conspirators in a trial in federal court.

Now it was up to Richards and his "sound men." Any entry from the front was precluded by Pope's forces, so Richards' attention focused on the rear of the store, entrance from the rear alley through the back window. Not only was the window barred, but it was protected by the security alarm. An iron grill had been placed around it. On close inspection, however, Richards found that, in accordance with the city fire laws, the bars were installed to swing out. They were locked from the inside, but, in order to allow for exit in case of fire, they could be swung out. There was no way to unlock the bars from the outside, however. The rear door had been bricked over. Robust had taken no chances.

The obvious answer was to "make" the janitor.

Small Hazziez was an older man who lived in Lawndale. Richards went to his home. A friendly conversation led Richards to believe he had an interest in good government and appropriate law enforcement. Richards took a chance. He asked Mr. Hazzicz to unlock the rear window bars and turn off the alarm when he departed Gentlemen's Attire the following evening.

The next night, a little after midnight, Richards and three "sound men" cautiously approached the rear window of Gentlemen's Attire from the alley. Quickly one of the sound men hoisted Richards up to the window. The bars were unlocked and the alarm was off. In quick order, the FBI was inside mob headquarters.

According to John Bassett's informant, Robust had been seated at the desk in the office and he had been placed on the sofa, with an easy chair in between the desk and the sofa. A tiny pin hole to contain the mike was drilled through the baseboard directly in front of the desk. The mike was voice activated and transmitted without need of wires.

Richards dubbed the mike "Bum's." Every FBI bug had been code named to prevent its identification. If an agent slipped and was overheard talking about a code-named mike, it would not have as much harm if he referred to it by its acronym. Richard thought it was a good play-in-words to code-name Gentlemen's as "Bum's."

Within the hour, the foursome was up and out the rear window. John Bassett, in a Bureau car, had signalled them on their walkietalkie that the alley was clear. A police car had been stationed in the front, on State Street, all the time they were in the store. Another had made regular cruises up and down the alley. But the FBI agents had been safely ensconced inside the soundproofed office, concealed from anybody outside the State Street or in the alley. Now if only Robust failed to notice that the lock on the bars was unlocked before Mr. Hazziez could lock it again the next evening, it would be the perfect "crime." To minimize that danger, the FBI team had gone in on a Saturday night. Richards had asked Mr. Hazziez to come to the store on Sunday morning to lock the window and turn the alarm back on. He was to excuse this unusual occurrence, if he were caught, by saying that he had felt ill the previous day and had not finished his clean-up. Mr. Hazziez did as requested and was not observed except by the squad car outside. The officers recognized him and made no effort to stop him. It was a *fait accompli!*

On Monday, Richards and Bassett hustled to the "sound room" in the FBI office in the Dirksen Federal Building. "Bum's" was working!

Just after ten o'clock, Rocco Robust arrived at Gentlemen's Attire. Throughout the day, each capo of the Chicago mob appeared. Rocco congratulated some for doing a good job during the previous month. A couple he tore into. To others he seemed non-committal. By late afternoon, Richards and Bassett had been able to identify, by the nature of the conversation, who four of the capos were.

The next day, Tuesday, Joe Ferriola appeared.

"Robust," Ferriola said, "we got a problem. Leo Manfredi, you know, that bookmaker in Cicero? He's holding out. I've given it a chance but there is no doubt he's holding out on us. I give him 10,000 a month to put on the street in Cicero and what I found is that he is using it to finance drug deals. Now we all know that's against all the rules. He's been a good guy for many years, that's why we had him in Cicero, a good territory. But he knows he can't do that."

Rocco was perturbed. "You sure of this, Joe?"

"Yeah, I wouldn't be here, Burly, if I weren't," Ferriola replied.

"What do you suggest?" Robust asked.

"We chop him," was Ferriola's response.

"Do it." Rocco Robustelli had not hesitated. It was cut and dried. Leo Manfredi had violated one of the prime rules of Tony Accardo's family. As long as Accardo was *consiglieri*, no made guy would be involved in dope. Not as long as Joe Batters was "The Man." Even if Rocky Robust had wanted to ease the rule, he couldn't. Not when he had to answer to Joe Batters. There was no need to consider his response to Ferriola.

But it caused a dilemma for Richards. It was established FBI policy to provide warning to an intended victim. To do so would jeopardize the mike at Gentlemen's Attire. If he followed Bureau policy and warned Manfredi of what Robust and Ferriola had in store for him, he risked jeopardizing "Bum's." At this point only Ferriola and Robust knew of the plot to chop Manfredi. If Manfredi was warned by the FBI and then made that warning known to the mob, that would be the end of "Bum's." All the hard work and risk down the drain.

Richards and Bassett took the problem to their supervisor, Vince Inserra, but, by the time it made its way through channels, it was too late.

Leo Manfredi's body was found in the basement of a closed pizza parlor in Berwyn. He had been shot four times in the head at close range.

Richards took the transcription of the tape containing the conversation of Robust and Ferriola to kill Leo Manfredi to Jeff Johnson, the assistant United States Attorney. He knew Johnson would have the savvy to understand what he would request.

"Jeff, let's hold this. We're just starting. If we go for an indictment for the violation of civil rights by Robust and Ferriola right now, we've got a real humdinger. We don't know who pulled the trigger on Manfredi, but we know it was ordered by those two. And they would be good catches. But I'm suggesting to you that we wait. We can always file on this later. Let's hold off and, in the meantime, keep on monitoring. Unless they find it, 'Bum's' could be the best mike we ever placed. Let's play this out for now, hold it in abeyance, and pick it up later. Who knows, by then we might have a whole bunch of stuff as good as this!"

Johnson didn't hesitate. He agreed. There would be no indictments for conspiracy to violate the civil rights of Manfredi—not at the present. Richards went home that night feeling very good. It had been a good day's work. He felt sorry for Leo Manfredi, but he felt some satisfaction that he had made a big drop in the bag of evidence he was amassing against his most bitter adversary.

It wasn't until morning that Bill thought about what Rocco's conviction for Leo Manfredi's brutal slaying would do to Rocco's children. Especially when it would be revealed that Richards was the one responsible. He had thought about it in the past, but now he had much more reason to shape up his thoughts in this regard. His efforts were beginning to bear some fruit.

Richards felt that someday soon, at the appropriate time, he should sit down with Linda and Ricky and explain just what was transpiring. They certainly had an idea by this time of the nature of their father's work and it wouldn't be a shock to them. They also knew of the deep feelings their father and Richards. They certainly wouldn't be shocked to learn that he was the guy mandated to put their father in prison, hopefully for the rest of his life.

He would simply have to find the right time.

On the following Monday, "Bum's" produced another bombshell.

"Lou, sit down. How was your trip? How's Loretta? Let's have dinner tonight if you're free."

Lou Lederer had returned to Chicago. Lou was the front at the Tropicana for Frank Costello, "the prime minister of organized crime." When Sam Giancana had attempted to make inroads in the Dominican Republic to initiate gambling there, it was Lou Lederer he sent to do a feasibility study. Later, when Giancana had bribed the Shah of Iran to permit his opening a casino in Tehran, it was Lederer who was placed in charge. Lou Lederer was the premier expert on casino gambling in the United States. He was highly respected by all who knew him, including Bill Richards.

Lederer was game. "Fine. I had a good trip. America West has good flights now from Las Vegas. I catch a plane from Reno to Vegas and then shot right in here."

Bill, on the other end of "Bum's," was interested. He knew Lou

Lederer as his own man. Legit or not, who wanted advice and counsel on casinos retained Lou. Although Lou preferred to advise the legitimate companies, he was not adverse to refuse if the mob wished to utilize his services. Having been raised in Chicago, he also knew better than to say no to the likes of Giancana–or Robust.

Bill wondered what Lou Lederer was doing in Reno. He would soon find out.

"So, Louie?" Robust asked, "what do you think of our operation there at the Lake?"

The news that the mob had something going in Lake Tahoe was out.

"It's good. You people have had better, at least as far as the overall operation is concerned, like the Stardust and the Desert Inn. But not much better. I haven't gotten involved in your skim there, but I can see that it gives you a good bite. I would think, without delving into it, as I say, that you're good for two, three million a year from the skim."

Lederer was obviously impressed.

"You think everything is going smooth there, Lou?" Robust asked. "Anything we should be doing or not doing there?"

"No, I think the guy you got in there as the casino manager, Silver, is a good man. As you know, I recommended him to you. He was with me in Tehran, as a shift manager. I raised him right. He's a good man for you."

"No suggestions you want to make then?" Robust queried.

"Yes, there is one. The guy you got in charge of the sports book. Frankie Molley. I ran into him in Atlantic City. At Trump's Castle. He wasn't in sports books there, of course, they got none. I really think he's out of his league there at your place. I know if you put him in there he's trustworthy, but he's in a sports book for the first time, never been in Nevada before, and I don't think he knows what he's doing. You know, the sports book has become a big money maker in a casino. When I started it was peanuts. Its hard to skim. Every hotel has one now and some are big. That's why I advised you to make ample room for a big one in your joint. That's fine. But I don't think this guy Molley is first class. That's just my opinion. He went out of his way to make everything available to me, all the books and records, but I just get the idea he's over his head in that spot."

Robust took it under consideration for a moment. Then apparently decided to level with Lou Lederer.

"Lou, Molley is not my guy. You know I mentioned to you that although we got 51% of that place, Gotti and the rest of those guys east, have got the other 49%. I got control since I got the majority, but what I haven't told you is that we alternate spots with New York and New Jersey and Philly. The casino manager is ours and then we alternate spots. So *we* put Silver in; *they* put Molley in."

"Oh, I didn't know that," Lederer said. "Well, I should have guessed that since he came out of Atlantic City. But I didn't know how the set-up was handled. Well, I told you. If I was you, though, I'd have Silver pitch in there. Silver knows what he's doing, he can slop over into that some."

"Yeah, that's a good idea," Rocco replied. "I'll send word out there to him. Matter of fact, I'm going out there next week. Connie is going with me, or at least she'll go on another plane and meet me there. You'll meet her at dinner tonight. Nice kid. Sharp. Attorney. You'll like her. OK, Lou, if there's nothing else, let's make it at eight tonight. How about the Cape Cod Room at the Drake? You like fish?"

"I don't so much, but Loretta does. That'll be fine. See you at eight."

Bill Richards had been aware that there was a new big hotel built at Lake Tahoe, but he hadn't been aware it was mobbed up. He didn't even recall the name of it. But there was no question about it now. Obviously the Chicago mob and the New York mob had a joint venture. For years there had been no hotel at The Lake which was owned by any mob. Now it was apparent that the mob had moved back into Lake Tahoe.

Not just the mob, however, the mobs.

First he called Chuck Thomas, a Las Vegas agent, and told him what he had learned.

"What's the name of the new place in Tahoe, Chuck?" Richards asked.

"Gotta be the Summit. The Tahoe Summit," Thomas replied. "The Gaming control Board had some questions about the casino manager there, guy named Silver. No mob connections that we could find.

"One thing, Chuck, I don't have to tell you that we got to keep this very tight. It comes from a very sensitive source. Don't mention it to anybody without a need to know. Mention it to the boss, but tell Joe what I said. You might also tell Yablonsky that I might want to come out there. Maybe the three of us could go up to the Lake and see what it looks like, if you know what I mean."

Chuck Thomas knew what Richards meant. Joe Yablonsky was the SAC in Las Vegas. It would be great to put in an undercover FBI agent in the Summit. Or develop a well placed informant there. Best of all, to put a mike in the executive offices of the Tahoe Summit.

"Bum's" was worth its weight in gold.

CHAPTER TWENTY FIVE

Connie's Compact

Connie didn't know how Lou Lederer fit in with Rocco. She know of his reputation as a shadowy figure behind the political scene in Chicago and it was common knowledge that he had been very close for decades with Eddy Barrett, a Democratic Ward Committeeman. At any rate, she was pleased that he and his wife would be around when she presented her big idea to Rocco.

She broached the subject soon after they were settled into the Cape Cod Room.

"You guys, I want to talk to you about something very serious. Something that's been on my mind for a long time."

Rocco, Lou and Loretta gave her their undivided attention.

Her opener was a startler. "I'd like to get started in politics here in Chicago."

Rocco was the first to react. "I don't know, Babe. There are some people who know you and I are very close. That would shoot you down right off the bat."

Connie knew that would be Rocco's first reaction.

"Yes, I've thought of that. We could continue as we are, but not be seen in public. I could dismiss our relationship as something that happened in my youth, when I was young and immature. And it might not come out anyway."

"No, Babe, I'm not for it." Rocco seemed ready to dismiss the thought out of hand.

"First of all, Buddy, I don't have to get your approval. You're not my father, you know. But I do want it. Lou, what do you think?" Connie was obviously going to use pressure.

"Connie, politics is a tough job for anybody. Especially, as

117

Robust says, you bring some baggage into this." Lou wasn't about to go against the boss of the Chicago mob on this.

Connie pouted like a young girl. Rocco was not happy with her. When the evening was over, he apologized to Lou Lederer, but Lou offered some unusual advise.

"You know, Rock, it may not be such a bad idea. You're always looking for good talent you can bring along, somebody who can help you. This girl seems to be a good prospect. An attorney, attractive as hell, articulate, intelligent. Good candidate. As she says, your relationship's not fatal. Keep a low profile with her and you could minimize that. You might think about it."

Unknown to Connie, Lou Lederer had become her ally. At least to some extent.

Connie was surprised when Robust brought it up later.

"Connie, I don't say no to you wanting to get into politics. Let's think about it. I still don't think its a good idea, but I'm willing to consider it. Let's just keep in it mind. I'll talk to someone about it."

The following Monday, Robust and Gus Alex had lunch. Robust brought up Connie Constable's ambitions.

"You know this girl I've had for the past couple years, Slim," Rocco stated. "Well, she's interested in getting involved in politics."

"Is that right?" Alex asked. "What do you think of that?"

"That's what I want to ask you. You're the expert on politics, you and Pat Marcy."

"Right off the bat, I'd be against it, Rocco. For the reason that it could be counterproductive. Somebody gets on to the fact she is your dolly, they'd hammer her with it and it would splash off on us."

"That was my first thought too," Robust rejoined. "But she sprung it on me in front of Louie Lederer. He's in town to report on the job I sent him on at Lake Tahoe. To evaluate what we're doing at the Summit. And Lou had the same opinion you did. At first. But, after thinking about it, he told me that it might not be such a bad idea."

Alex thought about that. "Well, Lou is a sharp old guy. Been around politics here for a long time."

"Well, what do you think?" Robust asked.

"I dunno, Rocco. What ward does she live in? She'd have to start out running there.

"She lives near Sandberg Village, on Dearborn, almost to North Avenue." But Rocco was unclear what ward that was.

"That'd be 42nd – or maybe 43rd. George Dunne. Or the old Botchy Connor ward."

Robust let Gussie think about it. If Gus put the kibosh on it, he'd go along, but, if Gus liked the idea, he'd endorse it. He was the boss, but this was Gussie's area of expertise.

Finally Gus replied.

"Tell you what, let me talk to Pat Marcy and John D'Arco. This is something in their sphere. If we was to help her, we'd have to go through them."

The two left it at that.

A couple days later Gus Alex, Pat Marcy and Rocky Robust met for lunch.

"Burly, Pat and I have discussed this thing with your girl," Gussie began.

Robust waited.

"Pat thinks it is a good idea. That's the 42nd ward. If we agree we want her to go for it, it's the alderman's job there. The guy there now is not with us. He gets up in the city council and works against us."

"That's right," Marcy chimed in, "we could use somebody good for us there. Gussie has explained how she is your girl. That's putting us off to a real slow start and when you first think about it you would not run somebody who has got fleas on her, right off the bat. But, Jesus Christ, we've run people with a lot more fleas than that. So she dated you once or twice, years ago? Hell, this is Chicago! And, if she's good, who knows how far we can take her? Think it over, and, if you decide, bring it to us. We can handle it."

Robust gave it some thought. Then he called Connie. "Meet me at Tiffs Too."

"Babe, I been giving it a lot of thought. I know you want this. I know how bad. So I've been discussing it with some people in our business who got a handle on things like this. Here's what I'm going to say to you. You want to do it, fine. But you got to understand that sure as hell Richards and Duffy will plant stories with guys like John Drummond and Chuck Goudie and Art Petacque and John O'Brien and Kup. All their pals. Probably Roy Leonard and Clark Webber too. It's gonna embarrass you that you and I have been together. Your opponent will use that against you. You understand that, don't you? And it's your own fault, you're the one who went to Du..y's brother."

Connie Constable knew it would be an embarrassment, one she could count on to tarnish her reputation. Top attorneys on La Salle Street would avoid her. Many of her friends and fellow lawyers would possibly scorn her. She had already considered the consequences. Rocco was right. But, nonetheless, she was determined to go through with it. She wanted a career in politics, to go as high as possible. She had made up her mind.

"Rocco, I know what you say is true. I've given it a lot of thought. I want to do it."

Rocco remained silent for a few minutes. Then he leaned over the table, in his usual serious manner.

"OK, Babe. It's your funeral. You want it, I'll give it to you."

It was settled. The career of Connie Constable as a Chicago politician was about to commence.

CHAPTER TWENTY SIX

"Mountain" Dew.

Joe Yablonsky, the Special Agent in Charge of the Las Vegas office, had an instant reaction to Bill Richards' news about the Tahoe Summit.

"Tell you what," Yablonsky said to Chuck Thomas, "let's get Richards out here on a temporary assignment. The three of us can go up to The Lake and see what we can do. Call Bill and see if he'd want to do that."

Richards usually left out-of-town assignments to his partners, but he and Jeannie were now empty-nesters. He was pleased to get involved at Lake Tahoe. Jeannie could spend the time visiting her aging parents in Cincinnati. Bill flew America West airlines to Vegas, where he quickly met with Yablonsky and Thomas to fill them in on all he had learned from "Bum's" about the Chicago-New York-Philadelphia mobs' venture in northern Nevada.

When the three reached Lake Tahoe, they checked in with John Norris, the Senior Resident Agent of the satellite office reporting to Yablonsky. Norris had arranged for a cabin as a command post. "Operation Pensum" (Penetration of the Summit) would be handled out of there.

Following procedures which has been successful in the past, Yablonsky intended to try a "elsur," or electronic surveillance. It would take some doing. Several "elsurs" placed in a Vegas casino in the sixties had resulted in a lawsuit against the FBI, a considerable embarrassment. Yablonski didn't want a repeat of that situation.

Yablonsky and Thomas were well known by the employees of Nevada casinos. Richards was not and was, therefore chosen to do the leg-work. He could think of no one who would know him by sight except for Robust, but he took no chances. John Bassett, back in Chicago, assured him that "Bum's" was reporting Rocco still there.

Richards found that the executive offices of the Tahoe Summit were located on the entire fourteenth floor. They could be reached two ways. By a bank of elevators and by a stairway. The stairway was guarded by a security guard. The elevator was guarded by two. Richards cased them both—once at ten in the morning, once at six in the evening and once at two in the morning. They remained guarded at all times.

Richards used a pretext to visit the fourteenth floor personnel office and found a security guard stationed inside the exit from the elevator. Another stood inside the door from the stairwell. A simple inquiry showed they were there around-the-clock.

It seemed impossible to penetrate the executive offices of the Tahoe Summit surreptitiously. There seemed to be no way to get up into the offices to plant a bug without alerting the guards. Yablonsky had been certain that this would be the outcome, but wanted Richards to find out for himself. He was prepared with another solution.

"Let's put an undercover operative in there," Yablonsky suggested. "Now that you're satisfied we can't do it your way, let's do it my way. I've got just the right guy. I trained him when I was conducting undercover seminars at Quantico. He got his feet wet in Los Angeles and Philly. He got 'inside' in Philly and he's still there. He's had sitdowns with Scarfo and Phil Leonetti, the underboss there, lives in South Philly with all the dagos and, I think, if he requested it, he could get moved out here. You've probably heard of him. "Mountain" Dew.

Richards had. "Mountain" Dew had become a legend inside the FBI in the past four years. He had been the most successful undercover agent since Yablonsky himself. "Mountain" Dew had not yet surfaced and his fame had, therefore, not spread except to the handful of FBI agents on a need-to-know basis. Richards had met him once when he had been asked to fill him in on a Chicago background. "Mountain" Dew was presently solidly in place in Philadelphia.

After Joe Yablonsky, with all his influence in the Bureau, convinced headquarters that the services of "Mountain" Dew would be more useful in northern Nevada then they were in South Philly, Yablonsky and Richards flew to Philadelphia. "Cappy," as he was now called, was glad to see them and took to the idea of relocating to Lake Tahoe. One of the guys he had gotten "in" with in South Philly was Sam Scafidi, an old time Philly wise guy who had been sent to represent Scarfo interests at the Tahoe Summit. He was sure Scafidi would honor his request to be relocated to Tahoe.

When Yablonsky and Richards left "Cappy," they called the Bureau and checked in with Marshall Rutland, now the headquarters supervisor who was the unit chief in charge of organized crime investigations in Las Vegas. "Maz" Rutland gave approval for "Mountain" Dew to arrange to be placed in a strategic spot in the Tahoe Summit through his close contact with Sam Scafidi.

Sam Scafidi arranged for his young pal, "Cappy," to take a spot at the Tahoe Summit. Scafidi vouched that "Cappy" had proved himself in South Philly at the Italian Market and that he would be a valuable addition to the crew operating the Summit.

Scafidi went to Mort Silver, the casino manager. "This is a good young kid. We're lucky he wants to come out here 'cause he's had a good deal for himself in South Philly with us. He's a worker. Where can we put him?"

"Mountain" Dew started as a floorman—not the most strategic spot for the purposes of the FBI in the "Pensum" Caper, but a good starting place. Clandestine meets were set up, so that he could make his reports to his Bureau associates. Bill Richards would be the primary contact with "Cappy," who came up with the idea of hiring row boats and meeting in the middle of the lake. "Cappy" worked the four to midnight shift. He would meet Bill every Tuesday and Saturday morning at one. In the meantime, if Bill needed "Cappy" for anything he would call, using the code-name, "Bucky."

It was all set up and ready to go. Now it was in the hands of "Mountain" Dew.

CHAPTER TWENTY SEVEN

Connie's Client.

Connie Constable was going to run for Congress. She had thought it over and come to a logical conclusion. Why settle for being a small-potatoes alderman? As long as she was going to have the unlimited resources of the Chicago Outfit behind her, why not go all out? Her residence put her in the 7th Congressional District. If she ran for alderman, her residence in the 42nd Ward would preclude much of the help she could expect from the First Ward. But, if she ran for Congress, she could expect such help since the First Ward is a big part of the 7th Congressional District.

With her decision made, Connie started her campaign. Money was no problem. That's where Robust came in. However, the money must be received legally. The mob couldn't just hand over a million dollars, or ten million, and say "here, use this." All contributions must be made public, periodically.

Pat Marcy and John D'Arco were pros at such shenanigans.

Connie quickly got seed money from the political action committees of the Teamsters; The Hotel, Restaurant and Bartenders Union; and Local 46 of the Laundry Workers Union. The cash was more than enough to get her campaign off to a fast start. Since about 98% of incumbents in Congress are re-elected, it was necessary for Connie to get going early. She started in the late fall, opening a campaign headquarters in the Lincoln Park area.

The signs read: "Connie Constable, the Citizen's Choice." No prettier candidate had even run in Chicago. The nice thing about Connie's beauty was that it was not flashy. She resembled June Allyson, not Madonna. Beautiful, but with a great hint of intelligence and charm. Femininity at its finest.

The first polls showed her running behind, 55% to 38% against the incumbent, with the other votes going to dark horses. One thing in her favor, they showed Connie would be the only challenger. Obviously, however, she had to come from far back. She would need something to catch the voters' attention other than her good looks.

You just couldn't get much more respectable or high profile in Chicago than Mr. and Mrs. Charles E. Banks. Charles Banks was one of Chicago's best known philanthropists. He and his wife, Diana, were prime benefactors of the Chicago Symphony Orchestra. Charles Banks was on the Board of Directors of the Union League Club. Diana Banks was on the board of Maryville.

Their house had come crashing down when their twenty year old daughter, Jayne, filed a civil action against her father for sexual abuse and molestation from the age of nine until she left her father's house at seventeen. Charles Banks and his wife hired the best: Joseph N. DuCanto, considered the best divorce attorney in Chicago.

Jayne Banks took her case and story to another well known attorney—Connie Constable. It was Connie's signs which attracted her.

Connie was skeptical about Jayne's allegations. Basically, they were that, from the age of nine, her father had "played with her private parts" and, eventually, when she was thirteen or so, he had commenced carnal knowledge of her. She even alleged oral sex. If Jayne's stories were true, Connie had a substantial case, exposing one of Chicago's highest and mightiest.

Connie took the girl to Northwestern Hospital and had tests run. The tests proved that Jayne had an enlarged vagina, a condition that indicated a great deal of sexual activity. Connie was satisfied.

When the trial opened in Circuit Court, the media had a field day. *The Chicago Tribune* assigned John O'Brien, normally its ace crime reporter, to the story.

Although not permitted inside, cameras besieged the participants entering and leaving the courtroom. Connie Constable refused client interviews before and during the trial, creating a profitable effect for herself. She became the only person available to reporters. She constantly granted interviews to the press. It was right up her alley. She even debated opposing lawyers on television programs. She was coming close to breaching the canons of legal ethics, but Connie was grasping at every opportunity to get her face before the Chicago public.

The trial opened on June 15. The first and only witness Connie put on the stand was Jayne Banks. Connie brought her along slowly, milking her story for its effect on the jury and on the press. She brought out that Jayne had several bouts of colic as a baby and that she also suffered from asthma in her very early youth. As a result, she had turned to her father for support and attention, her mother being very social and not always at home when Jayne needed her. The testimony was designed to discredit Diana Banks in the event she took the stand later on behalf of her husband.

Then Connie brought Jayne into testimony which would be the crux of the case. She slowly developed testimony that the distinguished Charles Banks began to take indecent liberties with his daughter around the age of nine. Connie had paced the testimony with an eye on the clock. She wanted to draw this out, but she wanted it all on the five and five thirty news on the television channels. She wanted that part of the testimony finished on the first day as a preview, so to speak, of what the public could expect the next day.

As Connie departed from the courtroom with her client, she had Jayne mouth the words "no comment." But Connie had a lot to say. The media found her to be, as always, a willing interview. She was as articulate as she was attractive. Television producers made her a lead item on the evening and nightly news.

The next day, after the cameras again caught Connie entering the courtroom for the noon news, Jayne took up where she had left off. Jayne was now 13 in her chronology. She began to become much more explicit on what her father had done to her.

Charles Banks had jumped to his feet.

"Enough, enough," he cried. "She is lying, lying! I can't go through with this. Enough!"

The courtroom was in an uproar. Judge Walter Biescke banged his gavel. "Order. I demand order. Counsel, calm your client!"

Joe DuCanto had jumped to his feet. He shouted to the bench. "Your honor, I request a recess!"

Judge Biescke quickly granted it.

DuCanto sent a message to Connie and requested a conference, which, much to the consternation of the press, cognizant of their deadlines for the evening news and the next morning editions, lasted the rest of the day. At the end, Connie agreed to settle. Jayne would get a settlement which would set her up for the rest of her life.

Connie announced it to the press.

Two years later, Jayne Banks would admit to *Rolling Stone* that her entire story had been a fabrication.

The exposé had no effect on Connie Constable. By that time, she had a lot more on her mind.

CHAPTER TWENTY EIGHT

Rick Responds;
"Candy Cane, The Courier"

Ricky Robustelli had again been assigned to Iowa. Although his first season had been a failure, the Cub brass was still high on him. After a good fall, he was added to the 40 man winter roster of the parent Cubs and trained with them at Mesa. He was finally called into manager Jim Frey's office.

Frey was optimistic.

"Rick, we like what we see in you. You seemed to disappear at Iowa last July and August, but you picked up again in Mesa last fall. We think you've got what it takes to make it big. You'll be at Wrigley Field soon. We'll be watching you carefully. Good luck."

Rick reported back to Iowa. He was happy to be designated to be the opening day pitcher against Omaha. Everything went right that April day and things were looking good for young Richard Robustelli.

Back in Chicago, "Bums" was continuing to produce quality information on a quantity basis.

Rocco Robustelli was pleasantly surprised. He had warned his confederates not to "give up" his headquarters by being careless, and he had certainly followed his own advice. The G must be backing off their investigation, he speculated. I never see them on me no more.

At the same time Rick Robustelli was having his success just a few hundred miles from Chicago, Joe Ferriola arrived to report and hand over the proceeds from his district. When Robust saw the totals, he was elated.

"Hey, Joe, that's great. Better than last month, you're doin' good."

"It's the fix we got with the Cubs," Ferriola said, explaining the increase in his profits for June.

Rocco Robustelli had little interest in the Chicago Cubs. He was busy inspecting Ferriola's income from gambling.

On the other end of "Bums," Bill Richards sat up.

"Fix on the Cubs? What the hell is that all about? Robust, you son of a gun, why didn't you ask him to enlarge on that statement." Richards could only file the statement away for future reference.

Following the Banks' trial, Rocco urged Connie Constable to get away from Chicago. Rocco was due to make a visit to Tahoe to check that the skim was proceeding as planned. Robust had no trust in John Gotti or his eastern "good fellas." He found Connie somewhat reluctant.

Connie had now become a "media star" and was making the most of it. She had always enjoyed the attention any beautiful young woman gets, but this was entirely new to her. It was an rare week she wasn't profiled in the Tribune, and the talk show hosts were featuring her. *Hard Copy* had done a profile of her, sending a production crew to Chicago.

As a result, Connie hated to leave—even for a fortnight. But she realized where her bread was buttered. She could not afford to do anything to upset her lover and mentor. The penthouse apartment of Rocco's in the Tahoe Summit promised to be a nice, relaxing interlude.

The night she arrived, "Cappy Capitano" rowed out to the middle of the lake and reported to Chuck Thomas.

"Things are going very nicely. Mort Silver had taken a shine to me. That's a big surprise to me since you guys told me Silver is Chicago's man at the Summit. He's moved me up. Now I'm a pit boss, got my own pit of crap tables. I haven't done anything to see what might be going on with the skim. I don't want to attract any undue attention. Pretty soon now, I can stick my nose in a little, try to catch the action."

Chuck Thomas had some news for Cappy also.

"Bill Richards called from Chicago. Rocky Robust will be comin' in from Chicago. Scheduled to arrive tomorrow. If there is anything you can do to get a line on him, Bill would especially appreciate it. Robust is his special target. Richards would like to climb into his back pocket if he could."

Cappy smiled at that.

"From what I hear from you guys, he practically is. OK, I'll keep an eye out. I've never seen him before though."

"Yeah, I figured that. Richards and his crew in Chicago took these surveillance photos about a month ago. They're good likenesses of the guy." Thomas handed Cappy eight photos, in color, of Robust, taken from the office at Marshall Field's.

It wasn't long before Cappy Capitano spotted Robust at the Summit. Although most of the casino employees at the Summit ate their meals at the buffet, Cappy made it his business to eat in the Spire, the gourmet restaurant at the top of the Summit. It added a touch of class to his act and was a small part of what had caused Mort Silver to notice him.

On the second day of Robust's visit, Cappy caught him in the Spire. With him was a beautiful girl Cappy didn't recognize from around the hotel. He had no idea who she was. Cappy had noticed that they had exited from the stairwell and surmised that Robust was staying in one of the two penthouse suites on the floor just below.

Cappy also noted a steady stream of sycophants who arrived, for a moment or two, at Rocky's booth. He casually mentioned it to Pierre De Soto, the captain who was in charge of his table.

"That's Gino, the man's driver," De Soto responded. Cappy noted Gino's appearance for future reference, but did not respond to Pierre's observation, as if it was of no consequence to him.

Cappy also noticed that the corner booth had been reserved for Robust and his quest. The next evening, he walked into The

Spire and, without asking, he quickly walked to the booth next to Robust's.

"The view is better from here," Cappy explained to De Soto.

Rocco and his guest arrived on schedule. Always alert, Rocco motioned to Pierre.

"Who's the guy in the next booth?"

"That's one of our pit bosses. They call him Cappy. He's from Philadelphia, been here almost from the start. He's a regular, eats up here every night."

Rocky was not only reassured, but impressed. So was his guest. "Nice looking pit bosses you have here, boss," Connie remarked.

Rocco was soon joined by "Little Nicky" Scarfo, the boss of the Bruno-Scarfo family in Philadelphia, and one of his capos, Sam Scafidi, the same guy who had sponsored Cappy at the Summit.

"Sam, hey, it's good to see you, Cappy shouted and planted himself in front of Rocco's booth."

"Good to see you too, Kid," Scafidi advised. "Hear you're doing nice things here. Silver says you're a good kid."

"Thank you, yes, I'm working hard, keeping my nose clean, trying to make sure you and Mr. Scarfo here are pleased with me." With that, Cappy reached out for Scarfo's handshake.

"You remember Capitano from The Italian Market" Scafidi said to Nicky. "We put him here on the floor. Now Silver has made him a pit boss."

Scarfo looked at Cappy. Then, turning to Robust, he told him, "This is a friend of ours in Philadelphia. He works for us here."

Robust looked at Cappy.

"I'm from Chicago. Robustelli."

Cappy looked dutifully impressed.

"Yes, Mr. Robustelli. In Philadelphia we've all heard of you."

He then turned to Connie. There was a moment of silence as no one seemed to want to introduce her. Finally, Connie introduced her self.

"I'm Connie."

To attempt to linger or join this party was out of Cappy's

league. He moved back to his own booth. As he sipped his wine, he cocked his ear to the conversation at the adjoining booth.

Robust and Scarfo seemed to be having a disagreement. Scarfo made some mention of someone he seemed to be calling either Peg or Pig. He didn't seem happy with this person's activity.

"The drop is always made to you first and then it comes east. We never know whether we're gettin' the right count or not."

At this point, Robust asked Connie if she had to go to "the can." Connie took her cue. She recognized Rocco's method of keeping her out of his business. They both wanted it that way. She wanted nothing to do with the mob—except, of course, what had to do with her political career.

After Connie departed, Cappy noticed Robust was getting tough.

"If you fuckin' mustaches from back there think I'm fuckin' you, then just piss off. I've got the majority interest here and that gives us the first count. How else you want it? The drop goes all the way east and then comes back to Chicago? In case you don't realize it, Chicago is on the way to New York and Philly. Those are the fuckin' reasons it goes first to Chicago. And that ain't gonna change!"

Just as Scarfo was about to reply to this, Connie Constable presented herself to Cappy's table. Darn it, he thought.

"I think my friend would rather that I dally at your booth for a few minutes, if you don't mind."

Cappy jumped up.

"It would be my pleasure," he said.

Cappy soon learned that Connie was an attorney in Chicago and that she was running for Congress. He didn't get her last name, but that should be enough for Bill Richards to identify her.

Robust noticed that Connie had stopped at Cappy's booth and motioned to her to return. He was finished with his business. He stood up and preferred his hand to Scarfo and Scafidi. He did not particularly care to dine with them that evening. They got the message.

Cappy soon had to get back to his job in the pit. He had been in exactly the right place at the right time.

Cappy reported to Chuck Thomas the next night and Bill Richards was soon aware that a candidate for Congress was still keeping company with the boss of the Chicago mob, probably in his penthouse apartment.

But Richards was not able to fathom the identity of "Peg" or "Pig." Obviously, Cappy had overheard a discussion of the skim from the Summit. But who was "Peg" or "Pig?"

Then it hit Richards. Years before, Sam Giancana had had a driver-body guard named Joe Pignacio.

Richards placed a phone call to Joe Yablonsky, now back at his desk in the front office in Las Vegas. He told Yabbo of his thought.

"Joe, you might have John Norris up there in Reno check out Pignacio. I have a very hazy recollection of him having an interest in a Reno restaurant. This may have nothing whatsoever to do with anything, but let's find out where Pignacio is now and what he's doing."

Yablonsky followed the suggestion. Norris discovered that Joe Pignacio still had an interest in a restaurant called The Western Outpost. It never seemed to have much of a patronage, but its balance sheet showed it did hundreds of thousands of dollars in business each quarter. Pignacio hadn't been seen on the premises for years. As a matter of fact, he was seldom at home. He seemed to travel a lot.

It all added up.

Yablonsky again asked the Bureau in Washington to have Richards temporarily reassigned to the Las Vegas Office for an operation: code name "TA-Tran."

Tahoe Transit.

Yablonsky himself would run it. Chuck Thomas and John Norris would also be on the crew. John Bassett, Richards' partner, would handle the Chicago phase. Jim Mansfield would head up the crew when and if it came to New York. Gino Lazzari would run the "fisur" from Philadelphia should it reach there.

Their problem was they were unable to find Pignacio. When he did reappear all he did for the next ten days was putter around his garden. Finally, Pignacio moved. His destination was the Summit.

Richards and his crew got there before him.

"Wait here and then follow him in, but from a big distance. If he's checking for a tail, pull off. I'm going in ahead of him and get in front to see what he does when he gets inside."

Richards felt he was safe inside the Summit. Just two people he knew would recognize him. Rocco was back in Chicago, and the other was Cappy.

When Pignacio entered the Summit, he noticed a young man come in a few seconds after him, but this guy walked right on by and started to play the nearby slots. He seemed to be a gambler, not somebody who had any interest in him. Pignacio did not see Richards at all. Richards was behind the "21" pit, obscured by six players who, even at nine in the morning, were hot and heavy looking for a big win. By putting himself in this position, Richards also put himself in place to observe the elevator to the 14th floor. Richards figured that the elevator would be Pignacio's destination. For a minute, it looked like he might be mistaken. Pignacio walked around the casino and entered the sports book, where he watched a replay of a previous day's race at Pimlico. Apparently satisfied he was "clean," he then hastily walked to the elevator and waved to the guards. They passed him without any questions.

Richards hustled back to the Bureau car and got on the radio. "He's upstairs. Let's assume he'll come out soon and get ready to take him back. We'll be way behind him and let you know when he's coming. Then you pick him up."

Richards had already decided that it was Pignacio's job to pick up a satchel of skim from the executive suit at the Summit, drive back into Reno to Cannon Airport and fly to make his "drops" in Chicago, New York City and Philadelphia. They would anticipate him and observe the identities of those recipients.

Pignacio hadn't wasted any time on the fourteenth floor. His "satchel" had been waiting for him. He was carrying a large grey attache case. Probably packed with hundred dollar bills. Maybe even thousand dollar bills, thought Richards.

It was soon apparent that Pignacio was heading for the airport. Richards made another transmission.

"Chuck, let's pass him and get there first. Let's assume he's headed for my home town and get on first." If Pignacio got on a plane, Thomas and Richards would board it also. The other two agents would put in a call to Yablonsky to let him know of developments. Yabbo would then call the Chicago FBI and let then know of arrival time so they could have agents available to pick up the tail.

Pignacio obviously had made a reservation ahead of time. Richards hunted down the chief of security at the airport and advised him of the problem. The supervisor wasn't a great deal of help.

"We have flights from here to Chicago on United, American, Delta and Continental."

Pignacio didn't have a great deal of space to roam around inside the terminal. The agents were able to keep him in sight without giving themselves away. Richards heard an American Airlines flight being announced. I'll bet that's it, he thought to himself.

Just as the gate attendant went to close the gate, Pignacio jumped. He was the last aboard. As he took his first class seat in the front of the cabin, he watched. Nobody else had boarded after him. He was clean. Away.

Richards called Yablonsky.

"Joe, he's a smart cookie. He got on last and there was no way we could get on without alerting him to the tail. Call Chicago and let them know. He's carrying a grey attache case and a grey suitcase. He picked an attache case up at the Summit. That's the target, to see what he does with that in Chicago. He's wearing a grey suit, red tie, black shoes and was wearing sun glasses when he left here. He's in first class, so he could be first off. He's tail conscious as hell, but he absolutely didn't make us. Tell them in Chicago that I'm on the next flight. Ask them to have an agent pick me up and to be ready to join the fisur."

When Pignacio arrived at O'Hare, he caught the first taxi in the cab line to the Midland Hotel in Chicago.

Within hours, Bassett, Richards and two "sound men" moved

into the room next to Pignacio's. Without alerting Pignacio, they drilled a hole into the base of the wall between the two rooms and inserted what is commonly called a "spike mike."

The next morning Richards and Bassett could hear that Pignacio had slept in. At 10:45 there was a knock on his door.

Richards called on his walkie-talkie to Burt Jensen and George Benigni, two fellow-agents in the lobby.

"Somebody is at the door. I'll call as he's leaving."

Jensen was an expert with surveillance photography and Richards wanted a shot of Pignacio's visitor.

The visitor turned out to be a lady. At least she had a lady's voice.

"Mr. Pignacio, I've been sent by Rocco Robust. I'm Candy Cane."

Pignacio had obviously been expecting the lady.

"Wait," Pignacio suddenly exclaimed, "that's the wrong package I gave you. That one is for New York. Here's the one for Chicago."

There were no further words. Richards and Bassett heard the door close.

"It's a lady; she calls herself Candy Cane," Richard whispered into his walkie-talkie. Bassett had cracked the door.

"She's wearing a green dress, blonde, about 32 or 33," he told Richards. Richards repeated it into the walkie-talkie.

"Carrying a grey purse," Bassett added.

"Carrying a grey purse," Richards intoned into his transmitter.

Downstairs, the agents were watching the indicator on the elevator. When the elevator reached the lobby, two people stepped off. One was a man. The other was about 32, 33. A very attractive blonde. Wearing a green dress. Carrying a very large grey purse.

Burt Jensen got a good shot of her exiting the elevator.

Agent George Benigni had located himself deep in the lobby. When he observed the girl who must be "Candy Cane," he hustled through the doors and jumped into one of four cars parked between La Salle and Wells on Adams. When the girl exited from The Midland, Benigni spoke on his car radio. "That's her," he exclaimed.

Since the agents had already gotten the description from the

Richards' walkie-talkie, they were familiar with her description. She stood out. Adams is one way, heading west. "Candy Cane" went east. One agent from each of the four cars jumped out. They would take her on foot. Jensen and Benigni followed. So would Bassett and Richards within a few minutes. Each of the agents had walkie-talkies. "Candy Cane" turned north on La Salle, crossed the street to the east side, and entered the La Salle National Bank Building.

She spent five minutes at a counter, presumably about to make a deposit. She was obviously "cleaning" herself. Then, "Candy" left the bank and re-entered the corridor leading the length of the building from La Salle to Clark. When she got half way down, she stepped into a bank of telephones located on the north side of the corridor and spent five minutes making a phone call. At that point she walked back into the corridor and proceeded to leave the Bank Building by entering Faber's Restaurant, finally exiting the building on Clark Street.

"Candy Cane" hustled up Clark Street to Monroe and walked rapidly, without once turning around, past Dearborn to the Monroe Street entrance to the Palmer House. She hurried up the stairs to the upper lobby and turned east, past the telephone bank, into the ladies room.

The agents thought they had lost her. Unable to guess where she might be headed, they had been unable to leap-frog her. They knew she was in the hotel, but where? They had no way of knowing where the final drop off would be made. The only thing they knew was that she couldn't have gone up to a room.

They finally figured it out. She must be in the ladies room. But they were far from certain.

"Candy" finally reappeared. Jensen spotted her from the mezzanine as she came back into the lobby and clicked off three photos as she walked to the down escalator and took it to the lower lobby. She then walked west to the stairwell on the south side of the lower level and then climbed back up to the ground level. She checked to see who, if anybody, was coming up behind her. She then walked to the State Street exit of the Palmer House.

At this point, "Candy" apparently decided that she was

completely dry-cleaned. She made no more precautionary moves. She crossed Monroe Street, walked past Carson, Pirie and Scott, and, at the corner of State and Madison, she crossed the street to the west side.

Richards heart almost jumped out of his chest!

Without a backward glance, "Candy the Courier" walked into Gentlemen's Attire.

Richards yelled into his walkie-talkie.

"Alert Bum's!"

Cici Guild, the FBI radio operator on the ninth floor of the Federal Building, didn't know what it meant, but she knew to alert Bob Dolan, Richards' supervisor.

There wasn't much to record. "Bum's" picked up the voice of Rocco Robust.

"Good, have any trouble? Just put it on the desk."

That was all. But it was enough. Testimony would now be available that "Candy Cane, the Courier" had picked up a package from Joe Pignacio at the Midland and, one hour later, at precisely 11:45 AM, after taking a most circuitous route from the Midland to Gentlemen's Attire, had given the package to Rocco Robustelli, aka Rocky Robust, the boss of the Chicago family of La Casa Nostra.

Identifying "Candy Cane, The Courier" was easy.

She walked out of Gentlemen's Attire directly to an office building on the west side of La Salle Street. Jensen and Benigni were right with her. She took the elevator up to the twenty sixth floor. When she exited she went directly to Suite 2600 and entered. Burt Jensen was right with her. When the door closed behind her, Jensen took one last picture. Of the door.

The sign read: "Connie Constable, Attorney At Law."

CHAPTER TWENTY NINE

Exciting Times For The Two Families

Rick Robustelli was being promoted to the major leagues. His first telephone call was to Bill Richards. Unable to reach his dad, he left a message on Rocco's answering machine. Bill and Bob Richards met the United Airlines Flight and drove him to Wrigley Field. He had met most of his new teammates when he trained with them that spring in Mesa.

Rick got a real tingle as he pulled on his Cubs uniform. As he jogged out onto Wrigley Field, he remembered how often he had sat in the bleachers. He looked at the familiar ivy vines on the outfield walls, the press box where he had watched and listened to Jack Brickhouse broadcast so many games. Now it was Harry Carey and Steve Stone who carried on the Brickhouse tradition.

The rooftops across Waveland Avenue were beginning to fill with fans and the gates at Clark and Addison were already busy. Rick wondered how many times Bill Richards would come to watch him pitch.

Rick wondered if his father would get his message. The news would probably be announced in the early editions of the *Tribune* and the *Sun-Times* which would be on the stands this evening, as well as on Johnny Morris' sportscast.

Rick watched his first game from the Cub dugout. The wind was blowing out and it was a high scoring game. The Cubs won 8-6. Rick was not even called to warm up.

After the game, Don Zimmer called Rick into his office.

"Rick, here's how we're going to use you. You start Saturday and then we'll use you in long relief for after 10 days or so and then you'll go back into the rotation. But you're our fifth starter. That's your role on this team. Fifth starter and long relief. Understand?"

Rick understood. He was happy. He realized that he had been brought up to the "show" at this time because the Cubs needed one more starter as they faced five games in the next four days but that after the All Star game they would have less need for a fifth starter in their rotation. He would have to produce if he didn't want to go back down to Des Moines. That wouldn't be the worst thing in the world, there was always next year, but he was 25 years old now and it was time for him to realize his potential.

The Cubs were in the race at that moment. They trailed Pittsburgh by 2 1/2 with the season almost half over and the Cards, and Mets and were right up there with them. The Cubs had not won a pennant since 1945 nor a World Series since 1908! They had come very close in 1969, but Leo Durocher, the Bruin manager at the time, had mis-managed them badly. They had been up by 9 1/2 games on August 14. They finished 8 games behind the Mets! Almost impossible to believe, but it happened. No Cub fan over 40 can ever forget the "'69 Swoon!" Durocher played the same lineup day after day, healthy or not. Ernie Banks, Glenn Beckert, Don Kessinger, Ron Santo, Randy Hundley, Billy Williams, Adolpho Phillips and Jim Hickman. For example, the catcher, Hundley, had set a Cub record by catching 160 games in 1968 and would come close to that again in 1969 by backstopping 155 games. By the dog-days of mid-August in Chicago, this starting lineup was dog-tired. More to the point, however, as far as Rick was concerned, it was the pitching staff which was done in. Leo the Lip, and what a loud mouth he was, a friend of some of the top "wise guys" when he had been the manager of the Dodgers and Giants, had stayed with a four man rotation all year, always using his pitchers on three days or less rest. There was no fifth man in his rotation. It was Ferguson Jenkins, Bill Hands, Kenny Holtzman and Rick Nye, day after day after day. "Twiggy" Hartenstein and Ted Abernathy, the sidearmer, in the bull pen. By late August the whole team was worn down. That was the year of the infamous encounter between Santo and Don Young, the seldom played center fielder who Santo believed loafed on a fly ball one day—and said so in no uncertain terms to

Young and to the press. By then, they were so fatigued they were fighting each other, not the other team. The moral of the story, however, was the four man rotation. The Cubs learned from that. They needed a fifth starter.

The "Swoon of '69" was uppermost in Zim's mind. He wanted his starters fresh for the September run. He wanted them on a four day rest routine all year. When the fifth starter he had begun the season with faltered, he asked Jim Frey for another out of the farm system or by trade. It was decided to bring up Rick. He seemed to be ready. Break him in easy, with spot starts and long relief. If he showed he deserved more work, then give it to him. If not, they hadn't lost anything by trading away a good player for that role. They would try somebody else.

Meanwhile, Ricky needed a new base. He found a bachelor apartment on Marine Drive. Ricky would be making a couple hundred thousand as a rookie major leaguer. His life was in good shape. He had a college degree from the University of Arizona, money in the bank, and a fine future ahead of him.

On Saturday, Ricky had his chance against the Cincinnati Reds. Although he wound up the loser of his first major league effort, it was a "quality start," seven innings with three or less runs. It wasn't bad. Not bad at all.

During the last weeks of July, Ricky pitched a total of 14 innings. He allowed three runs to score which were not charged to him and three that were. Again, not bad, not great.

In August, the Cubs started a long home-stand. It was now the dog days and Zim needed that fifth starter more than ever. As he has promised, he assigned the spot to Rick.

Rick had seen very little of his father. His one dinner with him had been a mistake. While Rick was recognized by many of the sports fans in the restaurant, his father was recognized by one—Bill Gleason. Gleason was a sportswriter who dallied in political overtones. It was no secret that Ricky Robustelli was the son of Rocco Robust. But, although it appeared in the press at the time Rick came up to the Cubs, it wasn't a major story. When Gleason observed father and son dining together, on good terms, at Ditka's, he decided to do a column on it.

When Gleason strayed to the world of crime, Bill Richards was his authority. When Gleason asked Bill if he had "two or three minutes to give me a quote on the background of Rocco Robustelli," he was very surprised to find that Bill wanted more than just "two or three minutes" to give a quote.

Richards knew that he couldn't ask Gleason to kill the story. That was out of his domain. He gave him essentially the same story he had used with the commissioner to get Ricky drafted.

The next day, Gleason's headline read: "FBI Investigates Robustelli's; Not Concerned." Done in Gleason's usual style, the column made it clear who Rick's father was and quoted Richards as to the exact position Robust held in the Chicago mob and that he was "evil." He talked about Rick's background in amateur ball and at Thornridge High School and at the University of Arizona. The gist of the column was Richards' quote: the FBI in Chicago had looked very closely at the entire situation involving the Robustelli family and had found nothing with which to be concerned.

Richards was hastily summoned into the front office. He had expected it. Bill Richards knew that it is hard-set policy in the FBI that only the "media spokesman," or the Special Agent in Charge, is authorized to act as a spokesman. Richards had done it dozens of times before, but only on "deep background," never for attribution. This time he had allowed himself to be quoted openly and directly. He knew that Gleason's column would be much more solid and convincing with a name quote.

He was lucky to escape a "letter of censure." Had he gotten one, he was in the frame of mine to accept it.

Rick became a celebrity overnight. So far, he had been a rookie pitcher of the Chicago Cubs. Now, without doing anything to deserve it, he joined the ranks of a dark Italian image most Italians resented. It was unfair.

On the day after Gleason's column, Bill Richards called Rick at his apartment.

"Meet me at Harry Carey's."

Rick was recognized immediately when he asked for Richard's table. He was now a curiosity piece: "The Cub rookie who is the son of the mob boss." That was what Bill Richards wanted to talk about. He also had another reason: he wanted to be seen with Rick.

It was important that Rick be seen at the most crowded sports restaurant in Chicago with his father's enemy. It would demonstrate that Rick stood on the side of law and order. Bill knew that Ben Stein, the owner, would spread the word. It was just the situation Richards wanted to create. And he couldn't have picked a better spot to demonstrate it.

The media would report that "Rick the Rookie," as some of the press had dubbed Ricky, was seen that noon dining at Harry Carey's with the lead FBI agent in Chicago.

It couldn't have worked out better from Bill Richards' viewpoint.

Cub fans are great. Rick was now an attraction. Good for the box-office. The outpouring was greater than usual on Saturday afternoon. When Wayne Messmer announced the name of the pitcher, the fans gave Ricky a standing ovation and, when the Cubs inched out the Pittsburgh Pirates 1-0, the fans gave them a rousing ovation. It had been one hell of a day in Wrigley Field and one hell of a day for the young "celebrity," Rick Robustelli. He had pitched a complete game shutout.

Rick had really burst into the consciousness of every Cub fan. The press crowded around him in the dressing room. With all the recent revelations about his background, now backed up by a great pitching performance, Rick was the talk of the town. Within a few days, Rick was as well known as any other Chicago sports figure.

When Bill, Jeannie and Bob Richards met him outside the dressing room, Ricky introduced the Richards family to his new battery mate, Sammy Watson. "He helped me through it all," he praised Watson.

That night, Rick met his father for dinner. Rocco had been in the ball park, in the left field general admission seats. He had been sorely tempted to attempt to purchase a box seat and especially regretted it when he saw the Richards family in a box.

"Fuckin' people, you'd think they was the family, not me. I don't like this at all. Rick is my son, but, the way this is all being handled, I'm some fuckin' asshole and Richards is some fuckin' saint! That's gonna change!"

Rocco brought it up that night at dinner at Ciel Bleu.

"Look, kid," Robust started, "I don't like the way things are going at all. It's great that you are off to such a great start here, but it's been done by putting me in a real fuckin' bad light here. This fuckin' Richards acts like he's your father, not me. That's not right, Rick. And you go right along with it. I can see your mother; it's a good thing she's not with us any more. She'd twist your fuckin' ear, boy. You ashamed of your family? I don't hear no protests that you stick by your father."

Rick sat still for a full minute.

"Dad, you know I'm not ashamed of you. I love you. I always have. You got to understand that."

Rocco made it clear, "I sure as hell don't."

"Well, I do, Dad," Ricky responded.

Again there was a period of silence. Ricky ended it.

"You must realize there is a very unusual situation here, Dad. I owe an awful lot to Bill Richards. If it wasn't for him, I wouldn't be where I am."

"You mean just because he went to the commissioner and got you off their blacklist? Well, hallelujah!"

Bill Richards had never told Ricky that he had gone to bat for him with Peter Ueberroth.

"What are you talking about?" Rick asked, very seriously. Robust shut up. He had always assumed that Richards must have told Rick, taken credit for what he had done for him. It was Rocco's estimation of Richards' character that he would have blown his horn to Rick, made himself a big man in Rick's eyes and taken credit for lifting him off the blacklist.

When Rocco refused further comment, Rick pressed him. But Robust would not say anything which would give his nemesis any credit. Robust had a deep hatred of Richards. The week's events only deepened his hatred.

Rick was not afraid of his father although he knew what he stood for.

"Dad, there is something I have to talk to you about. This is hard on me, but I feel I've got to say it. I told you I love you and I do. You're my father and, although you might be involved in something I know very little about, I still love you. That's what I mean. I think it isn't going to do either one of us any good to flaunt our relationship. You know what I mean?"

"No, what do you mean?" Robust wasn't making it easy for his son.

"I mean, because of what it is you do, whatever that is, I don't know much about it, but because of what the papers say about you, I don't think it's a good idea for us to be seen a lot together in public. That just raises the issue. I wouldn't even think it would be good for you."

Another period of silence prevailed.

Finally, Robust responded, "If that's the way you want it, Kid, OK by me. I don't need you."

Rick had anticipated Rocco's reaction. He loved his dad. He didn't want to hurt him.

"Dad," Rick exclaimed. "I don't want it to come to that. I want to stay close to you. So does Linda. I want to be with you, have dinner with you. Actually, a place like this is great. It's off the beaten track and the people who dine here are not sportswriters or athletes. They don't care much about your people or my people; they won't recognize us. I've met a nice girl; I'll bring her along. When Linda is in town, she can join us. You have a lady? Bring her along. We can have a great time and as often as you want. But let's not do it under some great big spotlight where it becomes the gossip of the town."

Robust said nothing. The logic of Rick's presentation, however, could not escape him. In his heart, he knew it was best for both of them. Finally, he nodded.

"Okay."

Rick reached over and grabbed Rocco's hand and smiled.

"It's best, Dad," he said.

Robust loved to walk. As he left Ciel Bleu that evening, he walked west on East Lake Shore Drive and then south on Michigan Avenue back to Outer Drive East. It gave him time to think.

"Richards can be seen with Rick at Eli's or Harry Carey's, but I can't. I got to sneak around with Connie and with my own son. What the fuck am I, some kind of leper?"

On the other hand, he could see the wisdom of Rick's thoughts. It was in his best interests as well. OK, he'd go along with it. But it grated on him that Richards could be seen with his son and he couldn't.

Eventually, Robust's resentment would put him in trouble with someone more dangerous than Bill Richards.

CHAPTER THIRTY

Connie, Rick and Sammy Make It Big.

If Ricky Robustelli was becoming a Chicago "celebrity," so was Connie Constable.

As August turned into September, Connie's campaign was off and running. The Banks trial publicity had been a great jump-start. In the space of a few days she had become well known. She couldn't have bought better publicity. All she needed to do now was prove to the voters in her district that she was a capable and worthy candidate.

Connie got the needed endorsements from the labor unions, a great boost in the blue-collar neighborhoods.

Connie's best asset was herself. She was attractive and articulate, a hard combination to beat. She exuded class. She was intelligent and well spoken, but not uppity. She mentioned her law degree and her membership in the Bar Association whenever she spoke, but in an understated way. She debated her opponent in the primary and held her own.

Connie prevailed in the primaries by a nice margin. She would now be a candidate for Congress in the general election.

Connie continued to meet with Rocco for dinner at Tiffs Too in the Sheraton Plaza. Their hide-away kept their affair in a very low profile. Rocco had obtained a suite at the Knickerbocker on a permanent basis. He and Connie were soon spending more time dining there than they did at Tiffs Too. In the meantime, both kept their apartments.

On the advise of Pat Marcy, Connie concentrated her efforts in the 42nd Ward. Pat took care of the rest of the district.

Ricky continued as the fifth man in Don Zimmer's rotation. Rick was living up to Jim Frey's every expectation and the front office of the Cubs was pleased. His record was a gaudy 8-2 when the season ended.

The Cubs did not fare as well, however. They dropped many games to the western division. When they played Houston and Atlanta, the two weak sisters of the western division, they lost. They finished three games out.

This time there was a good reason.

When Sammy Watson reported to the Cubs the previous year he quickly proved capable. He hit well, a real plus for a catcher. Very few catchers have ever led their teams, let alone the league, in hitting. Gabby Hartnett was the major exception for the Cubs. His "homer in the gloamin'" won the pennant for the Cubs in 1935.

Sammy was named Rookie of the Year and was the catcher on all rookie teams. He started strong and finished strong. His defense was good and his offense better. There seemed little question Sammy Watson would have a long, great career in baseball.

Sammy grew up in Watts, the riot-prone south-central Los Angeles community. He had signed with the Cubs as their number one draft choice two years before Rick Robustelli. Sammy made it to the majors in just three years, a great feat for a youngster signed out of high school. By the age of 21, he was the regular receiver for the Cubs.

Realizing what a long way he had come from Watts to Wrigley Field, Sammy worked hard. He was among the first to report every day and took batting practice before the other players showed up. After the games, he found it pleasant just to hang around the clubhouse. He seemed to have no life outside baseball.

Tommy Morgan, the reserve outfielder, was the other side of the coin from Sammy. Tommy grew up in Harlem. He loved the night spots. He had hated Geneva and Midland and Des Moines, his route through the Cub farm system. Once he got to Chicago, he felt like he had died and gone to heaven.

Tommy, however, was just a reserve. He needed a little reflected glory. He introduced Sammy to the Blue Note on the south side of Chicago, on 63rd street. Sammy had never been south of Madison Street before. When word spread that the Cubs favorite was at the Blue Note, the place soon filled to capacity. They all thronged around Sammy. He was treated as a hero.

Tommy and Sammy soon became close friends. They headed south after every home game.

Angelo Volpe ran the mob's numbers and policy operations on the south and west sides of Chicago. When it came to Volpe's attention that Sammy Watson had begun to frequent the south side night spots and was becoming a regular at the Blue Note on 63rd Street, Volpe immediately recognized the possibilities. This was just the kind of thing the mob was looking for.

Volpe had known of Tommy Morgan's proclivities for some time, but Morgan was just a reserve, a little used outfielder. Sammy Watson was a star, the regular catcher of the Cubs, an important cog in the team.

Volpe looked into the situation and, the next time he reported to capo, Joe Ferriola, to give his monthly "take" to the Outfit, he mentioned it.

Ferriola reacted immediately. He had been around when Tony Torts, a former Chicago mobster, was able to get to a Bear player. He knew just how Torts had handled it. He outlined the scheme for Volpe.

Volpe had just the person for the job – Galaxy Jones. Galaxy had recently arrived from Hattiesburg, Mississippi. She had quickly become the hottest new trick on the south side. Copper-colored, with a head of long brown hair, willowy but amply endowed, legs up to her neck, Galaxy was all girl. She knew what to do with what she had. Yet, she was still fresh meat. She had only been in Chicago for a couple months. She was still ripening.

Galaxy hadn't been a habitue of the Blue Note. Sammy had never seen her before. Now Volpe made sure she was brought to Sammy's attention.

Volpe made sure Galaxy would have a very nice place to entertain Sammy, and he soon was going home to Galaxy's place on Stony Island. Not the best neighborhood in town, but furnished very, very nicely.

Before he knew it, Sammy was so pussy-whipped he didn't know which end was up. He couldn't get enough. There had never been a girl quite like this in Watts. Galaxy was another planet. She was aptly named!

Volpe made his move.

Galaxy put it to Sammy one night in her apartment.

"Honey, I got a few bucks on the ball game tomorrow. The man told me, bet on Houston. You gonna be my baby and strike out about four times tomorrow?"

Sammy was shocked.

"No way! What you talkin' 'bout!" he exclaimed.

"Baby, the man told me. He told me to bet on the Astros and to tell you they better win."

Now Sammy Watson was really shocked. "What man, what you talkin' 'bout," he exclaimed once more.

"This Man, Baby, *The* Man! He told me he will make it so I never see you again if you don't lose tomorrow." Galaxy was whimpering. She was some kind of actress.

By the time the evening was over, Sammy was in a quandary. But he had not promised Galaxy anything. He left the apartment early. As he approached his new Mercedes, the kid he had paid to guard it was nowhere in sight. Two large men were lounging on the hood.

"Good evening, Sammy Watson," one of them said. Sammy tried to brush by. "You and Galaxy have a nice chat this evening, Sammy Watson?"

Sammy tried to open his door. He got his meat hand out just as the door crashed shut. "Listen, Sammy," one of the monsters said, "it's just Houston. What difference do they make? They ain't even in your division. What's a game here and there, especially against Houston. Go oh-for and have a passed ball in a tight spot. Who the fuck know the difference? Then you still got Galaxy and nobody gonna beat up on you. You understand us?"

Sammy had a lot to think about as he drove home.

The next day Sammy Watson went oh-for.

That night Sammy Watson never had it so good. Galaxy was all over him. Everything he had ever imagined in his wildest fantasies came true.

The Outfit had not bet the game. They wanted to make sure first that Sammy Watson was cooperating. Now they would place their bets. They made it as easy on Sammy as they could. For the rest of the year they told him to "pull up" only against Houston and Los Angeles. The mob was not greedy. They didn't want to ruin a good thing. Not until later.

When Joe Ferriola mentioned his "fix with the Cubs," the remark had gone right over Rocco's head. Ricky had not yet come to the Cubs and Rocco hadn't been paying any attention. It just didn't concern him.

One day soon, it would.

CHAPTER THIRTY ONE

"Operation Ta-Tran"

The agents working "Ta-Tran" had the foresight to leave an agent in the room adjoining Joe Pignacio's at the Midland Hotel and two more in the lobby.

About five minutes after "Candy Cane" entered Gentlemen's Attire, Bill and George Benigni were informed that Pignacio had checked out and was asking the doorman to hail him a cab. With the other FBI car a half block behind, they soon had Yellow Cab 143 in sight. It didn't take much to figure it was headed for O'Hare.

"Did he carry the same two pieces of baggage?" Richards asked the other agents. The answer was "affirmative."

When Delta Flight 3607 arrived at La Guardia and Richards deplaned very shortly after Pignacio, he noted that the NYO "fisur" team consisted of Jim Mansfield, Warren Donovan, Billy Kane, Jim Mulroy, Jack Bills, Guy Berado, Frank Gerrity, Tom Tolan, and two others Bill did not know. Mansfield had been at Notre Dame with Richards, had been in the Marine Corps in China with him and had served with him in the NYO. Gerrity had broken his arm once playing touch football at Quantico with Richards. The others were all good pals. More than that, they were the real pros on the Organized Crime Squad of the NYO. Jack Danahy, the supervisor, had picked them well, knowing that Richards would not forgive him if the NYO messed this up. More so than any other offices, there has always been a rivalry between the NYO and Chicago. Richards always felt justified in believing that C-1 in Chicago was the best O.C. squad in the Bureau. C-1 had developed the first top echelon criminal informant, inside the mob; had not only put in "Little Al," the first mob bug at Celano's, but two or three others, code named

152

"Mo," "Shade" and "Plumb" before the NYO installed any and had convicted the first four top bosses of the Chicago family before the NYO had convicted any. Richards was, therefore, sometimes a little too smug for the taste of his former associates in New York, but when all was said and done they got along just fine. Besides, the NYO had quickly caught up when Jimmy Flynn developed Joe Valachi, the highly publicized informant, and then later convicted so many of the top New York family bosses. At this stage it was about a toss-up in the minds of FBIHQ as to which was the better office, if not in the mind of Richards.

Pignacio immediately hustled through the corridor at La Guardia towards the cab line. Just before he got there he was accosted by a Arabic-looking man. Donovan was close enough, fortunately, to hear that the man was unknown to Pignacio and that he was dickering with Pignacio for a cheaper fare to Manhattan. A time honored custom at La Guardia. Pignacio accepted his offer for $25 to drive him to The Pierre. That was a stroke of luck; now the FBI knew where he was headed. They could tail very loosely and even be there before him.

Through Queens, over Northern Boulevard, they proceeded. Over the Queensborough Bridge, called the 59th Street Bridge in Manhattan, straight over 59th to Fifth Avenue and uptown a half-block to the Pierre Hotel. Mansfield, with whom Richards was riding, remarked: "If he had caught a cab, he'd have gone over the Triborough Bridge. Every smart ass cabbie in New York does that, it's almost as quick because of the usual tie-up on the Queens-borough, or the Midtown Tunnel, but they get a better meter run over the Triborough." Richards was offended that Mansfield didn't think he knew that. Whenever he took a cab from Manhattan to La Guardia he instructed the cabbie, before he got in, that he wanted to go to La Guardia "over the 59th Street Bridge." Many cab drivers in New York refuse to do that, refuse to accept a passenger under those conditions even though they can face disciplinary action from the Taxi and Limousine Commission for doing so. Richards has found that it is not unusual for a cabby to refuse the passenger, drive around the block and wait all over again in line for the next passenger rather than go to La Guardia over the 59th Street Bridge or even the Midtown Tunnel. They want that long ride all the way up to Harlem to take the Triborough to La Guardia.

When Pignacio arrived at the Pierre, one of the four or five finest hotels in Manhattan, on Fifth Avenue just uptown from Central Park South and opposite Central Park, Bill Kane and Guy Berado were waiting in the lobby. They watched him check in and made immediate contact with the chief of security at the Pierre, John O'Brien, a former New York Police Department detective, formerly assigned to Manhattan South. O'Brien quickly determined that Pignacio had registered as Mike Mitchell and that he was assigned room 1520. Luckily, on this occasion, room 1518, on one side of Pignacio's room, was vacant.

A call was made immediately to Danahy back in the office. "Get started on a Title III." Jack Bills, a "sound man," had all the equipment with him to handle the installation of the mike. Bills and Richards had worked together in Chicago before Bills had transferred to his "o.p.," his office of preference, to the NYO. Richards knew he was just about the best, while at the same time remaining partial to his pals in Chicago.

Before Bills could get set up, Pignacio reappeared in the lobby. He was carrying a grey attache case. Richards felt that it appeared to be lighter than it had been in Chicago when he was carrying it from O'Hare to the Midland, but perhaps that was because he knew that, in fact, it was lighter after the drop to "Candy Cane."

Pignacio exited the Pierre on the Fifth Avenue side. He cut right across the street and entered Central Park. Immediately upon entering the park, he took the stairway down to the pond in the southeast corner of the park. He stood for five minutes, in a position to watch the stairway from Fifth Avenue to see if anyone came down behind him. He ostensibly watched the ducks, but Richards and Mansfield, who had circled above him, were able to keep him in sight from Central Park South, directly across the street from the Plaza, Tony Accardo's favorite. They instructed by walkie-talkie that nobody follow Pignacio down to the pond. He was obviously "cleaning" himself.

After five minutes or so, Pignacio began walking once more. He cut west through the park, skirting the south edge of the pond. While still in the park, he walked past all the big hotels up above on Central Park South: The Plaza, the Ritz Carlton, The Park Lane, The Essex house, the old Barbizon Plaza which is now Trump Parc, the St. Moritz and then the New York Athletic Club on the corner of Central Park South at Seventh Avenue. There he exited the park and walked downtown on Seventh Ave. Past the Barnes and Noble bookstore, past Carnegie Hall, past the old Park Central Hotel, now an Omni, where Albert Anastasia and Arnold Rothstein had been murdered, past the Carnegie Delicatessen, past the Stage Delicatessen, past the Sheraton Centre and the Sheraton City Squire, soon to be known as the Sheraton New York and the Sheraton Manhattan. Then he cut back to the Sheraton Centre. There he remained just inside the lobby for five minutes, observing who might enter after him.

After those five minutes, Pignacio walked deep into the hotel, past the Cafe Fontana and then the registration desk and then down into the hotel garage. He then exited, not on Seventh Avenue where he had entered, but on W.C. Handy Place, 52nd Street.

Pignacio then walked the long block to Avenue of the Americas where he turned downtown once more. He walked past the fountains in front of the Time-Life Building and then cut across the Avenues of the Americas at 50th Street where he entered the lobby of the Radio City Music Hall. For the next three minutes he stood inside, again watching carefully for anyone who might enter after him.

After three minutes, Pignacio moved again. This time he walked to Fifth Avenue on 50th Street to St. Patrick's Cathedral. He walked up the dozen steps or so to the door of the great church and entered. He walked up and down the side aisles, past the side altars. When he got to the altar of Blessed Elizabeth Seton, in the middle of the side altars on the south side of the church, he paused and make the pretense of praying. At the same time he once again observed all around him. Finally, after ten minutes he left St. Patrick's and crossed Fifth Avenue once again. He walked to

Rockefeller Center through the promenade's Channel Gardens filled with palm trees and cactus. The Channel Gardens changes its flora frequently. When he came to the end of the promenade to the spot where the ice skaters skate in the winter and where the diners dine in the summertime, and where the gilded golden statue of Prometheus overlooks the skaters or diners as the case may be, he broke into what was almost a trot.

Pignacio darted into 30 Rockefeller Center, the GE Building, formerly the RCA Building. He hustled to the bank of elevators marked 52-69, jumped inside and punched the button to the 59th floor. Just as the door swung shut, Jimmy Mulroy jumped on with him. When he saw Pignacio punch the 59th floor, he punched the 58th floor. When Mulroy exited the 58th floor, he quickly found the stairwell and raced up to the 59th floor. Just in time to see the flash of a dark blue suit enter Suite 500.

Jim Mulroy hustled to see who the occupant of Suite 500 was. He recognized the name immediately. It was the law offices of John Walsh! Mulroy smiled and hurried back to the stairwell to send the message on his walkie-talkie to the rest of the crew while at the same time staking out the entrance to Suite 500.

Years before, Joe Bonanno, the godfather of his own Brooklyn family, had retained the services of John Walsh, the lawyer, who was a close friend of Bill Herlands, one of the prosecutors assisting Tom Dewey in the prosecution of Lucky Luciano for white slavery. Prostitution. Bonanno had furnished Walsh with information for Herlands and Dewey damaging to Luciano, his rival on the "Commission" and had also assisted them by supplying them with the two main witnesses against Luciano, the prostitutes "Cokie Flo" Brown and "Fancy Nancy" Presser. Warren Donovan had developed this information and Mulroy correlated it in the files of the NYO.

Billy Kane was immediately dispatched to the 59th floor stairwell to assist Mulroy. Half of the crew would stay in the G.E. Building while the other half would take Pignacio after he left. After all, it was expected that, although two-thirds of the "satchel" would now be empty, Pignacio still had a journey to Philadelphia in front of him.

It wasn't long before Kane and Mulroy spotted John Walsh exiting his suite of offices. He was much greyer than they remembered him, but they recognized him. There is no substitute for an old-timer in the Bureau. No computer would have recognized Walsh. Had not Kane and Mulroy been on the job – and Donovan waiting in the lobby – the FBI would have been out of luck. When Mulroy transmitted "he's out, getting on the down elevator, wearing a black pinstripe suit, red tie, no hat, grey hair, carrying a mahogany brief case," Donovan and the rest of the FBI crew were ready. Richards had decided to stay with Walsh in New York. He hoped he could catch up with Pignacio after Walsh had dropped off his package and before he left New York, probably over the Triborough, like he had caught Pignacio before he left Chicago.

When John Walsh arrived in the lobby of the GE Building, he appeared to be somewhat cautious. He started one way, stood at the elevator which goes only to the Rainbow Room on the top floor, an express elevator, and then walked back the way he came. He then walked to the corner of Avenue of the Americas, still carrying the mahogany brief case, of course, and walked into Hurley's on the southwest corner of Rockefeller Center. Hurley's had been a saloon since 1892 and was a famous speakeasy during the prohibition era. It gained great fame as "the hold-out bar" when John D. Rockefeller decided to construct Rockefeller Center in the early 1930s. He make a great effort to buy up the lease of Hurley's, just a four story structure, while planning to build his 70 story RCA Building immediately adjacent. But Hurley adamantly refused to sell to Rockefeller despite his most generous offers. Finally John D. was forced to redesign the RCA Building with a recess to accommodate the four story saloon at its base, dwarfed by the highest buildings in the world all around it in Rockefeller Center. When the NBC Studios were installed in the RCA Building, Hurley's became famous as Johnny Carson, Jack Paar, Steve Allen and David Letterman featured the saloon in their broadcasts. Henry Kissinger and his party were once asked to leave for being rowdy.

When Walsh entered the only entrance to Hurley's, just at the corner of Avenue of Americas at 49th Street, he stopped to chat with the owner-host, Adrien Barbey. Since Adrien's post was immediately inside the door, this gave Walsh the opportunity to observe anyone who entered after him. He then sidled up to the long bar, located just inside the saloon. He took a position where anyone who entered the saloon would have to pass him. He engaged in a long conversation with Michael Flynn, the bartender to whom he was obviously well known. He ordered a gin and tonic. None of the agents had entered Hurley's. They stayed outside and watched the only entrance. They peeked in one of the many windows and could see Walsh from the sidewalk on 49th Street. If he had met someone, then they would have entered and gotten pictures from their hidden cameras for evidentiary purposes.

After he took his time downing his gin and tonic, John Walsh, now code-named "Westie," after the New York mob of Irishmen on the west side of Manhattan who use that name, headed for the nearest subway station. It is located right tight up on the uptown side of Hurley's. "Westie" hurried down into the underground. The subway station is two blocks long. It is one of the busiest in the world since it empties into the bowels of the Rockefeller Center. The agents had no choice but to hurry down almost on Walsh's heels. They quickly immersed themselves into the hundreds of passengers there. They watched as "Westie" caught the first "B" train. Richards, Donovan, and Mansfield jumped on the cars immediately forward and back from the car Walsh entered.

When "Westie" reached West 4th Street, several stops downtown, he jumped off. He waited until the doors almost closed before he did so. Fortunately, the agents were on to this trick—an old one. They jumped off from their cars right after him and immediately got lost in the crowd of subway riders. Walsh then walked up the two flights of stairs and stood on the platform. Waiting and watching. Then, once again just as the doors were closing, he jumped onto a train. This time the "Q" train. The FBI trio, all veterans of surveillances like this one, were able to keep him penned in.

Walsh seemed unconcerned. He had picked up *New York Newsday* and appeared very nonchalant, reading it. The headlines read, "Steinbrenner Blasts Winfield." What else was new in New York?

When the "Q" train reached Chambers Street, Walsh made his move. He once more waited until the doors were about to bang shut and then jumped out. Fortunately, by this time, the agents had anticipated his move. The Bureau agents were being very lucky on the New York phase of "Ta-Tran." Mulroy had taken a big chance on the stairwell of the GE Building. Had Pignacio waited at the elevator bank for just several seconds he would have seen Mulroy leaping up the stairwell, the same guy who had just gotten off the floor below. That would have blown "Ta-Tran" to pieces. Likewise, Donovan, Richards and Mansfield, who had jumped off the "Q" train simultaneously with Walsh, had not been detected.

When Walsh exited the "Q" train, he walked the three blocks underground on the concourse which took him into the World Trade Center, the twin towers which highlight the skyline of lower Manhattan. Inside the lower level of the WTC, he walked past the scores of shops which inhabit the bottom of this piece of architecture which is renown throughout the world. When he got to the WTC branch of Alexander's, the big department store chain, he ducked inside. Just for a moment this time. When he seemed satisfied that he was not being tailed, he exited the store and hurried the hundred feet or so to the escalator taking him up out of the lower level of the WTC to the corner of Liberty Street and Church Street. He hustled east on Church which becomes Trinity Place at that point. When he reached Rector Street after two blocks, he turned left on Broadway and then quickly one half block to Trinity Church, the famous Episcopal Church located on the intersection of Broadway and Wall Street, two of the most famous streets in the world. Trinity Church, chartered in 1697, is a soaring Neo-Gothic building with a towering spire surmounted by a gilded cross. It dominated the skyline of lower Manhattan during its early years and was a welcoming beacon for the ships sailing into New York Harbor. The graves of many historic figures are located in the graveyard on the church grounds including those of Alexander Hamilton, William Bradford and Robert Fulton.

Walsh quickly ducked into the church. He sat in the last pew and once again observed anyone who came in after him. By this time Mansfield was able to regroup the entire contingent of agents by use of his walkie talkie. He had been unable to transmit from the bowels of the subway but now, once again on the surface, his message had reached the agents who had remained in Bureau cars on the streets of Manhattan. Now all had rendezvoused with Mansfield, Donovan and Richards at Trinity Church. In effect, Walsh did them a favor when he remained inside for ten minutes. It enabled the entire FBI team to resituate themselves.

After the ten minutes he spent in the famous church, "Westie" exited at B'Way and Wall Street and walked straight east, towards the East River. "This guy has a lot of energy for an old guy," Richards remarked to Mansfield.

When he reached the corner of Wall Street and Broad, right at the intersection with the New York Stock Exchange on one side and Federal Hall on the other, Walsh seemed to run out of gas. He took one step up on the stairs of Federal Hall where George Washington took the oath of office as the first president of the United States on April 30, 1789 – at 26 Wall Street – and hailed a cab. It seemed his walk was about to end.

As the cab headed east on Wall Street the agents were in perfect position to follow. They tailed Walsh's cab as it turned back uptown on Water Street, then west on Pearl Street, then east on Centre Street to Canal. At this point, Mansfield, driving Richards, allowed a big smile to light up his face. Richards didn't get it.

But the rest of the FBI crew did. Almost simultaneously, the Bureau car's microphones crackled. "OH, oh. Be alert now." Richards was the only one who didn't get it.

He didn't recognize that the cab was waiting on Canal Street, waiting for traffic to clear to turn left on Mulberry Street. If the cabbie would turn right at that point he'd be in Chinatown. But, by turning left, he entered Little Italy. Onto Mulberry Street.

When the cabbie made his turn, Richards caught on. The headquarters of John Gotti is on Mulberry Street, not all that far from Canal Street. It is the heart of Little Italy. Just as many of the "made" members of the Chicago family of La Cost Nostra grew up with each other in the "Patch," that area around Taylor and Halsted on the near south side of Chicago, many of the "wise guys," the "good fellas" of the five New York families of La Cosa Nostra, grew up with each other in Little Italy, on Mulberry Street or on Mott Street, adjacent to it.

All of the "fisur" agents now realized where "Westie" must be heading. Obviously, the expected recipient of the "Ta-Tran" skim was John Gotti, the Dapper Don, the Teflon Don. If that was so, it was only natural that the skim would eventually end up with him in his headquarters. Just as Rocco Robustelli had a headquarters, just as Tony Accardo had a headquarters, so every mob boss had one particular spot to headquarter. The place where he plots his strategy, meets his underlings and counts his money. John Gotti's headquarters was on Mulberry Street. The Ravenite Social Club. The FBI agents knew it well. They had been there many times. Sometimes late at night to plant a mike!

Sure enough, Jack Bills was on the scene when Walsh paid off his driver and ducked into the Ravenite Social Club. With his mahogany briefcase. Bills was able to get a shot of him with his camera, for evidentiary purposes, just as he disappeared into the white door of the red brick building. There were the usual three thugs at the doorway, watching carefully to see if "the G" or the Intelligence Unit of the NYPD might come by.

The trip from the office of John Walsh in the GE Building, to Hurley's, to West 4 Street, to the World Trade Center, to Trinity Church, to the New York Stock Exchange to Mulberry Street had taken almost an hour and a half the way John Walsh had negotiated it. But the FBI tail team stuck right with him.

Mulberry Street is one way going uptown. Jack Danahy, located in the Operations Center of the NYO in Federal Plaza, not that far away, was able to watch the action on Mulberry Street through the sophisticated equipment of the current day FBI. He was able to direct the cars so that when Walsh came out in just a matter of two minutes, Billy Kane was able to get a shot of his exit. Sans mahogany brief case! These photos would make the "Ta-Tran" operation one solid one when it came into court!

At that point the three thugs became excited. They had just seen the Bureau car with two suspicious looking guys go east. They stepped into the street and quickly copied down the license number of the Bureau car. It would do them no good, FBI cars are licensed to fictitious people and the plates are changed regularly. But it sure excited the thugs' suspicions.

Not that it mattered. As far as Richards and his pals from the NYO were concerned, they had gotten what they came for.

First they traced the skim from the Summit, to Chicago and right into the headquarters of the prime recipient. Then they followed the "bag" into New York City and into the headquarters of John Gotti, the boss of the Gambino family, another prime owner of the Summit.

Now hopefully, they could tail it to Nicky Scarfo, the third recipient, the leader of the Philadelphia family of the La Cosa Nostra.

To that end, Richards rendezvoused with his old pals from the NYO. "Thanks guys, you guys haven't slowed down a step. Great job. I've got to get back up to the Pierre and meet up with your guys on Pignacio. It's been fun being with you pros again. See you soon, probably in Chicago when we put this whole thing together for a RICO case on all these guys. Thanks again."

He was off. His old buddy, Jim Mansfield, drove him to the Pierre Hotel where it all started about two hours ago. Richards had experienced the excitement of working in the Big Apple once again with his old colleagues. Thomas Wolfe had once written that you can't go home again. Richards had never considered New York City exactly as home, but it had been enjoyable working there once again. Now he would see where "Ta-Tran" would lead him from here.

Richards found no time to relax. He found that Pignacio spent the night in his room at the Pierre ordering room service and, although Richards would have preferred dining downstairs at the Cafe Pierre, he had dinner in his room also.

The next morning, shortly after Richards woke up in the room next to Pignacio's, he heard Pignacio rustling in his bath room. He quickly showered, shaved and dressed, ready for another day of "Ta Tran."

Soon, Pignacio exited his room, took the elevator down and then walked across to the lobby. The Pierre is one hotel where the elevators are not located inside the lobby and one of the great hotels of the world which does not have much of a lobby.

When Pignacio had completed his check out, the bellman hoisted his suitcase—Pignacio would not let loose of the attache case—and carried it to the 61st Street entrance to the hotel where the doorman whistled for a cab. John Foley had been the doorman at that entrance for 54 years. When he retired in 1984 a plaque was inserted just inside the lobby renaming the door the "John Foley Door." Richards had come down, after alerting the NYO agents below, on the next elevator after Pignacio and was ready when he completed his checkout. Today there was a new set of NYO "Fisur" agents on the job. The "old pros" had done their job and had no desire to merely escort Pignacio out of town. It wasn't expected to be a difficult assignment and it turned out just that way.

Sure enough, the cabbie took Pignacio over the Triborough Bridge, not the closer 59th Street Bridge. Had he known who his fare was, the cabbie might not have been so quick to bilk him.

At La Guardia, Pignacio took a USAir flight to the City of Brotherly Love, again first class while Richards was able to use his FBI credentials once more to obtain the bulkhead aisle in coach, not a difficult task since the bulkhead is often held until the last for families with children, the ill and infirm. In the meantime, the agents had phoned ahead to the Philadelphia FBI Office to give them his ETA, estimated time of arrival, Pignacio's description and the fact that Richards would be close behind him when he arrived.

Once again, Richards was greeted by a crew of old pals. Gino Lazzari, Andy Sloan and John Osborne had all worked with Richards at one place or another. Gino would soon retire to go with the fine Pennsylvania Crime Commission as its top investigator and Andy had been as old hand-ball partner of Richards at the

Austin YMCA in Chicago, the brother of a couple of Chicago cops and an attorney. John had been on C-1 with Richards in Chicago. All were now assigned to Philly.

Richards had not been in Philadelphia for a couple years. While they drove, Lazzari filled him in on the situation in the Keystone State.

"Frank Rizzo, the old chief of police and a long time mayor here years ago, is making noises like he's going to run for major again. He's been out for years. Nicky Scarfo is the boss here, but now he's running things from prison. We got him just the other day for the murder of Frank D'Alfonso, "Frankie Flowers," and he got a life sentence. First LCN boss ever convicted of murder. We've been able to turn more CTE's here in Philly then anywhere. Wait a minute, I know, you guys in Chicago think you're the best, but we got seven guys who have testified and are now in the Witness Protection Program. We just turned Phil Leonetti, Scarfo's underboss, but that's not out yet. That's need to know. We've had more murders of LCN guys here than anyplace else. Scarfo even had his boss, Angelo Bruno, killed, and then he went on a rampage. I can't tell you how many LCN guys have been killed, but at least 15-20 in the last ten years, since Scarfo had Bruno downed. Two, three years ago, before Scarfo got convicted, it was a tough family, one of the best. But Scarfo ruined it. Inept, real bad killer. Of course, we had a lot to do with it too. We also had Scarfo and many of his top guys in a RICO case. We had turned two guys, one you remember, you met him when you came here two, three years ago. Del Giorno. And another guy, Caramandi. They were top guys. We played a tape for Del Giorno, you remember, of Scarfo plotting to kill him. That turned him. In a hurry. Then we recently got Local 54 of the Hotel Employees and Restaurant Employees Union on a RICO showing how Local 54 had a tight grip on them by the Bruno/Scarfo mob. The mob doesn't have a boss now, but Scarfo, as I say, is running it from prison. The action boss, we think, is either Tony Piccolo, who's about 70 or maybe Joe Ciancaglini. He's much younger, about late 50s or so. It's a good town, this is, and since we have put the LCN down so far, it's better. But we have a lot of emerging crime groups here too. They are becoming a bigger and bigger problem every year. All the time. The Outlaws, the motorcycle gang, the blacks, the Jamaicans, the Colombians, the Dominicans, the Puerto Ricans, and the Cubans. They're all here and all make big trouble. Mostly in drugs. The LCN here, unlike your people in Chicago, are much into drugs also. Drugs are a very big thing in Philly, even in South Philly where the Italians under Bruno tried so hard to keep them out. But Scarfo screwed that all up too. He was a real bum, still is, even in prison we can't shake him."

It had been a great precis on the current situation in Philadelphia. Now, as they neared the downtown on I-95, it was time to turn full attention on the situation at hand.

"He's either going downtown or over the Walt Whitman Bridge over the Delaware River into Camden and I doubt he's doing that," Lazzeri observed. Pignacio wasn't, he was going downtown. Soon his cab arrived at the Sheraton Society Hill on Dock Street, downtown.

There had been no chance to anticipate this. Therefore, no Bureau car or agent had been able to get there first. It didn't matter. Osborne and Sloan caught up with Pignacio at the registration desk. This time he registered as Mike McGee. He seemed to have a thing for the first name of Mike. It wasn't all that smart, although it wouldn't make a difference on "Ta Tran." He had been out-smarted all the way during this trip—so far. Richards made careful note that he was still carrying the attache case. It even seemed much lighter now, but Bill knew that was his imagination.

Again, arrangements were made with the hotel management, again this time with the security chief well known to Osborne, to obtain the room next to Pignacio. Again, arrangements were immediately made to set up a Title III with a spike mike. Once again, however, Pignacio made his move before that could be accomplished.

This time Pignacio disdained the cab. He walked. Over to Walnut and then to Chestnut. He was carrying the attache case. The agents stayed very loose but kept him in sight. Pignacio was obviously "cleaning" himself, according to custom. One trick he pulled was an old one—one that the agents had ducked many times in their careers. He stood on the sidewalk in front of storefronts and used the large plate glass windows, especially those slanted, to give him a view behind him using the refection as a mirror to scout his rear. It did him no good, the agents were alert for that.

Soon he appeared to be satisfied that all was clear. He headed towards the river, the Delaware.

Very quickly he came to what appeared to be his destination. The Chart House. A large, well appointed restaurant with a great view of the river and over it into Camden, New Jersey.

The agents found later that he had a reservation for two under the name of "Mr. Mertz"—or that somebody had. Richards and the Philadelphia Office crew were very alert at this point. And well they were served in being so. Because, as it turned out, "Mr. Mertz's" companion for that evening had been sitting at the bar in the Chart House watching him arrive and surveying the scene behind him to observe who might be tailing him. Another old trick, one the agents again were on the look-out for.

When "Mr. Mertz" had been seated, the man at the bar got up and joined him. Andy Sloan recognized him immediately. Again, luck played a part. Had Gino Lazzari followed Pignacio into the Chart House instead of staying behind in the car with Richards, he would have been immediately recognized by the man at the bar and the Philadelphia phase of "Ta Tran" would have been blown. This operation seemed to have a special blessing—from Chicago through New York City into Philly.

The man at the bar was Kevin Milligan. Kevin Milligan was well known to the Philadelphia FBI agents. He was a business agent of Local 54 of the Hotel Employees and Restaurant Employees International Union, sometimes called the Culinary Union. For over two decades this local has been under the influence, sometimes under the violent influence, of the Bruno-Scarfo mob in Philadelphia. As a matter of fact, the Philadelphia Office was then in the process of working up a RICO case, a civil RICO case. The suit would allege that the Philadelphia mob used murder and intimidation to attempt to control the local and that they plundered its health and welfare fund and used this local to extort money from bars and restaurants. The suit would attempt to put the Local under federal trusteeship. Local 54 has 22,000 members and is a great influence in the hotels and casinos in Atlantic City, the primary lever the Bruno-Scarfo mob has used to infiltrate the hotels and casinos on the Boardwalk.

Osborne was close enough to hear part of the conversation. However, what he heard was strictly "desultory." He assumed that all of it was, that none of it pertained to any mob business since neither participant in the conversation was actually a "made" guy. He heard Pignacio say that he liked Chart House Restaurants and especially "this one and the one up and off the Kingsbury Grade, above Lake Tahoe. What a view that one gives you. This one too. What do they call this, Penn's Landing, this spot we're on?" Milligan was seen to nod.

After a quick meal, Pignacio left first. Half of the Philadelphia FBI crew went with him, only to find that he cabbed back to the Sheraton Society Hill and apparently sacked out for the night. The next day another crew would put him on a flight to Reno. His job was obviously finished—for this trip.

When Pignacio departed the Chart House, Sloan, Osborne, Lazzari and Richards all immediately looked for one thing. Was he carrying the attache case? He was not. This was another indication that he was leaving what was left in it for the Philadelphia mob since in Chicago and in New York he had retained the case, apparently dipping into it and giving it to the recipients in those cities to carry what he had given them in their own "satchel."

Ten minutes after Pignacio departed, so did Milligan. Immediately the agents looked to make sure he was carrying Pignacio's attache case. He was.

Milligan picked up the tab, leaving a hundred dollar bill and not waiting for change. He walked to the parking lot of the restaurant and retrieved his own car. A bright red Caddy.

"Looks like he does pretty well for a business agent," Richards remarked.

"Doesn't matter to him. That's Local 54's car," Lazzari replied.

Milligan drove his car from Penn's Landing and immediately headed for the Walt Whitman Bridge. He didn't seem to be surveillance conscious at all. When he exited the bridge he was on the North South Freeway on the southern edge of Camden, New Jersey. He continued almost directly south until he reached the Atlantic City Expressway which connects with the North-South Freeway. It is a toll road. In about an hour he was in Atlantic City. Nothing fancy about his driving, he didn't seem to care if he were being followed or not. It was Richards' experience that such is the way things happened. Some hoods, like Gussie Alex, are cautious even if they're just going to the bathroom during the middle of the night. Others, even when they're on a strategic mission, never are wary. Milligan seemed one of the latter.

When it became obvious that Milligan was on his way to Atlantic City, Gino Lazzari gave Richards another run down; he was most knowledgeable about his territory and he didn't mind sharing that knowledge.

"I know you've been here before," Lazzari started, "but let me bring you up to date now. They've got 12 casinos here now. Compared to 351 in Nevada, so you can see its small potatoes. But they gross. Philadelphia is 60 miles from here, New York and Newark about 100. 60 million people live within 300 miles of here. Slots are the big money makers for the casinos here, more so than in Nevada because the great bulk of visitors here are older people who aren't interested in learning the intricacies of craps or blackjack or roulette or baccarat. They just push in the quarters or dollars and pull the lever. Most of the gamblers who come in here never leave the Boardwalk. They arrive by bus, stay the day and bus back in the evening. Like a day at the beach. They don't go a foot off the Boardwalk. In fact, the most dangerous part of the day is coming in and going back when a bunch of young blacks throw rocks and bottles at cars and busses coming in on this Atlantic City Expressway. You'll see the slums when we get into town. Gambling has done nothing for the people who live here, has not lived up to its promises at all. Since 1978, when gambling started here, street crime has gone up about 700%. What it has done is attract the drug dealers, the pimps, prostitutes, car thieves, pickpockets, thieves and burglars. One of the big things you notice right away is the dichotomy of the Boardwalk. There's the gaudy Taj Mahal and then next door there's an old hot dog stand that's been battered by the salty winds from the Atlantic Ocean for decades. Same way up and down the Boardwalk. You go from flash to fizz. From the new and beautiful to the old and dilapidated. Right next to each other. Another big thing. In Vegas or Tahoe or Reno, but especially in Vegas, the hotels are set off the Strip, back aways like Caesars or the Mirage or Bally's or the Trop or Excalibur. Way back where you can get a real perspective of them, a good look at their grandeur. Here, the hotels are flush up against the Boardwalk. You can't hardly get a perspective of them. To see them you have to look up, not out and up. Another big thing, of course, is that here you don't have sports betting, no sports books. That, of course, is a big money-maker in Nevada. They say the professional sports teams blocked that, got to the lawmakers, because they don't want gambling on their teams, baseball, football and pro basketball. Most of the pro teams are located in the east and midwest, not in Nevada. So that hurts. Guy wants to bet on games, he's got to go to Nevada if he wants to follow the action on the big screens. On Sunday afternoons in the fall, with the satellite dishes, at the sports books in Nevada, and every casino of any size has them now, a fan can watch any game in the NFL he wants—they carry every one of them. Another thing. In Nevada the casinos are open 24 hours a day. Guy gets on a roll, one way or another, he can stay and play it out. Here we're closed for four hours each morning. Also, here you can't cash a check in a casino. Against the Casino Control Commission rules. Another thing. Here there is no poker or keno. Big things in Nevada. And here the CCC doesn't allow those big kaleidoscopic outdoor neon lights that the Strip in Vegas is famous for. Now we got a new governor, Jim Florio, and he seems to be loosening the tight control that Tom Kean, the old governor, kept. But I was looking the other day at some figures. In New Jersey they spend sixty million dollars a year for enforcement. You know what they spend in Nevada? Eighteen million. In Nevada they've got 351 casinos. Here they've got 12. But in Nevada they've got just 394 employees of their Gaming Control Board. Here they've got 985 employees of the Division of Gaming Enforcement, same as the GCB. 394 employees in Nevada to police 351 casinos, 985 in New Jersey to police 12 casinos. Think that makes a difference? You bet your bippy. That's about 80 enforcement people policing each of 12 casinos against one employee policing each of 351 casinos in Nevada. Most of the casinos have had bad years here. Trump Castle is down 31% in revenue. Trump Plaza is down 21%. Bally's Grand is down 20%. Bally is in default on its corporate debt. One of only five casinos which is up is Resorts and that has just come out of bankruptcy protection. The Taj will have to do much better than it has to keep The Donald out of trouble. Harrah's Marina, the Claridge, Caesar's, Showboat and Bally's Park Place are holding their own but the Sands is down along with the rest I mentioned. And yet this is the most frequently visited resort in the United States. Las Vegas might be the fastest growing city in the country but more people visit here. Course, that's somewhat misleading too, because many of the visitors here stay just hours while in Vegas and Tahoe and Reno, and that new place out there where gaming is becoming so hot, Laughlin, there they stay for days."

Lazzari knows his Atlantic City. He had given Richards a real quick but concise summary of the situation there.

Richards had been vaguely aware of most of what Lazzari had said. He was especially impressed, always, with the figures on what the two states spend to keep the casinos from mob control. No wonder the mob has had a good thing in Nevada but not in Atlantic City. The Boardwalk swarms with cops. Not noticeably uniformed ones, but those of the Division of Gaming Enforcement, those watching the operations of the casinos so closely.

Now, however, it was time for Richards and the rest of the crew to pay strict attention to Kevin Milligan. Richards was not there for a seminar on the situation pertaining to Atlantic City, he was there to follow the bag, the booty, the skim from one great body of water to another, from Lake Tahoe to the Atlantic Ocean.

When Milligan approached the Boardwalk, he turned right, right into the covered parking lot of Trump Plaza. Richards left his car as did Sloan. They put themselves in the small lobby off the garage to watch Milligan as he approached, making sure he was still carrying Pignacio's attache case. He was.

Milligan walked into the lobby of Trump Plaza. He punched an elevator button. He got on the elevator. Richards hesitated. They had been so lucky so far. Should he press his luck? He did. He decided that this guy was by far the least cautious of anybody they had shadowed so far. He didn't seem to have a care in the world. Richards jumped on the elevator.

Milligan pressed the button for the fourth floor. Richards did just as FBI agents are taught in surveillance school at Quantico in such situations. Just as Mulroy had done at the G.E. Building. He got off on the third floor. He raced up the stairway to the fourth floor. Only to have Milligan standing in the hallway. Carefully watching the elevator door and the door to the stairwell!

"Missed my floor," Richards said to Milligan as he walked past him with a shit-eating grin on his face. Milligan merely nodded. He was not fooled. Richards, in desperation, went to room 401, in the corner and knocked on the door. A little old lady answered it and opened the door.

"Mam, your car is ready for you in the garage," Richards said. With that he turned quickly and hurried to the elevator. The lady looked at him as he departed, with a perplexed look on her face.

Milligan remained in the hallway, carefully eyeing Richards. When the elevator arrived and Richards departed, he continued to wait. Milligan had two choices. He could keep the attache case and return to the lobby and then return to Philadelphia with it. The safe thing to do. Or he could make the drop, say nothing about any suspicions, act as if he had successfully completed his mission and then return to Philadelphia. He thought about it for a minute. Then he decided, "what the hell, maybe the guy did miss his floor. I get well paid for this, I ain't gonna admit I fucked it up. Besides, what can they prove even if that guy is the G?"

Kevin Milligan, not as dumb as Richards thought he was on

the one hand, was as dumb as Richards thought he was on the other. He went to room 410, knocked on the door and entered. Five minutes later he departed the room, took the elevator downstairs, walked through the lobby to the covered garage, got into his red Caddy, quickly got onto the Atlantic City Expressway and drove back home to Philadelphia. Now he was cautious. He watched his tail all the way. He saw nothing. The FBI agents had let him go. As soon as they noticed he had not been carrying the attache case when he arrived in the Trump Plaza lobby, they lost all interest in him. Now, they would concentrate on the next piece of the puzzle. How to identify the person to which Milligan had passed the "satchel." The last piece of the puzzle to be solved before Ta-Tran could be called an unqualified success.

It was a big piece of the puzzle. The agents weren't sure that the drop had been made to a guest on the fourth floor. Even assuming it had, to which of the guests in the dozens of rooms on that floor?

They could only hope. That the recipient would soon depart, descend into the lobby—carrying Pignacio's attache case!

There isn't much room in the lobby of the Trump Plaza. The hotel is set right on the Boardwalk. Like all Atlantic City hotel-casinos, with the floor space almost identical in the casino, a visitor cannot walk off the Boardwalk into the casino. That is another difference between Nevada casinos and Atlantic City casinos. The law forbids entry from the Boardwalk directly into the hotel casino. It is designed to prevent luring the sucker into the occasion of sin—gambling. In the case of Trump Plaza, the lobby of the hotel, the registration desk and the elevator to the guest rooms are located in the back of the hotel, off the parking garage. Almost all hotels have their lobbys in the front of the hotel. That seems just natural. Not Trump Plaza, however. Besides, the lobby itself is cramped. If the lobby of the Pierre in New York City is small for a major hotel, the lobby of the Trump Plaza is minute in comparison. The agents found they stuck out like sore thumbs, standing around in the lobby. Being from the Philadelphia FBI office and not the FBI resident agency in Atlantic City, they were unacquainted with the security people at Trump Plaza. They knew only that, unlike the very best gaming hotels, like Caesars down the street, there was no former FBI agent in charge of the security at Trump Plaza. They put in a quick call to Dick Ross, the "R.A." of the FBI in Atlantic City. He quickly placed a call to the chief of security at the hotel and put him in touch with Lazzari.

Gino Lazzari was not a physical giant. Tough, but not huge. He was quickly outfitted with a uniform of a bellman at Trump Plaza. Now he could situate himself in the tiny lobby of the hotel and not be out of place at all. He carried his walkie-talkie, concealed. It had been a long day for Gino. He hoped it wouldn't be all night that he would have to stand on the marble floors.

He didn't. Gino saw the attache case. He hustled up to the man carrying it.

"Care to have me carry your luggage, Sir?" he asked.

The man didn't bother to reply. He just gave Gino a dirty look. He walked right past him. Into the garage area. Gino got on his walkie-talkie.

"He's on his way into the garage, carrying the case. You'll all recognize him!"

They did. All but Richards. Excited, Andy Sloan ran up to Bill.

"It's Patsy Caruso! He's a capo in the family! Top guy! He's right under Scarfo! Great!"

Richards recognized the name from the chart of the Bruno/Scarfo family of La Cosa Nostra. Pasquale A. Caruso, long time mob member and now a capo. He agreed. Great.

Lazzari ran to Richards' car and jumped in the driver's seat. Off the crew went after Caruso. The capo was crafty, however. He moved his car around and about. From Missouri Street to Arkansas Street to Mississippi Street, he was obviously as tail conscious as any target in "Ta Tran" had been from the start at the residence of Joe Pignacio in Reno.

Finally, Richards got on the radio.

"Screw it! We've got what we need. Let him go. Let's head for the barn!"

"Ta Tran" had concluded. It had been a long haul. A long lucky haul.

Richards had what he needed.

The next morning Gino picked Richards up and took him on a tour of Independence Hall and the Liberty Bell. Richards had been there before, but whenever he was in Philadelphia he would made sure he visited this great place where the history of the United States had been made.

Then it was back to Chicago. Back to touch base with John Bassett and find out what he had missed while on the "Ta Tran" phase of "Operation Pensum"—especially what he might have missed from his pal, "Bum's." One more piece of the great impending RICO case against Rocco Robust and his associates in La Cosa Nostra had been put in place.

CHAPTER THIRTY TWO

"Bum's" Best.

"Bum's" was about ready to reach its crescendo. The mike was about to deliver much of the evidence Richards and the FBI had been looking for to put together a RICO indictment.

Several days after Connie delivered Chicago's share of the skim from the Summit, the upper echelon of the outfit gathered in the haberdashery office. Tony Accardo, Rocco Robustelli, Joe Ferriola, Rocky Infelice, Gussie Alex, Al Tocco, and the other top brass were in attendance.

Accardo, never one for "desultory" conversation, started it off.

"Rocco, we got the skim in from Tahoe, you say. What's it amounting to now?"

Rocco responded to his boss and Bill Richards, at the other end of "Bum's," perked up.

"This month it was, rounded off, $110,000. That's not like in the old days when you guys had five or six casinos in Las Vegas, Joe, but it's picking up. I expect we'll be a couple mil a year next year."

"OK," Joe Batters replied. "We got spoiled in the old days, the sixties and seventies, but that's good. Now what you got comin' in from gambling, Joe."

Joe Ferriola, in charge of the lifeblood of the Chicago mob, answered this.

"We got about three million this past month, September. That's about it. Pretty good. About what we expect these days. The Illinois state lottery has cut into our play, as you know, and the off-track parlors from the tracks, but it's been pretty consistent. About 35–40 million a year, from gambling."

"OK, how about juice?" Accardo inquired.

It was Infelice who answered.

"About average in September. We had a couple big guys duck out on us, but we'll catch them. Rocco gave me the OK to break legs on two welshers this month and they'll pay off next month. We got about a million seven."

"Good," Batters said. "What about the street tax?"

Robust answered this one. "About 800,000. That's been down ever since there haven't been as many abortionists to lay on. But it's evened out now. That's about what we can expect."

"Chop shops?" Accardo asked.

Tocco answered this one. His people put the arm on the "chop shoppers" and it was good money for the Outfit.

"About 350,000. Up and down, but that's not all that bad."

"What else, anything unusual?" Accardo asked.

Joe Ferriola started to jump in.

"We got this kid on the Cubs. Angelo has an. . ." He got no further. Rocco cut him off.

"I got a rumble from Pat Marcy that the G is looking into my hit on Jimmy Catuara. You remember, Joe, I got the order from Pilloto to take over Jimmy's territory years ago and that if I had to chop him I could. Well, Pat tells me he got from one of his coppers that the G is hot on that right now. I told Pat to keep close to that copper; he's from homicide, downtown, and he's one of Pat's guys. After all these years, I don't want to go down for what I did to The Bomber. That's past history. Any of you guys picked up anything on that? Al, that's your territory, Blue Island. Any rumbles on that out there?"

No one spoke up.

"Anything else," Accardo asked.

Gussie Alex spoke up just as Ferriola tried to get back to "the kid on the Cubs."

"We're going along well on the lady lawyer. She's helping herself a lot and, with the help of the First Ward—which is a big slice of her district—it looks like we might have one of ours in Washington in a couple months. She's a hell of a campaigner. She's so good, she might have been able to do this all on her own. So I'm optimistic on that. Other than that, we made a new commander this month. Chicago Avenue. They moved that fucking Mike O'Donnell out of there, finally, we could never do anything with him after all these fuckin' years of trying, but the new guy Dancewicz there, we moved right up all these years and now he's in a real good spot. So it finally paid off. One other thing, this captain down south, the watch commander, Lou Sabella? It looks like Pat has pushed the right button on him and he's gonna be moved out of there. He was Duffy's right hand for so many years then they put him out south where he was hurtin' Angelo Volpe, but now it looks like Pat has the right connection at 11th and State to make a move there."

"Good, good," Accardo agreed.

"Bum's" had had a good day. Maybe the best. As Richards rode the Metra home that night, he felt pretty good. He didn't know what Robust had been talking about when he discussed a new investigation of the age-old clip of Jimmy Catuara, but that was fine. Let Rocco worry about it. Probably some police officer who was light on what he had to furnish to Pat Marcy and wanted to beef up in order to justify his envelope that month.

Things were going well, especially since "Ta Tran" had been successful. It wouldn't be long before there was enough to put together a RICO case.

CHAPTER THIRTY THREE

Gaming On The Colorado

The Summit was doing so well that Robust decided to look into an expansion. Since Lake Tahoe was now filled to capacity with casinos, he directed his attention elsewhere.

Robust sent Pat Tuite to see Donald Angelini at the federal prison in Minnesota. As Angelini's attorney, he had no trouble visiting him.

Donald Angelini was once the capo in charge of the western part of the country, including Nevada. What Robust wanted was to pick his brain concerning the "pockets of potential" he had surveyed several years before. Angelini had been in contact with all of the people the Outfit had done business with in Nevada through the decades. People like Moe Dalitz, Charley "Babe" Baron, Al Sachs, Lefty Rosenthal and many others who had operated for years in Nevada. Angelini had the results of his study stored in the top of his head. His advice to Tuite for transmittal to Robust was short, succinct and to the point.

"There is just one place I'd think of expanding to right now. That town on the Colorado River across from Arizona."

"That town" was Laughlin. Located in Nevada, right across the Colorado from Bullhead City, Arizona.

Years ago, Don Laughlin founded the little community he named after himself. He landscaped the first street in town and named it Casino Row. Laughlin build a hotel and gaming casino— the first in the remote southern Nevada outpost—and called it The Riverside. Basically, he put in a full size gaming casino and emulated Las Vegas, Reno, Carson City, Lake Tahoe, Sparks, Minden and other gaming hot-spots in Nevada. He put in a great buffet on the second floor so that tourists would have to pass through it to the gaming pits and slot areas. His son, Pat, was the casino manager.

Others soon realized the potential. There were now ten hotel-casinos in Laughlin, all on Casino Row with the Riverside situated in the best spot. Visitors had the unique pleasure of going from one casino to another by boat, with docks in front of each hotel offering ferries to connect the gamblers from one hotel to another.

The hotels featured class entertainment in their showrooms. They didn't get Wayne Newton, Frank Sinatra or Paul Anka, but they did get Al Martino, Paul Revere and the Raiders, Helen Reddy, Allen and Rossi, Redd Foxx, Charley Pride, Willie Nelson, Mickey Gilley, Waylon Jennings and Mel Tillis.

Laughlin had begun to live up to the potential foreseen by Don Laughlin when he founded the small river town.

Donald Angelini had also seen the potential. There was still room for one more major hotel-casino. Robust got the word from Tuite and began to give it his utmost consideration. If Angelini thought it had potential, it was worth a look.

As Robust and Gino Martini drove south from Las Vegas, Robust got out a map.

"You know," he said to Martini, "this place looks on the map like it's only about 200 miles from Los Angeles. It's in Nevada, just across the river from Arizona and yet it's not all that far from Los Angeles. You'd be up here in a little over three hours, three and a half hours if you crawled along. Looks like good interstate from LA almost all the way."

Rocco hadn't even gotten there yet and already he was feeling great about the place.

Then they arrived.

"It ain't The Lake; it ain't the Strip; it ain't even downtown Vegas. But it's kind of—what would the word be—quaint. Sort of like Virginia Street in Reno, but with the river yet. Look at those ferry boats. I bet a lot of those hokey tourists like them. Look at all the old ladies on the boats. Jesus, look at all the RV's and campers and vans and whatever they call all those things. Lot of tractors and trailers too. I think one thing is obvious here, Gino, right off the bat. I bet before we even walk into a casino that what we are gonna find is that this is a low-roller place. You won't find many high-rollers here, They're up in Vegas." Gino nodded as his boss expounded on his early views on what he was seeing.

Robust had made arrangements to meet Herb Newman at the Riverside. "Speedy" Newman was an expert on just about everything when it comes to gaming. His business card read "the sports investor." He was not a mobster, but he had known a few in his time. There were few people of any magnitude in the gaming industry that Speedy didn't know.

He gave the pair a fast run-down on Laughlin, suggesting they concentrate on a piece of property on the southern edge of Casino Row. They left immediately to look it over.

It seemed a natural.

Robust would need a front for finding out who owned the property and how much they wanted for it. He could not be associated on record. He'd have to do in Laughlin what he had done in Tahoe with the Summit. Get a "square john" to front for him. One who could withstand scrutiny and had no record of association with the mob.

Rocco knew just the guy who might be able to help him find a "square john." And he was only a stone's thrown away from Laughlin. Robust made a phone call and then he and Gino headed south to Indian Wells, California.

Since Rocco didn't want to be seen at the condo of Tony Accardo along the fairways of the Indian Wells Country Club, he and Gino drove past the country club, checked into the Gene Autry Hotel, and made a phone call.

Joe Batters had no idea what brought Robust to the shadow of the San Jacinto Mountains. Rocco had merely called, identified himself, and asked if it would be convenient for Accardo to meet him "at the cowboy's lounge" at 3:30. Joe had dry cleaned himself, or his driver had, and here he was.

After a few amenities, Rocky got right down to business.

"Joe, we're expanding into Laughlin, you know, that town on the Colorado across from Arizona where gaming is booming. You might remember that years ago Donald suggested to expand there. He still thinks it's a good idea and so I've made a feasibility study there the last couple days and I like it."

Robust had reached a position in the mob where it was a sign of his maturity that he was now telling "the man" what he had in mind. Not that Accardo didn't have the wherewithal to countermand any of Robust's decisions. But, as time had passed, Rocco was the one who was making the decisions.

"Sounds good," Accardo responded. "Years ago we had so much going for us in Las Vegas, now that's diminished. We need something to pick up the slack there, to go with what you told me about at your place when I was in Chicago last. I gather you feel that what you're taking out of Tahoe will support your venture in Laughlin?"

"Not altogether, no, not by a long shot. But, with all the other income from Chicago, we can do this easily." Rocco seemed confident.

"What about Gotti and Scarfo? Are they coming in on this too?" Joe asked.

"No, no, this one will be all ours," Rocco replied.

"Well, you're the boss. Do what you think is best. I'll back you up."

"OK," Rocco said. "Now, I wanted to come here and fill you in on our plans there. And I need something else. We need a front. A guy who can pass anything the Gaming Control Commission can throw at him and be licensed. Also, he has to be able to convince the Game Control Board that he can support any outlay of funds by previous earnings. I can't come up with a guy like that right off hand. Do you know of any?"

Joe Batters pondered a minute. "I might. There is a guy we helped years ago. Put him in business when he didn't have a pot to piss in. Now maybe we can call in that marker. He's a multimillionaire now and we haven't ever asked him to do nothin' but pay us back. Course, he paid back a lot, he went on juice from us to start up. That's fifty years ago when he was just a kid."

"Who the hell is that? I'd thought I would have heard of a guy like that."

"Peter Twist, he runs Fast Track Sanitation," Accardo replied. "Fortune 500 company. In Miami. In the waste handling and disposal business. Garbage, we used to call it. Next to Waste Management they are as big as anybody. I was just reading about them the other day in the *Wall Street Journal*. An article about recycling. That's why Twist is on my mind now, I guess. The *Journal* says they're expanding all over the south: Atlanta, Birmingham, Tampa. When I read that, I thought to myself, here is a guy we got started, now he's got as much money as I have, a fucking billionaire, maybe more, and we never have gone near him since he paid off the juice loan."

"Well, let's do it. If need be, put a little squeeze on him if necessary. You're saying, of course, that he can stand any scrutiny. Nothing in his background that the G or the GCB can turn up?"

Accardo replied, "Nothing that I know of. He come to us fifty years ago. Wait a minute, he came through Jake Guzik. I wonder if Gussie was with Guzik then? I wonder if Gussie would know this guy? Matter of fact, I'll put in a call to him. I know he's at his condo on the ocean there in Fort Lauderdale. Twist is in Miami. Right next door. I'll meet you about nine, that ought to give me time. By then, I should have talked to Gussie. Tell you what, let's not meet here again. There's another good spot. Hank's Café Americain. Why don't you guys go there, have dinner, and I'll catch up with you at nine."

Accardo showed at Cafe Americain promptly at nine. He got right to the point.

"Gussie says he remembers the guy and was with Guzik when he came to him for the juice loan. In fact, Slim was the guy who picked up the payments for a short time. Says the loan was for about 50 thousand—a lot in those days—and Twist paid it every week, right on time. Gus says he sure as hell would remember him. Gussie could probably talk to him. I told him you'd be calling and that you might want to go down there and talk to him about it. He'll be expecting your call. Just call him at home, here's the number, and don't even tell him it's Burly, just say when you'll be there. You know Gussie, he's as nervous as they come. They got a zoo on Key

Biscayne in Crandon Park. He meets by the tiger cage. Just call him and tell him to meet you. Give him a day and time and don't mention the place. It'll be the zoo at Crandon Park on Key Biscayne."

Shortly thereafter, Rocco met Gussie Alex in Crandon Park. They walked slowly around the park, Gino following them from about fifty yards, watching everything and everybody.

Robust explained his problem to Slim.

Gussie was obviously not anxious to get involved, and said so. His intent to remain out made Rocco angry.

"Gus, that's the fuckin' problem with you. You're gonna give me the same shit you gave Aiuppa? He warned me about you. We lined your pockets, filled your belly, since you was a snot-nosed little kid hangin' around your father's restaurant at 21st and Wentworth. Not even a dago for Christ's sake and look what we've done for you? Now, you're a fuckin' nervous nelly, afraid of your own shadow. Even been in a clinic for hypertension. Shake yourself, my friend, or I'm gonna shake you!"

"Rocco, this is not the way we do things. One of us don't go to a guy like Twist. The G turns him some day, makes a snitch out of him to save his own hide, he blabs, gets immunity. Testifies we intimidated him. Then anybody who went near him goes to the can. Don't you understand that? I'm not being nervous, I'm being smart."

Robust wasn't buying it.

Alex persisted, "The way to handle this is to have a lawyer make the approach. Lawyers got attorney-client privilege. They are 'representing a client.' That's their out. That's the way to handle this."

Robust, exasperated, could see he wasn't about to change Gussie's mind. He still didn't like it and still felt Alex was exhibiting his lack of guts in refusing to make the contact with Twist.

Alex then clinched it.

"We have a guy down here who would be perfect. He was with Lansky here for years and Twist would know that. Twist is a smart cookie. I haven't talked to him for forty years, but he was always a sharp kid. Had to be to get where he is today. This attorney's name is Nathan Zuckerman. He is an old time G attorney and he's been representing Meyer Lansky's interests for years."

"That's no good, then!" Robust exclaimed. "He'd smell to the Gaming people in Nevada."

"You don't understand, Rocco," Gussie said, "It don't matter. He's not going to show in this. I'm not suggesting he be a owner of record of your joint. All he does is make the contact here. Then, if they come to him, the buck stops there. He claims his privilege. But, if you or I make the contact, we got no privilege. They haul us before a grand jury, give us immunity and we go to the can. But not a lawyer. That's what I'm trying to explain to you, that's how it's done."

Rocco wasn't convinced. He still felt that Alex was weaseling out, but he would contact Zuckerman.

Twist wasn't easily convinced until two thugs appeared at his house when he wasn't home. One was Gino Martini. Mrs. Twist was perplexed. They asked some questions about some place called Laughlin, Nevada. She had never heard of the place. They weren't really polite; they stood very close to her, not the way strangers with any manners act. They asked about her children and whether there had been any fires in the neighborhood. She thought it was very strange, but was not anywhere as upset as Mr. Twist was when she casually mentioned it.

As soon as Nathan Zuckerman arrived at his law office the next day, he got the message from Peter Twist.

"Come see me immediately!"

Peter Twist informed Nathan Zuckerman that his company had been contemplating the purchase of a casino for some time. They would seriously consider Mr. Zuckerman's proposal.

Fast Track Sanitation Company, one of the Fortune 500 companies, applied for a license to operate The Safari, designed as the most beautiful hotel-casino in Laughlin. Fast Track would control the hotel, even the casinos, under the plan.

Rocco Robust, however, figured to control the skim.

CHAPTER THIRTY FOUR

"Work and Effort Down the Drain."

Connie Constable's campaign had been moving along at a nice, clipped pace. She had won the primary and the polls showed that she was a contender, moving up as her name recognition grew. The publicity from the Banks trial had thrust her into the limelight and she had built on it.

Now, everything was about to come tumbling down.

Richards had been bothered for some time knowing that Connie Constable, the candidate for Congress, had been dating the top boss of the Chicago Outfit. "Mountain" Dew's report from Tahoe, putting Connie in the presence of Robustelli, Scarfo and Scafidi, led him to believe that Ms. Constable would soon be more than just a part of Rocky Robust's romantic life.

Soon after, Connie Constable was identified as "Candy Cane" and was the main topic of conversation at Gentlemen's Attire.

Now that he was fully cognizant of Connie's role in the plans of Rocky Robust, Pat Marcy and Gussie Alex, Richards felt it was time to neutralize Ms. Constable.

Bill Richards and Johnny Bassett put their heads together.

"Johno," Bill said, "this has gone on long enough. If we allow her to get to election day without disseminating what we know about her, she just might win. Then we'd be in a hell of a mess. We just can't take that chance. We can't let the Outfit get another congressperson in Washington."

Bassett responded. "You going to take it into the front office and let them handle it?"

"Hell, no," Richards replied. "We take it in there and we have no control of how they would handle the info from 'Bum's.' First thing you know, 'Bum's' would be compromised. We're the guys responsible for those sources. We've got to do this so that enough gets out to the public, but not anything which will hurt 'Mountain' Dew or Bum's."

"What do you suggest?" Bassett asked.

"I suggest you and I sit down with some of our friends in the media, guys who can be trusted not to go into how and where they got the information."

Bassett laughed. "I agree, Hotshot, but whenever you get in trouble it's because you go over the heads of your supervisor and your SAC. You've been warned about this, how many times? And just recently when you went to bat for that Cub rookie. The front office warned you emphatically at that time not to go to the press. This time you'll wind up in Butte, Montana. I'd give this a lot of thought before I went way out on the limb again."

"John," Richards sighed, "I guess that's why I'll always be a street agent. This is the way I've been since I started and I can't see changing my ways now."

John Bassett shrugged his shoulders. Richards was a craggy old veteran of the mob wars; he wasn't going to change.

"We could give it to Kup," Richards said. "He might even do a whole column on it. That'd be great. Or to Art Petacque. He'd be just as good. I think though this would be right up Steve Neal's alley at the *Sun-Times*. Let's go see him first. Then maybe we could give it to John O'Brien at the *Tribune*. He's the best!"

"How about TV, on the evening news?" Bassett asked.

"Mike Flannery at Channel Two might be best. He's their political editor. What do you think? Agree on O'Brien and Flannery for this?"

"It's your show; you do what you think best." Bassett had resigned himself that there was no way to stop Richards.

The result was everything Richards had expected. The combination of the Chicago metropolitan dailies with the television exposure caused a terrific reaction.

"Candidate More Than Just Robust's Girl," cried the front page headline of the *Chicago Tribune*. The *Sun-Times* spotlighted Steve

Neal's column by highlighting it on the top of its front page. It was the lead item on the "News at Five" and again on the "Five Thirty News" and "Ten O'Clock News."

Richards was again called onto the carpet.

The Bureau had, indeed, considered a transfer to Butte, the disciplinary office of the FBI. In the end, however, Richards was merely reprimanded. He had anticipated all of this; it was nothing new to him. He accepted the criticism once more and promised to be a good boy in the future.

When he left the SAC's office, he joined Bassett in the tech room. Bassett was delighted to learn that he still had his partner. About the time Richards had finished filling Bassett in on his encounter with the SAC, "Bum's" announced the arrival of Marcy and D'Arco at Gentlemen's Attire.

Marcy, who had apparently decided that the best defense was a good offense, started the conversation.

"Jesus Christ, Burly, how the hell could the G have learned so much about Constable? The sons of bitches sure have ruined her. They know a hell of a lot more about her relationship with you than I ever did."

Rocco replied.

"I wish the hell I knew. We got a leak somewhere in this outfit and I'm gonna find it. But, right now, what are we gonna do about Connie? I had dinner with her last night at Tiffs Too and she's sick. It's taken the heart right out of her. She wants to quit."

Marcy responded immediately. "Quit? I don't think she's got any choice. Fuck, she's ruined. We could run a Chinaman now and have a better chance."

Rocco Robustelli was not sure.

"John," he said, obviously to D'Arco, "what do you think? Any chances we could pull this out? Recover from this?"

Not a word was heard for almost a minute.

"OK," Robust said, "if that's it, I guess I'll tell Connie it's all done. Fuckin' shame. She would have been a good one for us back east. Lot of work and effort down the drain." He did not recognize his redundancy.

"Bum's" went quiet. All seemed to have left.

Bassett reached out for Richards' hand. "Well, you got your tit in the wringer, but it looks like it was worth it."

Richards smiled. You lose some; you win some.

CHAPTER THIRTY FIVE

John Gotti Comes To Chicago.

"Bum's" was one of the best bugs the FBI had ever installed. Its information had been the best.

It was about to get better.

With only a few days of monitoring left, one of the major figures in organized crime appeared.

At first Richards and Bassett, monitoring, didn't recognize him. They had never heard the voice before.

Robust had obviously gone out into the haberdashery itself to greet the visitor. The conversation had been initiated outside, but continued inside Robust's office.

"Things goin' good back there, huh"? Robust said.

"As good as can be expected, I guess. The G stays on us, but that's nothin' new," the new voice replied.

"Been out in Tahoe recently?" Rocco asked.

"No, not for several weeks. But our people out there seem to be on an even keel. Your man made another drop to us just the other day, as you know. It's gettin' better and better as time goes by. That was a nice move for all of us."

Richards and Bassett now knew that the voice must belong to one of the eastern mob leaders. But which one?

Robust bragged a little, "I want you to know, we're movin' into Laughlin. I was out there recently and it's a good spot for one more joint. So we're gonna take it."

"Is that right? Why didn't you come to the Commission with that? Seems to me you have to take that up with the Commission before you go into that by yourself. You got no right to do that without offering it to us!" The visitor seemed animated now.

"Bull shit. We got Nevada. We got everything west of Chicago. We let you guys into Lake Tahoe as a concession. We want anything out there, we have the right to glom onto it. You guys want anything, you got to come to us, but we don't come to you. That was decided years ago, you know that. You and I weren't here then, but that was what the Commission decided. We gave you Atlantic City and we kept what we had in Nevada and you was out there. Capish?"

"Bum's" reported no response immediately. Then the visitor replied. "You fuckin' guys are so fuckin smart! You got one guy who was at that Commission meeting, Joe Batters. I often wonder if we had somebody left from then what he might remember different about that fuckin' meeting. Well, I'll tell you what, Robustelli, we'll just add that to what I'm here for. I didn't want to handle this by the phone what with the G tappin' so many phones. I ain't never been to Chicago before, and I thought I'd take the trip and get a little vacation at the same time. We'll just add this little item onto our agenda. The Commission is gonna have an expanded meet. The main thing is to figure out how to handle the G. They seem to have all the tools now and we got to figure out how to deal with them. Fight fire with fire. We have just been sitting around and watchin' all our guys go down. As you know, they hit at me three fuckin' times and now they're comin' at me again. I'm here to suggest to you that you meet with your best lawyers in the next two weeks and get their ideas. Then come to this meet, and, if we think we can beat them with the law somehow—which I don't see how that is possible because we haven't had much luck with that—then it is my feeling we got to try something else."

"Something else? Like what?" Rocco was obviously perplexed.

"Fight fire with fire, a little rough stuff. Do what they do to us—what do they call it?—leverage. They make deals with some of our weak guys, they must have some weak guys too. We haven't looked hard enough to find them. They had this fuckin' pussy-whipped agent in Los Angeles who turned over documents to the Russian broad he was fuckin'. There must be some other FBI guy like him; he couldn't be the only weak sister in the whole fuckin' organization.

I know, you're gonna say you've looked for those kinda guys. But we haven't looked hard enough. And you're gonna say if we get tough with them it will be counterproductive. That's the old school of thinkin'. Where has it got us? In the fuckin' can, that's where. What have we got to lose? We're losing now; we can't lose much more. I know all the old bosses figured that to get tough with the FBI would be our ass. Maybe so. But what do we have to lose that we aren't losin' already? I'll tell you this. A lot of guys back east are thinkin' that way. So we want to sit down among all the Commission guys and anybody else we think should be there. You want to bring your top guy or two with you, fine. But, as always, you get one vote."

"Yeah, one vote and you wise guys in New York, you get five." Rocco didn't think this was equitable.

"We get one each. Not five." The visitor thought it was.

By this time Richards and Bassett had figured out who the visitor was. It wasn't hard. Only one guy had beaten prosecutions against him on three consecutive occasions—John Gotti. Probably the most high-profile mob leader of the day. The flamboyant Teflon Don, who headquartered in the Ravenite Social Club where John Walsh had delivered the Tahoe skim.

Richards jumped up. "John, keep this tape rolling and I'll be right back. I want to run down over to our office at Marshall Field's and verify that this is Gotti, get a photo or two as he comes out. Then I'll jump right back here and we'll transcribe this."

As Bill hustled the six blocks to their Marshall Field's office with his trusty Leica, Gotti continued.

"Now here's what we're gonna do. We're gonna take no chances with this sit-down. We thought where we could put it without the G seeing 25 guys coming into their territory. We had too many of these sit-downs busted up. Or bugged. We ain't gonna take no chances this time. No fuckin' chance at all!" Gotti hesitated, apparently for effect.

"We're gonna hold this one in Europe!"

Robust seemed surprised. "In Europe? What the fuck? Why do we have to go all the fuckin' way to Europe?"

"To be safe, that's what the fuck for! Can you guarantee we could meet out here some place? 25 guys, the top guys from all over the country bein' followed every fuckin' minute by the G? How do you know we ain't bein' bugged right this minute?"

Robust laughed. It seemed a big joke.

Bassett shuddered. "Don't get him suspicious, John," he thought.

Robust counted. "How do I know they didn't follow you all the way from New York? Might be outside watching you right now?"

Bassett shuddered again.

"That's just what I'm talkin' about. I watch my tail. I'm careful, but too many of us guys aren't careful enough. 25 of us guys show up in, say, New Orleans or Denver, what do you think the odds are the G in those places don't catch on. 25 guys comin' into one town? At the same time? But who's watchin' in Europe? We all go out of the country at different places—Miami, Dallas, Los Angeles, you come to New York, I come to Chicago, Boston. We all get out different locations and we're not noticeable. Then, when we meet up in Europe, there's no fuckin' G watchin' and seein' 25 guys sittin' down in one spot. Who the fuck cares over there? Who knows us over there, who would spot us? Some guy named Rocco Robustelli registers in a hotel over there, even by his own name 'cause he's got to use his passport, who the fuck knows Rocco Robustelli over in Europe?"

Robust made no rejoinder.

"Now," Gotti resumed, "where to go? My first thought was Rome. Italy. Some place, 'cause we're all Italian, we wouldn't stick out like a sore thumb. But then we think. Yeah, but the one place our fuckin' names might be recognized would be in Italy. They're very conscious of the Mafia over there. Bunch of strange dagos comin' inta one spot, the carbinari might latch onta that. Make sense?"

Rocky must have nodded.

"OK, so then this Dom Cirillo gets an idea. Incidently, you'll meet two new guys there. Chin Gigante is no longer the boss of the Genovese family there. This Cirillo replaced him. Anyhow, this

Dominick Cirillo gets an idea. We all got secret accounts in Switzerland, let's go there. He heard that's a nice spot with the Alps and all. But then I say no, same thing. Interpol watches Switzerland just because of that. We got accounts in the banks in Zurich and Geneva and Lucern and all. It's a small country, I been there, there ain't much place to hide there with Interpol watching the banks there and all. So then somebody says well, let's make it in some spot close where we can all get to our banks before or after the meet. So I sent a guy to our travel agency, guy we set up in Queens. We don't tell him what we're thinkin' but we lay out what they call a hyper-critical. What if? This guy comes up with the Black Forest. In Germany. It's close to Switzerland but not in Switzerland. Who the fuck would know Rocco Robustelli in the Black Forest? OK? With me so far?"

Rocco seemed to be.

"OK," Gotti went on. "Now our guy tells us in this wilderness there is a place where no fuckin' Americans or even Brits or French or Swiss or nobody goes. It's strictly for the Germans themselves. Perfect! They don't even talk a little American there, he says. He says you will be the only Americans at this place. It's a lake. Here, I wrote it down, I can't remember it or pronounce it. Anyway, that's it. Now what we done is buy out a whole hotel. All to ourself. They got a restaurant in there and a bar. We can stay as long as we want. They even have a holiday while we're there. Octoberfest. It'll be a nice thing. We're all get to know each other and we can hammer out everything as long as it takes. One thing, they got some rooms we can't use. Be sure you get a shower and a toilet. If you don't get a dopplehammer, you got to go down the fuckin' hall to take a shit. But they got enough dopplehammers. For all of us."

Robust said just two words. "OK." He seemed to be catching on that this was a good idea.

"Now, here's what we do," Gotti picked up. "We all go out different spots. You go out from Dallas. Make your own arrange-ments. Just be at the hotel at that lake I got on that piece of paper. You can keep that. There will be plenty of room, we got the whole hotel and so we don't register when we get there and we don't need no reservation so nobody knows who is comin'. Just be there on October 24th and be ready to get down to business the next morning."

Richards got his photos of Gotti when he emerged onto the State Street Mall. He didn't try to follow him. Gotti had said he was in Chicago "on vacation" and it was hard-set policy not to surveill anybody in or out of Gentlemen's Attire.

That night Robust met with Connie Constable at Tiffs Too as usual. Connie had been very despondent since she had taken herself out of the race for Congress. She had let her law practice diminish as she had concentrated on the campaign and, at the moment, had little to keep herself occupied.

"Babe," Rocco said, "I got a thought. I got some business in Europe in late October. Why don't you and I go over there now and have a nice vacation for ourselves and then, when it's time for my business, I'll go on and you can come home alone?"

Connie thought it was a nice idea. She could use something to pick her up at this point in her life.

"Where would we go?" she said.

"I'll leave it up to you," Rocco said. "Take two weeks and we'll go where you want, see what you want to see. You got a passport? Good. Go to your travel agent. Better yet, go see mine. I'll call Nick Nitti and tell him you're coming to see him to arrange a trip to Europe and then you and him settle all the details. Surprise me. Just make it so I'm free to leave from wherever we are early on the morning of October 24th. Put us in first class and put us in the best hotels. Whatever you want, don't worry about what it might cost. It's all on me. Tell Nick, or I'll tell him, to use your credit cards. But then I'll make it up to you. Matter of fact, here's enough to get you started."

Rocco reached into his pocket and pulled out a wad of bills. From the bundle he extracted 25 hundred dollar bills. He put the rest back in his pocket.

It figured to be a fun time in Europe.

CHAPTER THIRTY SIX

Odyssey In Europe

While the FBI didn't know when Rocco Robustelli would leave for the meeting of the Commission, they did know that he would leave from Dallas. A "watch" was placed with the United States Customs at the international terminal of the Dallas/Fort Worth Airport.

But they didn't know that he would leave early with Connie Constable. Rocco and Connie left Chicago for Dallas unaccompanied and landed at Gatwick with no welcoming party. Nitti had booked them into the Britannia on Grosvenor Square–just around the corner from the home of the resident FBI, the American Embassy.

Unobserved, the pair spent two days as normal tourists, dining at La Gavroche, gambling at the International Sportsman's Club and nightcapping at Annabel's. The second night they dined at "Best of Both World's" in the Britannia after "a pint of bitters" at the Waterloo Station in the hotel.

On the third day they arranged for a limo, drove to Heathrow and flew to Munich, checking into the Vier Jahreheitzen. That night they dined on bratwurst and sauerkraut, drank large steins of Hof Brau beer and danced to an Um Pa Pa Band. The next day, they caught the Eurrail to Vienna, checked in at the Bristol, and took in the Emperor Franz Josef's Holburg Palace, the State Opera Building and St. Stephen's Cathedral. The following day they walked all the way, maybe four miles, to the Prater where Rocco was amused to find a small replica of Las Vegas.

The next day they visited the Festung Hohensalzburg and drove to Bergesgaden, the headquarters for Hitler during World

War II. Coming down from Bergesgaden, they sped on their way through the Swiss Alps to Innsbruck and to the suburb of Hungerburg and its beautiful view of the Alps.

In the ensuing days, the couple visited Zurich, Lucerne, Pilatus, Lake Lausanne and Montreux.

At this point the odyssey ended. Connie returned to Chicago. It was time for business.

Robust forgot the fun and games. These jerk-offs from New York wanted to get tough with the G and wanted to come into the western United States without sanctions from Chicago. Rocco would oppose the wise guys on both counts. There was no way he could allow them into Nevada or California or any place else west of Chicago. He was certain the FBI would exert extreme pressure on the mob if they tried rough stuff with them. He recalled that placing explosives under the floor mat of Bill Richards' car years before had not caused Richards to back off.

Rocco would fight their effort to enter the west without Chicago approval and he would use whatever influence he had to discourage any overt action against FBI agents. He could care less if the New York good fellas wanted to try it in their territory, but he would fight the concept that it should be a national policy and that Chicago should be expected to involve themselves in that craziness.

It was on to the Black Forest.

CHAPTER THIRTY SEVEN

The Black Forest

Whereas Lake Tahoe has the distinction of being located near the base of the Sierra Nevada Mountains, Lake Titisee is located in the heart of the Black Forest. Titisee is not as large as Tahoe, but it is just as blue and almost as pure.

Rocco Robustelli's first thought was "this must be the German Lake Tahoe." The similarities are striking; both lakes are surrounded by miles and miles of tall pine trees.

I wonder if they got a casino here, was Robust's next thought. He had allowed Connie to plan the European agenda. Looking over the lake, he wished she could have been able to see this.

Business would allow him little time to inspect the wonders of Lake Titisee and the surrounding Black Forest.

Rocky had driven himself from Geneva and found the hotel where the sit-down was to be held—the Hotel Seehof am See—sitting on the far end of the lake, more or less by itself, separated from the lake by a large meadow with several cows. When he presented himself at the registration desk he found that he had been assigned a suite overlooking the meadow and the lake. As he started up the stairs, he recalled John Gotti's instructions and returned to the desk.

"I hope I got a dopplehammer," he asked.

The clerk laughed and said, in pretty good English, "Yes, you have a dopplezimmer mit Bad oder Dusche and WC." Rocco wasn't quite sure of what she had assured him, but he smiled and nodded. He found his suite was a double room with bath and what the Europeans call a water closet. Gotti had misunderstood; dopplehammer had nothing to do with bath or the toilet, but instead referred to a "double room."

Robust then took a short nap, enjoying the Black Forest air through the open doors of the balcony. When he arose, he dressed and went downstairs to the small restaurant in the Seehof am See, called The Vesperstruble. Three men, obviously from America, were enjoying the German beer. Since Gotti had advised him that the mob would be leasing the entire hotel, Rocco introduced himself. The three represented the New England family and introduced themselves as Biagio DiGiacomo, Antonio Spagnolo and Vincent Gioacchini. DiGiacomo was the underboss of the Boston family representing Raymond Patriarca, Jr. who was then confined in the Metropolitan Corrections Center in Boston awaiting trial. DiGiacomo referred to the other two as "Spucky" and "Dee Dee."

DiGiacomo, who seemed to do all the talking for the Boston contingent, advised Rocco that the group intended to drive to Baden-Baden that evening, less than two hours away, and "check out" the casino there. Rocco accepted the invitation to join them.

They left shortly thereafter and soon were out of the Black Forest and in Baden-Baden. But, when they attempted to enter the casino, they were blocked by the host and informed that they were "out of dress." No one was admitted to the casino without stylish suit and tie. They were directed to the haberdasher in the luxurious Brenner's Park Hotel, where they bought sports coats and ties and then returned to the casino.

The Kurhaus was a big cut above anything in Las Vegas, Lake Tahoe and, especially, Laughlin or Atlantic City. Rocco went to school on the ambience and the amenities, wondering if he could duplicate it in the United States. He wondered where all the high-rollers came from. There didn't seem to be any low-rollers in Baden-Baden.

Returning to their own hotel that night, the group was challenged by two men in the parking lot and two more inside. Gotti obviously wasn't taking any chances.

The next day Robust noticed from his balcony that guards had now been placed at the foot of the road alongside the meadow, keeping all but the guests of the hotel from approaching it. He had been told by the guards the night before that breakfast would be available at nine. As he munched on his mueslich which was heaped with fat walnuts, dates and banana slices, he was joined by more than a score of men. He quickly determined that the New England crew had not been alone in bringing along more than one mobster. Gotti had advised him that he could bring others from Chicago, but there was only one other he would have wanted here – Joe Batters. But Batters was in his mid eighties now and not up to this type of travel. He had considered bringing his underboss, Joe Ferriola, but decided his odyssey with Connie prior to the meet would dictate against that. He realized he would be badly outnumbered at the meeting.

What the hell's the difference? They're gonna do what they want to do anyhow. They got about eight families represented here, I got one. Even if I brought ten guys with me, I got only one vote, so what the fuck is the difference.

The meeting then moved into the Vesperstruble. The moderator turned out to be John Gotti, no surprise at all. He had brought along his two top guys: Sammy "The Bull" Gravano and Frank Locascio.

The first item on Gotti's agenda turned out to be how to deal with the FBI. Gotti himself gave the presentation.

"It's time we got tough with these cocksuckers," Gotti started. "As I been tellin' all of youse as I came to see you lining this up, they been beatin' the hell out of us. They got all the fuckin' weapons now. First, it was this Interstate Travel, what they call it? In Aid of Racketeering. Bobby Kennedy passed that when he came in. Then it was this Omnibus Act where they got the right to plant bugs. Then it was RICO. In 1960 they had none of them. By the end of that decade they had them. First, they bugged us, than they started finding finks in our thing, like this fuckin' Valachi in New York, Bombacino in Chicago, Frattiano in California, Lonaro in Cleveland, Cantalupo in New York, Cullota and Romano in Las Vegas, DiGiornio in Philadelphia, Teresa in Boston, Henry Hill in New York, Ito in Chicago, Christ I can't name them all. Then they put their own guys into our thing. Undercover. Like this Yablonsky in

Miami, Christianson in Arizona and especially Pistone who called himself Donnie Brasco in New York. Dirty fuckin' rat he was. That I think went too far. So now I think we got to fight back. We ain't never done nothin' heavy to either back them down or to find a weak fuckin' sister inside them or put one of our guys in their job. It seems to me that instead of puttin' up money to send guys to college so they can get into politics for us when they graduate, we ought to find some clean kid, in high school or even grade school. Go to his pop. Give him some money. Keep that kid clean. Send him to college and then when he gets out, have him apply for the FBI, get our congressmen to sponsor him like they do for the military academies, and then we got a guy inside them like they do to us. Do I have any thoughts anyplace on that?"

Robust recognized the opportunity. He knew that most of what was going to go down at this sit down he would forced to oppose. This was his chance to show all these eastern good fellas that he would not be unreasonable, that he wouldn't be against everything on the table here this week. Rocco jumped to his feet from his table near the rear of the Vesperstruble.

"I like this idea," he exclaimed. "That's a good idea. In Chicago we've had guys we found in school, gave them some money and then got them jobs in labor and as clerks of courts and that kind of thing. We've had guys we've put with judges as drivers and bailiffs. Now I think it would be a big jump from there to get inside the FBI and it ain't a thing we could do overnight, we have to bring a guy along slow. Their rules are that you got to have a college degree before you can get in. We have to get a guy started before he got far along in college and he'd have to be clean as a whistle, no drugs, no gamblin', no traffic arrests even I would guess. They even investigate his mom and pop and his brothers and schools and his neighbors. Yeah, it could be done. I like your idea, Gotti. Good one. Count on us in Chicago."

Gotti looked pleased. So did the rest of the gumbas. They had been led to believe that Chicago was going to be a big problem. But here, right out of the box, he was seconding the proposal of New York.

"OK, good Robust," Gotti said, standing again behind the bar. "Now, if we agree on that, who will ramrod that for us? We want to appoint one family to be in charge of finding the right kid or kids. Who will step up for that?"

Robust was on his feet again.

"We'll spearhead this. What I think is that every one of the families should be assigned one kid. From their city. To groom for getting inside the FBI. And, while we're at it, why not the United States Attorney's office too? Get somebody in those places. We'd have the investigators and the prosecutors, know what they're doing, who they're doing it with, who the snitches are, where they put bugs in, where they got some agent undercover, we'd have it covered from both angles. But Chicago will be responsible. I'd even set a deadline. Each family got to come up with a prospect in the next three months. Then whoever's assigned by each family to run this, they all meet in three months and give a progress report. A family don't come up with at least one in three months, he's out of this. We learn something about the family from our guy inside the G down the line, we don't let that family in on it. They don't deserve any help if they don't help first."

Gotti stood inside the bar again. "OK, anybody got any objection to Chicago running this?"

Nobody stood up. Nobody objected."

"All right. Our first order of business is settled. Good start. We still haven't decided whether at the same time we look for sissies. For weak FBI guys."

The session continued. Robust went along with the proposal that the La Cosa Nostra follow the same agenda that he had outlined for penetrating the FBI by locating a suspectable FBI agent for intimidation. The Bonanno family in Brooklyn would spearhead that effort.

Then it was time for a lunch break. Rocco decided he would rather go for a walk around the lake in the Black Forest. When he told Gotti of his plans, Gotti cautioned him to make sure the guards on the road at the end of the meadow would recognize him in order to pass him in when he returned. The sit down would recommence in two hours. Rocco took off by himself on the trail leading to the other side of Lake Titisee. The spot reminded him of Lake Tahoe. He returned just in time to rejoin the assembly in the Vesperstruble.

He would soon wish he had stayed on the other side of Lake Titisee.

CHAPTER THIRTY EIGHT

"Operation Dark Woods"

When Bill Richards reported to FBI Headquarters in Washington that "Bum's" had reported John Gotti in Chicago making arrangements for a meeting in Europe, the Bureau quickly went into action. A meeting between the bosses of the most powerful La Cosa Nostra families, the Giancana's and the Gambino's, would have been an attention-getter, but a meeting of all the top bosses was top priority.

But in the Black Forest? To the knowledge of the law enforcement agency, there had never been a Commission meeting anywhere outside the country except in Havana in 1946. The meeting looked like another Apalachin.

The agenda item of the possibility of finding a "sissy" inside the FBI was especially intriguing. The Bureau had been aware of attempts before, but only in rare incidents. Now, however, it seemed that the mob was trying to decide whether such attempts should be standard operating procedure.

The other part of the agenda didn't particularly concern the Bureau. It didn't matter who controlled organized crime in the western part of the country; the FBI would attack it no matter who ran it.

The first problem was jurisdiction. If the mobs run to Europe and sit down with each other, what was the crime? What statute had they violated? Luckily, the legal history of the Interstate Travel In Aid of Racketeering Statute, passed in 1961, would apply. Although no crime would be committed while the potential defendants travelled interstate in the United States, when they arrived in the Black Forest and conspired to bribe or assault an FBI agent they would have travelled over state lines. It would be a violation of the statute.

The next question was the absence of an overt act. In any conspiracy case there has to be a act made in furtherance of the scheme. What would it be here? That was a sticking point.

"What the hell," Richards explained, "do you mean we can't bust them in the act? We've got to wait for weeks and months before we can get them and then maybe never, if we can't show they've taken any action to further their plans?"

Richards realized that unless the public was exposed to the evil of organized crime—and given graphic illustration—that they tend to lose interest in law enforcement's fight, easing pressure on their lawmakers and causing a cut back on the appropriations needed to do battle. Here was a perfect chance to illustrate for the public the insidious nature of the mobs.

"Twenty five of the top leaders of the Mafia going all the way to the Black Forest to meet in secret to conspire to assault or bribe an FBI agent? Or to cut up territory for their crimes? Come on," Richards argued, "it's a once in a lifetime chance to bust their balls and show the country that the FBI and Interpol is right on the top of these guys, completely aware of what they're up to, what they're planning. And we're going to forego that opportunity, know they're meeting and let them do so, uninterrupted? Give me a break! What are we working our butts off out here for? You guys will have a lot of unhappy campers in Chicago if you don't let us bust this up, you'll dampen a hell of a lot of enthusiasm out here!"

The Bureau and the Justice Department finally decided to rest their case on the fact that the overt act would be the fact of the travel itself. A weak argument, for sure, if the travel could not be shown to involve a crime.

Washington has bent over backwards to accommodate Richards' view. He would try to not let them down.

The New York office was designated OO, the Office of Origin, in this investigation. Knowing that this would happen, even though "Bum's" was his source, Richards dubbed the mission "Dark Woods" in the first airtel he sent the Bureau. The jurisdiction being settled, Jim Mansfield was chosen to be the case agent. Richards was designated case agent in Chicago with Johnny Bassett alternate agent. Along with Warren Donovan, the alternate agent in New York, the street agents were summoned to FBI Headquarters in Washington to meet with Larry Heim, who would handle any press, Paul Dingen of the Justice Department, who would handle the murky legal aspects and Inspectors Frank Pulley and Rene Dumaine of Interpol.

Dingen advised that the Justice Department had come up with an idea.

"Go as originally planned, but, if we're successful in rounding these birds up, we'll have Interpol put subpoenas on them calling for a grand jury in Germany, maybe in nearby Frankfurt. Then when they are questioned over there they have no right to any American Bill of Rights, no Fifth Amendment. If they refuse to answer, put them in a damn dungeon. If they answer and lie, it's perjury. If they answer, and tell the truth, they then admit they conspired to assault an FBI agent and we got them."

Richards immediately had some questions about this plan.

"First of all, Mr. Dingen, it doesn't appear there is any crime under German law to assault an American law enforcement officer. And second, how can we prove what they conspired to? Can we bug them in Europe under German laws and is anything we get admissible? If not, then how can we prove perjury if we can't show what they talked about?"

Dingen had the answer to both questions.

"In answer to your first question, it's a crime under any nation's law to assault anybody, any person at all, or to conspire to do so. Again, we have the problem of the overt act. But let their attorneys raise that. All we want is the fact of this grand jury over there. As to your second question, I'll let Frank Pulley answer that."

Frank Pulley had been an inspector with Scotland Yard for years.

"Under certain conditions having to do with the public safety, the Germans' laws permit eavesdropping and wiretapping. They generally are allowed to do it in terrorist investigations, against such as the Red Army Faction or The Baader-Meinhof Gang. Although something like this is unprecedented, since we never had your Mafia coming over to us before—it's always been the other way around—it's believed that the theory of the law in this regard could be extended to apply to this. It's been checked out with the Ministry of Justice in Bonn and they agree."

It was settled. They were off to a good start. All they had to do was bug the mob's meeting place.

First, they had to find out where it was.

CHAPTER THIRTY NINE

Into the Cow Dung.

Rocky Robust was a voice crying in the wilderness of the Black Forest.

John Gotti was attacking the issue of whether the Chicago family should be allowed to continue to control the western part of the country. The rule of the Commission had existed since the day of Al Capone.

Returning from his walk on the trail around Lake Titisee, Rocco quickly learned the cards were stacked against him. There were 13 families represented at the Black Forest sit-down. Five from New York, and one each from New England, New Jersey, Philadelphia, Pittsburgh, Buffalo, Cleveland, Detroit and Chicago. Robust found Chicago stood alone. The other families had obviously caucused before they left America and agreed to join forces in order to gain territory in the west.

"OK, fellas," Gotti started, "the next item for discussion is what we do about Chicago trying to keep us out of Laughlin, Nevada by going in there alone, without talking to nobody, just planning to open a big hotel there."

Rocco could see that Gotti would be using the situation in Laughlin as a crack to open up the whole west. If he could force Chicago to give in on this matter, it foreshadowed a next move by the eastern families into California. Robust decided that it was important to make a stand in Laughlin. He jumped to his feet.

"The Commission has decided, time and time again, that Chicago has got the west. Now that ain't gonna change. We were kind enough to let you in with us at Lake Tahoe when we opened the Tahoe Summit. Now you fuckin' guys are getting greedy. I've got all the plans set for a hotel we are calling the Safari in Laughlin. I got the financing; I got the company that's gonna front for us; I got the blueprints; I've hired the contractors; it's all set to go. I don't need no help from any of you; I've done it all myself. There's no fuckin' way any of you can get into that now, not after I done all the work. Explain to me why I would now give up a piece to you people?"

Rocco knew he could make no concessions. Eventually, he was going to have to go home to Chicago and explain all that had happened at Lake Titisee to "The Man." Robust could imagine how Accardo would react if he came home from this meet and told him that Chicago no longer controlled the west.

The cards were stacked against him, however. One by one the "representato" of the other families on the Commission arose to criticize Robust and the Chicago family. Philadelphia called it "selfish." Detroit called it "a situation which has no reason to exist." Buffalo called it "something that has gone on too long." Pittsburgh called it "time for a change." The Bonanno family of New York called it "a disgrace." The Columbo family called it "no reason for even being in the first place." The Genoveses called it "an example of what happens when one family gets too fat."

Gotti had obviously primed the pump. Rocco noticed he was not saying a word. He was letting the other families do his work for him. After the exchange which Rocco had with him at Gentlemen's Attire, Rocco knew that Gotti was not neutral on this matter. He knew where Gotti stood.

When every family had had its say, Gotti stood up behind the bar.

"I propose we settle this in a democratic fashion like we do all matters which comes before us. Let us put it to a vote."

Robust was on his feet in a flash.

"Fuck that! There ain't gonna be no vote!" He well knew that the vote would be 12-1.

He was shouted down.

Rocco looked Gotti in the eye.

"This fuckin' sit down was rigged right from the start. Talk about democracy. You fuckin' wise guys set this all up long before we got here. I ain't participatin' in no fuckin' vote!"

With that, Robust strode out of the Vesperstruble. For him, the sit down in the Black Forest was over. He rushed to his room, intending to pack and leave.

In cooperation with Frank Pulley, Rene Dumaine and the other representatives of Interpol, the FBI had made a quick survey of the situation and soon targeted the Seehof am See as the intended site for the mafia meeting. Agents assigned to "Operation Dark Woods" had arrived at Lake Titisee a week before the sit down.

The FBI-Interpol team established headquarters at the Schwartzwald Hotel. With the cooperation of the owners of the Seehof am See, Familie Berger, they entered the Vesperstruble after midnight a few days before the arrival of the American mafia and installed bugs in all four corners. They also installed a video camera and operated it from a small storage room adjacent to the Vesperstruble. The microphones fed the FBI-Interpol team at their headquarters and would monitor, record and transcribe from the Schwartzwald.

Although far away from the Seehof am See, the FBI could see and hear everything that happened in the Vesperstruble—as it happened. They had even observed Rocco Robust hiking on the other side of the lake. They had even accompanied him and the New England family to the Kurhaus.

As Rocco Robust made his unexpected and premature departure from the Vesperstruble, the team reacted. Bill Richards and Johnny Bassett did not want Robust absent when they made the raid on the sit down. They had not come this far, and worked this hard, to see him escape.

Located about a mile from the mobsters, the team jumped into their cars and raced to the Seehof am See. Right through the guards at the foot of the road leading to the hotel and into the Vesperstruble.

Hans Weidemann and the Germans on the Interpol team had

the authority here. They loudly announced, "You're all under the authority of Interpol! Sit very quietly." Nobody had pulled any guns. It was not necessary. Gotti and the "representatos" of the other families were shocked! Here they had come all the way to the Black Forest of German to escape detection and look what happened!

Gotti's first thought was of Rocco.

"That bastard, he leaves before we get hit!"

Rocco was also the first thought of Bill Richards and John Bassett. Unaware of which room he occupied, Richards posted guards at the foot of the stairs and around the hotel in case Robust was in a first floor room or jumped from one of the balconies on the second floor.

When Rocco heard the commotion downstairs and realized what was happening, he realized there was only one way out. As Richards and Bassett were searching the rooms in the hotel, he make his move, leaping from his balcony on the second floor onto the meadow in front of the hotel. Disregarding the pain in his left knee and ankle, he sprinted for a herd of cows and flung himself on the sod in their midst. Right into a large pile of cow dung!

Richards, searching a room on the second floor, observed Rocco when he jumped from the balcony and landed on the cow dung. He raced from the room, down the stairs and out into the meadow.

By the time Rocco, in pain and covered with cow shit, out of breath from his dash and prone on the ground, looked up, his hated adversary was grinning down at him.

Richards hauled Rocco to his feet.

"You smell like the shit you are!" he hissed at Robust, prodding him towards the hotel as several Interpol men ran up.

Rocco took one step and fell to the pasture. One of the Interpol people gave him a hand and he limped back to the Seehof am See where he was herded in with a sullen John Gotti.

It was too late to reach a magistrate for bail. The magistrate for the district Donauescingen is located at Lake Constance, many miles away. The American mobsters would spend the night in jail.

Robust was glad that Tony Accardo had not accompanied him.

Accardo has never spent a night in jail in the sixty five years he has been a member of the Chicago Outfit. What a jolt it would have been had he been forced to spend his first such night in the lockup on the edge of the Black Forest. Robust would have a lot of explaining to do when he got back home to Chicago. He shuddered when he thought about it.

The newspapers broke the news. The European press thundered that "the American Mafia" had been caught "conferencing" in the Black Forest. *The International Herald Tribune* headlined the episode, labeling the mobsters "the Black Forest Bumbling Fugitives."

The ministry of justice swung into action. The magistrate at Lake Constance refused to set bail, stressing a fear that once the defendants were freed they would cross the ocean and never return to meet their justice. Rocco and his fellow commissioners remained in the lock-up.

It was the end of the year before they would be hauled before the dock. With no recourse to the American Bill of Rights, they were unable to take refuge behind the familiar Fifth Amendment. When their attorneys found that they had not only been bugged, but filmed, they gave advice that they should not perjure themselves. The evidence to substantiate what they were conspiring over would come from their own mouths, in living color yet.

But it was no crime in Germany to conspire to infiltrate the American FBI or to look for "sissies" inside that foreign agency. It was certainly not a German crime to conspire to allocate mob territory inside America.

When the American mob chiefs threw themselves on the mercy of the German court, the authorities could find no crime at all. In January, the members of the Commission and their underlings were finally released.

Bill Richards was basically pleased with the success of the mission, although, by forcing the abortion, the Bureau had not developed any evidence of violation of a statute over which they had jurisdiction. Bill only regreted was that he hadn't had a chance to visit Baden-Baden.

Rocco, on the other hand, was furious. He had been forced to spend seven weeks, including Christmas, in a moldy cell. When he heard the church bells of Christmas-loving Germans as they rollicked in celebration, it galled him even more.

When the mobsters arrived en masse at Immigration at Kennedy Airport, they were all served with subpoenas and hauled before the Senate Permanent Subcommittee on Investigations. The American public watched them grovel.

CHAPTER FORTY

A Seed is Sown.

Connie Constance returned to Chicago refreshed. The vacation had left her in a happy frame of mind and she was ready to settle down and reconstruct her law practice. When she returned to her office and found the many messages from her clients, she realized she would never be able to throw off the stigma of her relationship with Rocco. She did not contemplate it with relish, but she expected the only clients she would attract would be defendants in criminal actions. Her corporate clients had dropped their retainers and had looked elsewhere on La Salle Street for representation. When she returned the calls she found that they were no longer her clients.

When the headlines about the meeting in the Black Forest hit, the full weight of who she was hit Connie. She wasn't able to disregard the stares and smirks of Chicagoans as she walked down La Salle Street or around Lincoln Park. The "Celebrity" was now "Rocky Robust's girl, the broad the mob was going to put in Congress."

Connie realized she had fallen a long way.

At this point, Connie decided to reevaluate her life. She took a chance that Tom Foran might be willing to let her cry on his shoulder.

Tom Foran is a respected attorney in Chicago. A former United States Attorney for the Northern District of Illinois, he has the reputation of being a tough little guy, wound tight, always looking for a complicated case he could attack. Certainly not a guy looking to assist anybody in any way associated with the mob.

Since Connie had graduated from DePaul Law School and

began her practice, however, Tom Foran had been like a father, or at least an older brother, to her. Whenever she had a problem with a precedent, the ethics of a situation or whether there might be a conflict of interest involved, it was Tom Foran to whom she turned.

Connie was fearful that Tom might be aware that she had been travelling with Robust just prior to the Black Forest. She would not have been surprised if she had been told that "Mr. Foran is in conference."

Tom Foran came hurrying out of his office into his reception room to greet her. He had a wistful smile on his face. He put his hand on her shoulder and said, "Come on in."

It was the biggest boost she had gotten in days.

"Tom, I don't know what to do," she said. "I feel like an outcast when I go to court and see how the other attorneys look at me. My case load is way off. I can't even walk down La Salle Street without feeling, real or not, that the pedestrians recognize me as some kind of sinner. I really feel depressed with my whole life."

Tom Foran gave her his shoulder to cry on, figuratively. He was much kinder than she had any right to expect.

He suggested what he called a "dangerous but courageous course of action for you."

"Let me call a friend of mine. You might know his name although I don't think you've ever met. He'll treat you right. His name is Bill Richards."

"Tom!" Connie exclaimed. "I know who Bill Richards is. He might be the last person I could go to."

"Connie, what we have here is a loss of personal respect. What you have lost is your confidence that you belong in the society of decent people. The only way you are going to regain your respect for yourself is to earn it by undoing what it is that caused you to lose your self respect and by making amends for that."

Connie was not the least bit convinced. "By becoming a stool pigeon against Rocco Robustelli?"

"Let me arrange a meeting, right now if possible, and you can make up your own mind about how far you want to go. You'll like Richards. He's a decent man and a friendly one."

Connie had never, in any of her most confused moments, considered talking to Bill Richards. She had heard Rocco discuss him on dozens of occasions and clearly recognized that Richards was Rocco's nemesis, a hated foe. Rocco had never let her in on much of his business, but his animosity towards Richards was one thing she was sure about.

Connie wouldn't even think about it.

But Tom Foran had sown a seed.

CHAPTER FORTY ONE

RIC-K.

The Chicago Cubs reported to spring training in Mesa as a even favorite to win the eastern division of the National League. The Cubs had made a great showing the year before. There were two shining stars in the Cub's galaxy. One was the star catcher, Sammy Watson, the All Star from last year. Still young and improving, Watson had demonstrated in the past couple years that he was one of the finest ball players in the majors. The other reason for optimism was Ricky Robustelli, the young rookie who had come up from Iowa in mid-season. His fast ball was clocked in the dry Arizona air at 97 miles per hour.

In Rick's first outing of the spring he went three innings and fanned six Cleveland Indians in Tucson. Then he went four innings against Oakland and fanned six more. The next time out he went five innings and struck out eight against San Francisco. His ERA out of spring training was a solid 1.50. Obviously, he was ready! The Bleacher Bums in Chicago had their hopes high.

Even Rocco Robustelli caught pennant fever. After his return from the Black Forest, he was more high profile than ever. Only Sam Giancana had been better known to the public than Robust now was.

Rocco bought a full season box at Wrigley Field. It wasn't easy, but the First Ward had come through for him. Rocco dined with Rick at their usual spot, Ciel Bleu, the night before the season would open.

"Kid," Rocco told Rick, "I'm all excited about you and your team. What do you think it looks like?"

"I am too, Dad," Rick responded. "Gee, we dominated in the

Cactus League. I don't see any other team which should beat us out. A lot of things could happen, we all know that, but we've got a great manager and coaching staff, our offense should be great, so should our defense. Our pitching should be solid, the guy behind the plate may be MVP in this league this year, Sammy Watson. He should have 35–40 home runs, 120 RBI's. Everybody is very optimistic. I shouldn't say this, but if I were a betting man, I'd take those odds on us."

"How about you? What do you think you're gonna do this season?"

Rick hesitated.

"Honestly, Dad, just between you and me now, I don't want to sound cocky, but I got a good taste of what it takes up here last year and then again this spring. As I say, a lot of things could go wrong. But again, if I was a betting man, just son to father, I'd bet I will win 20 this year. With over 200 K's."

"By K you mean a strike out, right?" Rocco wasn't an insider, but he had watched his son pitch since Little League and knew something about the game.

"Yes," Rick smiled, "a 'K' is a strikeout. That's why they call Dwight Gooden, the ace of the Mets, 'Doctor K.'"

"Well, I'm glad you're so up about all this because I just plunked down several thousand bucks for box seats right along the third base line." Rocco smiled at his son.

"Dad!" Ricky exclaimed. "I thought we had an understanding! I thought you were going to keep a low profile on this. You remember the discussion we had right in this room last year? Where we agreed to be careful about being seen together after all the trouble we had then?"

Rocco scowled. "Yeah, I remember that. But this is different. We ain't gonna be seen together. You'll be in the dugout or on the mound. I'll be in the stands."

"Dad, you must be smarter than that!" Rick said, very seriously. "I'd bet that you'd be on television more than I would. The TV cameras would be shooting you every inning. 'There's Rocco Robust, the father of Rick, the boss of the mob in Chicago, rooting.'

'There's Robust, the Al Capone of Chicago, drinking beer.' 'There's Rock Robust, just back from the Black Forest where he met with all the big boys in the gangster world, eating a hot dog.' It would be a media spectacular. The ball game would be secondary!"

Robust growled. "You're overdoing it!"

"The heck I am, Dad. I'm just telling it like it is."

"Listen, Kid," Rock said, leaning over the table, "this is a free fuckin country the last I heard, although you wouldn't know it sometimes the way your friend, Richards, goes about it. If I want to come out to Wrigley Field, enjoy the fresh air and sunshine, watch my kid play ball, I got the same right as any other father, any other citizen. I got rights too, you know, although this fuckin' G tries to take them away from me. Bull shit, young man, Tuesday I'll be in my box and nothin' is gonna stop me!"

The dinner ended on that note. Rick knew that nothing he could say would influence his dad to change his mind. Rocco was used to dealing with the likes of John Gotti. He had just come from a battle with guys a hell of a lot tougher than his son. Rick wasn't about to change his mind.

Returning to his apartment on Marine Drive, Rick made a phone call to Bill Richards.

"Can we have lunch tomorrow? We have a workout at Wrigley Field at ten. Could you meet me at one?"

Rick and Bill met at their favorite restaurant, Eli's, "The Place For Steaks" on Chicago Avenue. Rick obligingly signed autographs for the owners, Esther and Mark Schulman, hostesses Gail and Bea, and for Paul, the Maitre'd before facing the same questions from Richards about his potential for the coming season. Rick finally got down to business.

"Look, there is a big reason other than touching base with you for us to have lunch. I had dinner last night with my dad. Would you believe he has purchased a full box, a season box? I can't believe it, I though we had an understanding."

Richards was upset. "Rick, he can't do that. A lot of people have put their necks out to keep this situation sub rosa. If he shows up in a box opening day—any day—it'll undo all that's been done!"

Rick finally grabbed his opportunity to discuss an old matter.

"My dad let it slip some time ago that I had been blacklisted in the draft because of him and that you went to New York and straightened that out for me. I want to thank you. I wouldn't be here today, I guess, if it wasn't for you. I owe you a lot."

Richards passed it off gruffly. "Back to our problem today, Rick. You tried to talk him out of this?"

"I sure did. I agree with everything you say. I talked until I was blue in the face and it didn't do any good. He intends to be in that box tomorrow—and probably most days of the season!"

Bill gave it some thought. "I could have Bill Duffy, the deputy superintendent of the Chicago police department, harass him so much he'd go any place but Wrigley Field. But that would be counterproductive. The press would surely pick up on it. I might just have one other ace in the hole though."

Rick looked at Richards expectantly.

"You don't want to know," Richards said. "I'll do what I can. I can't promise anything, But I'll give it my full attention."

Richards went directly from the restaurant to Gentlemen's Attire and pushed his way past the thug at the door.

"Robust here?" he asked.

When Rocco left Chicago for the Black Forest almost six months before, "Bum's" had died. The extension of the Title III authority from the federal courts had expired. While "Bum's" was alive and producing conversation on a daily basis as it had, the FBI stayed away from Gentlemen's Attire. Now, there was no reason to, especially if there was something to be gained. Still, Richards was taking a chance. It wasn't official business and, if it became known, he would probably be reprimanded—again.

Richards busted through the store and into the rear office. Rocco Robustelli was hunched over his desk, examining the mob receipts from the month of March.

"What the fuck?" Rocco exclaimed.

Without any greeting, Richards got right down to brass tacks.

"Robust, I'm told that you brought a box at Wrigley Field and that you intend to watch games there this season?"

"What the fuck business is that of yours, Richards?" Robust responded, rising from his chair and glaring at the G man.

"I was given to understand that you had some brains, Robust. You know full well how much your presence at Wrigley Field this year would hurt your son. Don't you have any more regard for your own son than that? Don't you know what a media circus that would create?"

"First of all, wise guy, what the fuck business is it of yours? Rick is my son, not yours—although some times I wonder if you understand that. If I want to watch my son play ball I don't see one fuckin' reason in the world I can't. You guys act like the Gestapo or something. You were over there in Germany too long, Richards. Go fuck yourself, Richards, and get the fuck out of my office. You got no right to be here. I could sue you for trespass or somethin'!"

Richards backed off.

"OK, Rocco, sure you got every right to watch Rick. Just like you did in Little League when we were in South Holland. Just like you did on Cape Cod. Just like in the Finger Lakes. Nobody is questioning your right. All I'm asking you, and I'm going to ask you in a nice way, one father to another, one man to another—with no reference to our situation otherwise—please don't go through with your plans to go to Wrigley Field."

Rocco almost whispered. "Fuck you!"

Richards tried one more time. "OK, Rock, let me ask you in another way. Do it as a favor to me. You do this for me, I owe you one. You get a marker in your favor. Favor for me?"

Rocco assumed his usual pose. He leaned across his desk. "You got a fuckin' lot of nerve. Comin' in here and asking me for a favor. I'll tell you this, Richards. I'll be at Wrigley Field at one o'clock tomorrow afternoon, come hell or high water. There ain't no way in the whole fuckin' world that you can stop me. I guarantee, fuckin' guarantee, asshole, that I'll be there. There is no fuckin' way you can stop me. Now, stick your big finger up your ass and get the fuck out of here!"

Richards looked Robust in the eye for ten seconds. He realized it was useless. He slowly turned on his heel and left.

Richards realized there was just one recourse at this point. The ace in the hole he had mentioned to Rick. He pointed the nose of his car towards Congress Parkway and its extension, the Eisenhower Expressway. When he reached Harlem Avenue, he turned north to North Ave and then pulled up in front of a luxurious home on Park Avenue in River Forest. He walked around to the back, to the guest house next to the pool. He was lucky. He found Butch Blasi at home in the afternoon.

Blasi was the bodyguard, driver and appointment secretary for the upper echelon of the Chicago mob. Richards and Blasi had known each other for decades. They were not friends, but they acted civilly towards each other. They could talk. Richards told Blasi what he wanted.

Richards then drove back to the FBI office on the ninth floor of the Dirksen Federal Building. He was waiting for a telephone call.

At seven o'clock it came.

Richards and Accardo had met before. He knew Joe Batters was a man of few words and got right to the point.

"Joe, I need a favor, but it's a favor for you guys too. You know that your man, Robustelli, he's got a son plays for the Cubs. Now I find out Robust has purchased a season box at Wrigley Field and that he intends to use it often this year including opening day tomorrow. I think you see the wisdom of thinking that is very unwise. The publicity which will attach to his presence, particularly when his son is pitching, will spotlight you people. I know you think that is very unwise. I know because I have heard you criticize Sam Giancana when he was running around the country with the McGuire Sisters. I know because I have heard you tell Robustelli to keep a low profile. Keep your head down is how you put it, I believe, Joe. Well, this action by this man tomorrow will be about as high profile as you can get. I can just see Harry Carey telling Arne Harris, his director, to put the cameras on Robust. I'm going to leave this in your hands, Joe. But let me say this. You're doing it for both of us. Your good and mine, since I don't want to see this kid get hurt. The more the media focuses on his parentage, the more it hurts his game. I went way out of my way for this young man once before and I'm doing it again. He's worth it."

Joe Batters remembered his sit down with Rocco. He knew what Richards was referring to. He had discussed Richards' trip to New York to see Peter Ueberroth with Rocco.

Batters didn't say a word. He hadn't spoken the entire time. He nodded, reached out, and shook Richards' hand. Then he turned and walked back to his car.

The next day, Richards filled out a leave slip and took the El to the ball yard. It was 1:30 and Wayne Messmer was singing the national anthem. He would soon be announcing the starting lineups. Richards walked up and down the box seats.

Rocco Robust was not there. Not that day or any other day the whole season.

As the season commenced, Rick, the "celebrity" from the year before, solidified himself with the sportscasters and fans, not as the son of the Chicago mob boss, but as a quality pitcher. The Cubs have some matinee idols on their team: Ryne Sandberg, Greg Maddox and Mark Grace, but Rick matched them in physical attributes. He was fast becoming a crowd favorite. The feature of his game which grabbed the fans especially was his ability to strike batters out. The strikeout for a pitcher does for him what a home run does for a batter.

Although it was only early May, attendance at Wrigley Field was up. Much of the reason was attributable to Rick. On the days he was scheduled to pitch, the bleachers were full. He was beginning to be a gate attraction.

The Cubs, however, were sluggish. Some well pitched games were going down the tubes in the late innings. The Cubs just couldn't seem to make the good pitch when it was needed.

The fans solved their problem.

On a day when Rick was scheduled to pitch, Moe Greenberg, one of the most fervid of the Bleacher Bums, and three of his female admirers brought a large, blue and white sign to the top of the bleachers and hoisted it in full view of almost anybody in the park and of the TV cameras. It proclaimed one word in large letters, one hyphenated word: "RIC-K"

The sign caused a media sensation. Television crews first spotted it before the game. When they came on the air, just prior to game time, cameras focused on it. About the same time, the fans caught sight of it. A loud murmur began throughout the reserved, general admission and box seats, all facing the bleachers.

When Rick took the mound to throw his warm up tosses, the fans began to chant.

"Ric Kay, Ric Kay, Ric Kay." Rick, concentrating on his warm-up, looked up. With that, the fans roared. The chant intensified. "Ric-K, Ric-K, Ric-K!" Rick shivered. He had never been so touched. He reached down for the resin bag to regain his composure.

The Cub fans had found a new hero. Rick determined not to let them down.

The opponents that day were the Dodgers. Strawberry, Butler, Samuel, Scioscia, Murray, Daniels and the rest. Not an easy lineup to face. When the game was over, "Ric-K" had fanned 16 Dodgers and won the game with his own sacrifice fly—1-0. A 1-0 shutout with 16 K's!

The mystique which had attached to Ricky the previous season because of the combination of his parentage and his potential had now blossomed into full bloom. He was still "Robust's kid," but his background had now been superseded by his pitching. He had become a full fledged star.

The media clamored for Rick's attention. Rick refused. He wanted to stand on his own as a professional baseball player.

Spearheaded by Rick, the Cubs should have been living up to their expectations. They weren't. Something was not quite right.

And Bill Richards started to wonder about it.

CHAPTER FORTY TWO

Sammy "Understands" — What Else?

Sammy Watson had remained in Chicago following the conclusion of the previous season. There was nothing for him in Watts or South Central Los Angeles, and Galaxy was supplying everything he needed on the south side of Chicago. Angelo Volpe made certain that "Charley Bones," the worker who had first brought Sammy to his attention, was on the top of the situation and Galaxy knew what was expected of her. Galaxy had been in Chicago long enough to grasp to be aware of "Chicago methods."

Volpe let Sammy alone for the layoff, but, when Sammy was preparing to leave the cold of Chicago for the air of Arizona, he had "Charley Bones" sidle up next to Sammy and Galaxy one night in the Blue Note.

"Sammy," Charley said to him after a few drinks, "I think you know I am the "man" on 63rd Street. That's pretty powerful stuff. But there are a lot of people on the other streets. I think you know what I mean. White folk. Mafia. They be very happy with you last season when you did your favors for Galaxy and didn't play too hard in a couple of games. Now I'm gonna tell you, Sambo, what me and my friends want this year. The Vegas books got the Cubs even to win the division. So do the books here in Chi town. My friends and I are gonna take some of that money. A lot of that money. A lot more money than you will make with the Cubs if you play until you're forty years old! Now, my friends and I don't want to lose that money, Sam. We expect to make it, not lose it. You understand where I'm comin' from, Sambo?"

Sammy had a very good idea where "Charley Bones" was

comin' from. He didn't know exactly who the friends were, but he certainly knew that "Charley Bones" was their enforcer on 63rd Street. He also knew there was a man who could reach him right from the pitchers mound, through his son, if he didn't do his bidding. Sammy Watson was well aware who Ricky Robustelli's father was. He assumed the son was an extension of the father.

Sammy Watson looked at Galaxy. She kept her eyes on him. There was no doubt that Galaxy was a part of this. Try to extricate himself from "Charley Bones" and all he represented, and he would not only jeopardize life and limb but his life with Galaxy. Life would not be worth living without Galaxy. He could just see some of "Charley Bones" boys taking him into the alley behind the Blue Note and stepping on the knuckles of his throwing hand. Just for starters.

"Charley Bones" resumed his talk.

"Now, Sammy, what I got to be takin' back to the boys is this. They want to make sure you understand what I'm sayin' to you here. I want you to be clear on this, Sambo. If my boys put their money down that the Cubs don't win the division this year, they will make some good money. Some of that will be yours. But if they put their money down and the Cubs win the division, then there are gonna be some sad people here. They want you to understand that. And if there are some sad people because the Cubs win the division, Sambo, they want you to understand that not only Galaxy here be very sad but you, Sambo, will be saddest of all. They want you to understand that, Sambo. Do you?"

Nobody had called Sammy Watson "Sambo" in many a year. The only guy who had done that had gone back to Compton with a big bump up alongside his head. The name wasn't bothering Sammy now, however. He hardly noticed it. He knew he was at the crossroads. If he indicated he "understood" now, he was off the hook. Until the season started, and then he would be caught in the web he couldn't get out of. He did a quick calculation. He was dammed if he did and dammed if he didn't. He made a quick decision.

"I understand," he said, quietly.

"Charley Bones" put his hand under Sammy's chin. He lifted it so that Sammy was looking right into his eyes, from a distance of about four inches.

"There's no backing out now, Sambo!" he whispered.

After "Charley Bones" left, Galaxy put her hand up tight inside Sammy's crotch.

"You done the right thing, Baby," she smiled. "Let's go home, you make me horny."

For some reason Sammy couldn't get it up that night.

The Cubs had been good to Sammy and he was close to almost all the players. He knew he figured to let a lot of people down. He had been an honest person all his life. While many of his friends in Watts, some of them dead now from drive-by shootings and from drug overdoses, had joined the Crips and the Bloods, the black street gangs, Sammy had spent his free time on dusty ball fields and poorly lighted basketball courts. He had stayed away from anything else — not an easy thing to do in Watts. He had made it in the world outside Watts. Just as Daryl Strawberry and Eric Davis had done. Now, however, in another ghetto, many hundreds of miles from home, he had found a parallel danger. This time he hadn't avoided it.

Sammy had a hard time getting to sleep, even cuddled with Galaxy. Usually his night's exertion put him to sleep almost immediately. This night he slept little.

"What else can I do?" Sammy thought.

CHAPTER FORTY THREE

The "170" Case

Something had been gnawing at Bill Richards. He had followed the Cubs since the days of Gabby Hartnett, Dizzy Dean, Phil Caveretta, "The Mad Russian," Hack Wilson, Big Bill Lee, "Swish Nicholson, Augie Galan, Andy Pafko and the other fine stars of the thirties and forties. Not that they had been his favorite team. He rooted for the Gashouse Gang with Pepper Martin and the Cardinals. When courting Jeannie in Cincinnati, he had even switched his loyalties to the Reds.

But now, because of his interest in Ricky, he was watching the Cubs more than ever. And something was wrong. In spite of their promise, the Cubs were lagging. There was more than enough blame to go around, but it just didn't seem right.

His unease brought him back to "Bum's" and Joe Ferriola's two mentions of something about a "fix with the Cubs." He went back to the transcripts he and Bassett had made from the tapes. Ferriola, reacting to Robust's praise for a good month of receipts from gambling, had once started to say something about a fix. Then, again, later when Tony Accardo, Gus Alex and several other top echelon leaders were in the conversation, Ferriola had seemed to want to discuss something about a fix on the Cubs. That particular conversation had been so ripe with other information that Richards had not focused his attention on "the fix." Ferriola obviously had been cut off by Robust and Alex, impatient to get his own two cents in.

Listening to the tape, Richards almost swore.

"Gussie, you jerk, why didn't you let Ferriola talk?"

Richards dictated a memo suggesting that a "170" case be opened and assigned to him. In the FBI each violation is assigned a case number. A "170" case is a Sports Bribery case. He entitled the case "Unsub; Chicago Cubs baseball player, Sports Bribery." Sports Bribery was one of Richards' specialties.

However, he had no specifics at all. Where to start?

His first step was Jack Brickhouse. Richards wanted to stay away from the actual team members and officials until he got some semblance of what to zero in on. Brickhouse had retired from the Cubs, but kept an active role with WGN, the station which carries the Cub games. He also stayed close to the team and was one of the faithful who believed an athlete can do no wrong.

Jack cautioned Richards to go slow, stressing that even the best pressure players had more occasions when they didn't produce than when they did.

"Don't get carried away, Bill, by something that is probably just coincidental. When you've been around as long as I have you'll know that this is an honest game. I've never found any reason to believe otherwise. I've been following baseball since I came to Chicago from Peoria over 50 years ago. I've seen a lot of things which would raise your eyebrows, but not one of them proved to be dishonest. Listen to advise from an old friend. Go slow."

Bill vowed to take the advise of Jack Brickhouse. He cautioned himself not to say anything to anybody which would either make it either appear he had some concrete information or compromise "Bum's." He would be very cautious. Careers were at stake here.

Richards went to other experts, but only to those who were not directly associated with the Cubs. In order to be of assistance, however, those had to be close to the Cubs and the game. He talked to all of them on "deep background" and off the record.

None of the interviewees were able to offer anything of value. All had observed the same thing Bill had and were saddened when the Cubs did not live up to expectations. The Cubs simply seemed to be playing lackluster ball.

As a result, the investigation languished. It seemed to have no place to go.

CHAPTER FORTY FOUR

Rocco's Burdens.

Rocco Robustelli was learning that there was a big price to pay for being the boss of the Chicago mob. Almost all of his predecessors had learned that lesson. Most of them were either in prison or in exile. Even Joe Batters, although he has escaped conviction, had had close calls.

Now the G's were bringing their big guns into play against Rocco. With the "170" case at a dead end, Bill Richards assembled all the evidence compiled against Rocco Robustelli and took it to Fred Foreman, the United States Attorney. Foreman knew the status of every case in his office at any moment. This would be the major case of his administration.

Knowing Foreman well, Richards took his evidence right to Foreman himself. Foreman gave it a quick once over. He then picked up the phone and called Jeff Johnson, the most capable assistant into the office.

"Jeff," Foreman said, "Bill had gotten all the evidence together on Robust and I've taken a quick look at it. It sure looks solid for a RICO case. Lot of years of hard work here and now it looks like we've got the makings of a successful prosecution on our hands. I want you to handle it. I'll put a major portion of my time on it also. We'll both handle it on trial. I'd like you and Bill to go over all of this and then, say next Monday, first thing, nine o'clock, both of you come into my office here and the three of us will give it a thorough examination. See where we're strong and where we might need something shored up. OK?"

Richards and Johnson agreed. Foreman then cleared off everything from Johnson's caseload and assigned him full time to preparation of Rocco's impending RICO indictment and trial.

Several major items were to be presented to the federal grand jury. Primary would be the transcript of the conversation wherein Rocco talked about the killing of Jimmy "The Bomber" Catuara. Although murder is not a federal crime, it can be shown as one of the "predicate" acts in a RICO case.

"RICO" stands for the Racketeer Influenced and Corrupt Organizations law, passed in 1970, making it a federal crime to conduct the affairs of an "enterprise" through a "pattern of racketeering." A pattern is said to exist when members of such an enterprise have committed at least two "predicate acts," of racketeering within 10 years of each other. These acts can include murder, robbery, gambling, securities fraud, using the telephone or the mail for illegal purposes or almost any other crime, state or federal. It can be applied criminally, as in the case Richards, Johnson and Foreman would now prepare, or civilly, and can result in confiscation of the ill gotten goods.

The crime of the murder of Catuara, although a state offense, could, therefore, be added to the menu of offenses to be included in the charges. Murder has no statute of limitations, so there was no impediment there.

Another item on the menu was the overhear of Robust by "Mountain" Dew in The Spire of the Tahoe Summit when Rocco informed Ricky Scarfo and Sam Scafidi that he owned the majority interest in the Summit and that, therefore, the skim would come first to him in Chicago before it went on to New York and Philadelphia.

Added to the menu would be the "Ta Tran" phase of "Operation Pensum," the surveillance of Joe Pignazio from Reno to Lake Tahoe to Chicago to New York City to Philadelphia to Atlantic City. Hooked up with "Mountain" Dew's testimony and the observations of the Las Vegas, Chicago, New York and Philadelphia FBI agents, it would be a major charge.

Another item would be the frequent instances picked up by "Bum's," when the monthly proceeds from the mob operations were delivered to Robust and counted.

Still another would be the evasion of taxes on the income from the skim and the proceeds of the Chicago family of La Cosa Nostra as they flowed to Robust.

The evidence looked ample and solid. The tapes from "Bum's" would consist of evidence from the mouth of the defendants themselves. "Mountain" Dew, aka "Cappy" Capitano, would be an excellent witness, an undercover FBI agent. Richards himself would be the star witness. He would testify about how he put the microphone into Gentlemen's Attire and what he heard from it. He would testify, after being qualified as an "expert witness" in the law, as to the interpretation and analysis of the overhears.

What Richards liked most about the "menu" was that it didn't hinge on testimony from a witness who had "turned" after being a mobster. Such evidence is great when there is no better available. Richards had won major cases when such evidence was the major item on the "menu." Richards, however, had gone through trials where such witnesses have recanted on the stand and thrown the case into a tizzy.

When the evidence was all assembled and the conference with Foreman completed, Richards punched the elevator on the fifteenth floor with a grin on his face. He was contemplating a final victory over Rocco Robustelli.

The FBI and the Justice Department weren't the only ones on Rocco's tail. The U.S. Senate Permanent Subcommittee on Investigations was about to commence their hearing on "Operation Dark Woods." Cass Weiland, Chief Counsel, had come to Chicago where he had debriefed Richards concerning the entire operation, from conception to fruition in the Black Forest. Weiland had enlisted the aid of Richards and Bassett in Chicago, Mansfield and Donovan in New York, Lazzari and Osborne in Philadelphia and other Bureau agents throughout the country to serve subpoenas on those who were apprehended at the Hotel Seehof. It was not easy to find all 25 attendees scattered all over the eastern and midwestern parts of the United States.

For Richards and Bassett it had been easy. They merely

walked over to Gentlemen's Attire. Robust had moved his head-quarters, but Richards left a message. He had no sooner returned to his office than he received a telephone call from Pat Tuite, the well regarded Chicago defense attorney, advising Richards that he was representing Robust and understood that the FBI had a sub-poena for him. He advised that he had been authorized to receive the subpoena on Robust's behalf. Richards advised him that such was not good enough. He suggested that he would be glad to serve Rocco in Tuite's office, but not without Rocco being present. Tuite knew that he could argue, but agreed to discuss it with Robust. When he called back, he advised Richards that Rocky would be in his office in an hour.

The two foes did not speak a word. Richards handed the sub-poena to Robust, exchanged a few friendly words with the highly respected Tuite and left.

The easy part was over for both Richards and Robust. Now would come a most enjoyable time for Richards and an uncom-fortable time for Robust.

Although he would obviously hide behind the Fifth Amend-ment of the Constitution when questioned by the Senate commit-tees, Rocco's appearance exposed the inherent danger of organized crime to the public. It put him under the kleiglights of public at-tention whether he answered questions or not.

Bill Richards spent three hours on the first morning of the Chicago hearing, defining organized crime as "that self-perpetuating, structured and disciplined association of individuals or organizations who have combined together for the purpose of obtaining monetary or commercial benefits, or power, wholly or in part by illegal means, utilizing a pattern of corruption, violence and threats of violence to achieve their goals and protect their interests." It was not quite the official FBI definition.

Other hearings, involving Gotti and DiGiacomo from New York and Boston respectively, were being held in the other cities where the citizens were delighting in seeing their mob bosses in living color.

Following Richards' testimony, Senator William Roth of

Delaware, who was presiding, called Rocco to the stand. There were several senators present that day including Warren Rudman of New Hampshire, the co-chairman; Sam Nunn of Georgia; John Glenn of Ohio and William Cohen of Maine. Also present were Cass Weiland, the Chief counsel, and Katherine Biden, the Chief Clerk.

The scowling Robustelli took his place at the table alongside his lawyer, Pat Tuite. Weiland had prepared the senators well. Each had five or six questions to hammer Robust with. Rock took the Fifth Amendment on each.

The purpose of the hearing was achieved. The Chicago press got a good look at the Chicago Outfit boss. The television cameras, the radio microphones and the print media were there in full force.

As Robust left the witness table, he scowled again at Richards. He seemed more subdued, as if he was in the eleventh round of a fifteen round championship prize fight–and knew he was losing.

The Cubs were in Montreal that day. As *The Chicago Tribune* and *The Chicago Sun Times* carried the stories about Rocco, Ricky was out of the country.

Back in Chicago, however, Ric-K's aura rose.

"If Attila the Hum had a kid who set out to save the world, would I hate the kid?" Moe Rosenberg announced.

When Mike Royko, the *Tribune* columnist, quoted Rosenberg, Robust angrily hissed to himself in his condo.

"Attila the fuckin' Hun, huh!"

Robust had begun to understand that the "celebrity" of Ric-K was having a reverse effect on Rocco's own notoriety. It hadn't been bad enough that he had been hauled before the United States Senate and exposed to the world.

"Now some low-life is calling me some dirty names in the papers."

It was not a high point in the life and times of Robust.

Rocco decided he needed to get away from it all for a while. That night he suggested to Connie that they take a long weekend in their favorite hideaway, the Tahoe Summit.

It would be a trip he would not soon forget.

CHAPTER FORTY FIVE

Without Him.

Connie Constable and Rocco Robustelli could travel together now. There was no reason that the world shouldn't know that they were lovers. The damage had been done and Connie was no longer a candidate for Congress.

Connie knew it must be love. Why else would she put up with the public embarrassment? Even in the newly renovated public concourse of United Airlines at O'Hare, she could feel the stares of the passengers who recognized Rocco Robustelli. Some even recognized her. She could hear the whispers.

"There's that gangster who was on television when the Senate hearings were here last week. And that's his mistress with him. The one who was running for Congress until the newspapers learned who she really was."

Some of it was her imagination, but all of it was based on some reality.

Some girls enjoyed such public attention, and even dated mobsters because of it. Connie didn't. She had made it on her own in the legal profession. She had graduated from one of the finest law schools in the country, had passed the tough Illinois Bar exam and had gained considerable success as a La Salle Street attorney. At one time she had been a highly respected candidate for one of the highest offices in the land.

It was all over now. Her association with Rocco had ended it.

That was her dilemma. She should have left Rocco a long time ago. On the other hand, her heart told her he had been good to her and deserved her love. It didn't make much sense to her, but there it was. She was hooked on the man.

When they arrived at Cannon Airport in Reno, Gino Martini was waiting for them. Soon they were perched in their penthouse suite at the Summit, enjoying the beautiful sight out over the Sierra Nevada.

Next to her, Robust shook off thoughts of his balcony at the Seehof am See and the mountains beyond. He quickly dismissed thoughts of the cow dung in the meadow. Even enjoyable times now reminded him of past problems.

After a short interlude in the bedroom, Rocco and Connie walked up the flight of stairs to the Spire.

After Rocco had ordered his Absolut tonic, Connie got serious.

"Rocco," she said, looking him directly in the eyes, "I have something I want to tell you."

Robust could see she was very serious.

"The other day I had a talk with Tom Foran."

Connie could see Rocco raise his eyebrows. She had talked with him in the past about her regard for Foran. Rocco also knew that Foran had been the United States Attorney who had directed attacks upon some of his predecessors.

"I went to him just to talk. You know how much I appreciated the use of his law library and his paralegals to do some research for me," Connie told Rocco. She paused, to gauge his reaction. Rocco remained impassive.

"One thing led to another and he told me that I have a problem with the other attorneys in Chicago. He told me there is only one way I can fix that. He suggested I talk with a friend of his." Connie hesitated again at this point, fearing that when she identified Tom Foran's friend, it would cause an explosion.

Then she went on. "Bill Richards."

Rocco's head jerked. But he said nothing.

Neither did Connie.

Rocco looked out over Lake Tahoe. He continued his silence. Finally he said, "Go on."

"That's it," Connie said. She hesitated again for a few moments. Then she said, "You know, Rocco, I wouldn't do anything like that."

Rocco maintained his silence. Her next words were like a shot. He jerked upwards.

"Without you," Connie said.

Now Rocco spoke up. Many of the other diners could not miss his words.

"Without me?" Rocco shouted. "Are you fucking nuts!"

Connie was not accustomed to Rocco in this frame of mind. She was startled, but not cowed. She reeled from the explosion, but quickly regained her composure.

"Rocco, you don't have to use that word around me! What I am telling you is that I have remained loyal to you. I am trying to tell you that I would never go to the FBI or the United States Attorneys' office or anywhere else—without you."

Rocco hissed it again. "Without me. What, Babe, makes you think I would ever consider such a thing?"

Connie didn't say a word. She changed the subject. She waved to the captain and framed her hands indicating they were ready to see a menu.

She had no need for a menu; she knew the fare at the Spire by heart.

All of this had been observed and overheard. Rocco had noticed the Philadelphia pit boss in the next booth, but he had paid no particular notice of him. After Connie mentioned her talk with Tom Foran, he lost all interest in everything.

"Mountain" Dew had been observant, however. "Cappy" Capitano would have something to report that night when he rowed out past the middle of the Lake. He told Thomas that he believed Connie Constable had been attempting to feel Rocco Robustelli out—to find out whether, with all his troubles, he might have some inclination to give some consideration to turning to the FBI.

"Cappy" reported that Robust's reaction definitely gave him the impression that Rocco would not.

CHAPTER FORTY SIX

The Mob Gives Up Sammy

The Cubs were slipping.

When Jim Essian replaced Don Zimmer as manager, it appeared, for a while, as if their chances had improved. Ric-K, especially, was sharp, running off a string of three wins with a total of 36 strikeouts.

Then things went wrong again. The team began to slip into their losing ways, not winning the games in the clutch. Rick had as much or more bad luck than the rest of his teammates. His won-lost record continued to hover around the .500 mark, but his games were not resulting in wins.

Every time the Cubs seemed about to get going with a sustained winning streak, something happened and they fell back around the .500 mark. Jim Essian had a tough time keeping his spirits up.

The Associated Press broke the major story over its wires, datelined Chicago. "Reliable sources" reported that the FBI in Chicago has made official inquires to determine whether some Chicago Cub games have been fixed. Bob Long, FBI spokesman in Chicago, didn't deny or confirm the reports, stating that, "the FBI does not comment on pending investigations."

The story set off a firestorm. Sports writers and crime beat reporters alike scrambled in an attempt to verify the story. *The Chicago Tribune* and *The Sun Times* alike covered the story on both the sports page and the front page. Television covered it on newscasts and special reports.

Even the suburban newspapers carried lead stories on the allegations.

The front office of the Cubs issued hourly reports condemning the story and the Associated Press. Bill White, National League President and Fay Vincent, Commissioner of Baseball, both denied the rumors. Vincent made a public demand that the Associated Press reveal its source. The Associated Press refused.

Privately, Fay Vincent reviewed the file on the decision of his predecessor, Peter Ueberroth, to remove the blacklisting of Rick Robustelli.

What a bad decision that was, he thought to himself. The press will soon be focusing on Ricky because of his background. It was a big mistake!

It didn't take long before short accusations began to appear in the gossip columns.

"Don't be surprised if it comes out that the alleged investigation by the FBI of a possible fix on the Cubs is focused on Rick Robustelli, the son of Rocco Robustelli, aka Rocky Robust, the boss of the Chicago Mob."

"In view of the allegations flying all over town, isn't it suspicious that Ricky Robustelli, the son of Rocky Robust, has lost so many close games, especially one-run games in the late inning?"

The Bleacher Bums soon picked up on the accusations.

"Do you really think Ric-K is throwing games? It sure is suspicious how many games he loses when the going gets tough."

"You got to wonder whether Robustelli's father put him up to throwing games?"

"Do you think the mob is behind Ricky Robustelli?"

There were all kinds of rumors, and not just in the bleachers.

The rumors had finally reached Rocco Robustelli. Rocco remembered Joe Ferriola had been trying to tell him once about "a fix on the Cubs." He was angry—very angry. He didn't need any more problems, especially in his backyard.

Robust sent for Ferriola.

"What the fuck is goin' on here, Joe?" he yelled. "Tell me about it!"

Joe Ferriola finally got Robust's attention.

"Robust, I been trying to tell you about this for a year or so

now, but you didn't seen interested. Here's the deal. You know
the catcher of the Cubs, Sammy Watson? OK, about a year ago he
started hangin' around the Blue Note on 63rd Street. 'Charley
Bones,' who is one of Angelo's guys, he come to Angelo and told
him. Angelo thought it offered some possibility so he come to me.
I agreed. So this 'Charley Bones,' Angelo's guy, he puts the ball
player in tight with one of the black broads, a pro 'Charley Bones'
has in the stable down there on the south side. Pretty soon this
Watson is head over heels for the broad. Can't get enough of her.
So then Angelo comes to me and we decided to make our move on
the ball player. We test him out first. This is in the middle of last
year when I first mentioned it to you, but you didn't show any interest so I just went ahead with it. Don't seem like it's anything I
needed your OK for, so I went ahead. We got the kid to lay down
on some games that didn't mean much to the team or him. Tested
out good, so we started holding on to all bets on the Cubs bet
against our books when the Cubs were playing those teams, first
two and then two more. By the end of the year we had cleaned up
pretty good. We weren't laying off to other towns when we overloaded on the Cubs on those teams. We held on to those bets even
though we were overloaded and stood a big chance to lose a bundle
if those other teams lost to the Cubs. But almost always they won.
OK? Now, comes this year. We see the Cubs are the favorite to win
the division. So Angelo comes to me and says instead of havin' this
kid lay down on just some of the teams why don't we bet against
them, wheel the other contenders, the Pirates and the Mets, and
we should have a very nice outcome. We talk to Donald Angelini,
'the Wizard of Odds,' who is followin' the game even closer now
he's got nothin' better to do in the can in Minnesota, he's our ace
handicapper as you know, and he tells us not to worry about the
other teams in the division, Philadelphia, Montreal and even St.
Louis although they are playing good ball right now. So I tell Angelo
to make sure of this fucking thing. If we're gonna put a big slice on
this we gotta make sure of the kid. But I tell Angelo don't you go
near the kid. Insulate him. Don't make it so if things go sour the ball
player can say the mob done this, or Volpe done this because

Volpe, of course, would splash back up on us. Everyone knows Volpe is us. So Volpe sends this 'Charley Bones' to see this hooker with Watson and together they put it to the kid. To make sure he understands that if we go on the hook for several million on this that there ain't no turning back once the season starts. So when Volpe comes to me and says 'Charley Bones' put it to him and the kid says he understands, then I put the word out to all offices to hold on to all the bets they get on the Cubs, don't lay them off out of town. And the Cub fans this year, as you know, went wild for the Cubs when the season started. So they bet real big on the Cubs to win the division. We hold on to all those bets instead of laying them off. So now we got three, four million of those bets so if the Cubs don't win the division this year and they sure as hell don't look like they are, then we win. So right now I'd say we're sittin' very pretty."

Joe Ferriola grinned. He was proud of himself, especially since his scheme was working so well.

But Ferriola hadn't reckoned with his boss.

"You fuckin' imbecile!" Rocco screamed. "You done all this without clearin' with me? You risk all this money without clearin' with me? You fuckin' idiot! Don't you see what's happened now? Now my kid is the one gettin' the blame for all this! You're ruinin' my kid's whole career! Why you no good fuckin' cocksucker! You got no fuckin' brains whatsoever. I got a good fuckin' mind to . . ."

Rocco seemed about to explode.

Ferriola tried to make his excuse. "Robust, I tried to tell you a couple times. Once when we was countin' the money at your place on State Street and again when Joe B and Gussie and all them were there. But you didn't seem to want to hear about it. It don't concern your kid, so I didn't think you gave a shit. If it concerned your kid, I'd sure as hell come to you first shot out of the box. But it has nothin' whatsoever to do with your kid. He ain't involved at all!"

"What the fuck you mean, he ain't involved at all? Don't you read the fuckin' papers, Ferriola? The papers say it's him the FBI is lookin' at! They don't even mention this fuckin' Watson!"

"But that's who it is, Rock! It ain't your kid!"

"You should have known, Ferriola, that it would splash back

on my kid! You shoulda had the brains to come to me first. I never woulda fucked around with the Cubs with my own kid on the team."

Ferriola said it again. "Burly, I tried. You wasn't interested."

"Don't give me none of that, asshole! You didn't try very fuckin' hard, don't give me that shit!"

Rocco Robustelli had to make a major decision.

"Give up Watson," he said.

"Give up Watson? Burly, that's crazy. We stand to lose millions if we lose our in with the Cubs. We can't do that!"

"I said, give up Watson! We got to clear my kid. If the FBI knows it's this catcher and not Ricky then that clears my kid."

Ferriola was aghast. "But Rock, we might go down the drain to the tune of three, four million!"

Rock stood up again. "As long as I'm fuckin' boss of this Outfit, Ferriola, you'll do as you're told. I'm tellin' you to give up this Watson. And you tell Angelo to tell Watson that if he don't hit a home run every time up we cut off his balls—and we cut the tits off his broad too! No, wait, not Angelo, we don't want this to reach back to us in any way. You tell Ang to tell this 'Charley Bones,' whoever the fuck he is, tell him to tell Watson. If he don't hit a home run every time up, especially when my kid is pitchin', then we cut his balls off—and his broad too! You got that? Go do it. This fuckin' minute!"

Ferriola didn't like it. Robust was putting personal interest ahead of his responsibilities to the Outfit. That was a cardinal sin. Ferriola's first thought was to go over Rocco's head to Joe Batters. As he left Rocco, he reflected that the Cubs got about as much chance of winnin' the division as a fly in a web. Better to let it go and not make waves. Going over Rocco's head could have serious consequences.

Ferriola sat down with Angelo Volpe.

"Ang, we got a big problem here. The G is investigating the fix with the Cubs. It looks like they think we got Robust's kid. Robust don't want that. He has ordered me to have you tell 'Charley Bones' to go to the FBI and tell them it's Sammy Watson. As if he's a rat. Make it look like he's a fink. Give them that tip from a guy who is in a position to know. Then tell Bones to tell Watson to play his very best the rest of the season. Understand?"

Volpe had some trouble understanding, but he passed the orders on down to "Charley Bones." Charley had great trouble with both of his tasks.

"How am I gonna get to the FBI? I just call 'em on the phone and tell them I gotta story?"

Volpe gave that some thought. Then he told Charley.

"Listen, the guy who's on us all the time for the G, that's a guy name Bill Richards. You call him and tell him you want to talk to the FBI agent who is runnin' the case on the Cubs. Make it plain you want to remain in the clear, what they say, anonymous. Don't act like you've been ordered to do this by anybody. And, sure as hell, Charley, if you know what I mean, keep me and anybody else out of this. You don't tell them you're involved or the mob is involved. Do that, my man, and you're dead meat! All you know is you hang around the Blue Note and you see Sammy Watson there all the time and that somebody got to him and he's throwing games. Don't tell him nothin' about Galaxy. Just quick, in and out. That's all. You understand?"

"Charley Bones" didn't, not exactly. He did understand, however, what he had been ordered to do and he knew what was best for him. He knew better then to go against his boss, Volpe. Besides, the pay was good. Very good. "Charley Bones" would do as he was told.

"Bones" made a call to the Chicago FBI office and asked for Bill Richards.

"I've got some news for you guys," "Charley Bones" said. "If you will put me in touch with the agent who has the case on the Cubs I can help you. A lot."

Bill Richards agreed to meet "Bones" that evening, not knowing who he was or what he might have.

When Richards arrived, he found "Charley Bones" waiting for him. Richards exhibited his FBI credentials and they went for a walk.

"Do you want to give me your name and how you might know

what it is you want to talk to me about," Richards asked.

"Bones" had given this some thought. Volpe hadn't instructed him on this. If he was to be credible, however, as Volpe made clear he should be, he had better.

"My name is 'Charley Bones,' I got some things going for me on 63rd Street. The Cubs player you are looking for is Sammy Watson." "Bones" had gotten right to the point.

"The catcher?" Richards responded. "How do you know that?"

"Sammy hangs around the Blue Note. Some of the people there have gotten to him. Last year he started dropping games a little and now this year he is dropping more. Just enough so the Cubs won't win the pennant."

"How can you prove that?" Richard asked.

"I'm not tellin' you I can prove it, that's your job. I'm just tellin' you I know." "Bones" wasn't about to divulge that information. Volpe had clearly instructed him not to.

"Who at this Blue Note is involved?" Richards inquired.

"Charley Bones" had anticipated this question. He wanted no investigation at the Blue Note. It was his hangout and he didn't want it disturbed by the FBI hanging around, asking questions. Besides, any such inquiry might well turn up Galaxy Jones and Volpe had specifically instructed him not to get her mixed up in this investigation.

"I'll make a deal with you. You stay away from the Blue Note. You jess go see Sammy. He's kinda straight. He comes outa Watts, but he is unusual since he doesn't seem like he comes outa Watts, know what I mean? He would not seem to be street smart. I betcha you go see Sammy and he will crack right away. Don't waste your time at the Blue Note. I'm doin' this for you and you do that for me. If Sammy don't crack then go to the Blue Note, but make a deal with me, go see Sammy first. Deal?"

Richards hesitated. Then he agreed to the "deal."

When Richards left, after just ten minutes or so, he told Charley he'd like to be in touch in the future. "Charley" refused. He had indicated to Richards, however, where he might be found.

The Cubs were in the late stages of a long road trip, winding up a four game series over the weekend against the Mets at Shea. Richards found out where Watson lived. He didn't want to approach him at Wrigley Field.

With George Benigni, Richards made the contact. FBI agents aroused Watson from his sleep. He had gotten into O'Hare late Sunday night. With him was a light-skinned black girl. Richards and Benigni made her identify herself and then told her she could go.

"Looks like Whitney Houston," Richards said to himself. "Galaxy Jones? Wonder if she fits into this?"

It didn't take long to find out. Just as "Charley Bones" had prognosticated, Sammy wasn't up to sparring with two FBI agents. His story soon came tumbling out.

"Listen, I'm going to tell you straight out what I done. I'm gonna tell you the truth, all of it, and I hope you will believe me. There is a place I been goin' to. On 63rd Street. Called the Blue Note. That's where I met Galaxy. Last summer. I guess she was a workin' girl. She had a guy who I suspect was her pimp. Named 'Charley Bones.' He come to me and his reputation at the Blue Note is he's with the people. I don't know who and how, but everybody at the Blue Note say that. So pretty soon 'Charley Bones,' he ask me to lay down on some games last year. Against Houston and Atlanta and then Phillies and Expos. Then this year he come to me again. Wants me to lay down for the whole season, so the people can bet against the Cubs to win the division. So we don't win it. They ask me, do I understand. I don't wanna lose Galaxy and I know the people could break my arm or leg or do worse to me if I don't say I understand. So I say 'I understand.' I figure we will lose enough games anyway so I don't have to do nothin' intentional. So I don't. Sure enough, we lose enough. I know they think I lay down, but I don't. It just seems when things get into a tight spot, either me or somebody else screws it up. So I see 'Charley' at the Blue Note and he says 'good work, keep it up.' And I smile and don't say nothin'. But I'm not trying to screw up, it jess works out that way. That's the truth, Mr. FBI men. I'm not lying to you. I figure that when September comes then I got to make up my mind what I do. But so far I don't. So I jess go along and I keep Galaxy and the people don't break my arm or leg and everybody is happy with me. But I don't deliberately do nothin' wrong. I don't have to yet. That's the God's honest truth. You believe me?"

Richards and Benigni looked at Sammy. He did seem to be a straight kid. Caught so quickly this morning, he didn't seem to have time to make up such a story. Besides, he had given up "Charley Bones," and that jived with what they could believe.

Richards looked Sammy right in the eye and leaned to within a foot of him. "How about anybody else on the Cubs?" he asked. "Anybody else fixing games?"

"No way, nobody. We all try hard, we jess screw up when it seems to count the most." Sammy seemed sincere.

"Not Sandberg or Grace or Robustelli or any of those players?" Richards wanted very much to clear Ricky, but he wanted to be impartial also.

"No, nobody, especially not those players, especially not them, but nobody," Sammy said, looking Richards right in the eyes.

That seemed to do it. Richards asked Watson if he would come down to the office the next morning to give the FBI a signed statement, incorporating what he had just told them. He also suggested to Sammy that he might want to retain an attorney before he came. Sammy asked if he was under arrest. Richards replied he was not.

The next morning Sammy Watson appeared and executed a signed statement detailing the essence of what he had told Richards and Benigni the previous day.

Richards believed Watson's story. Sammy had created immense pressure on himself. He was trying his best, but couldn't handle the strain which had been created. The overall result was the same as if there was a fix. It just worked out that way. The Chicago Outfit had attempted to fix Sammy Watson and they had inadvertently achieved their purpose.

The Chicago office of the FBI issued a news release.

"Based on what was believed at the time to be reliable information, the Chicago Office of the FBI instituted an investigation under the Sports Bribery Statute designed to determine whether investigation would develop whether there was any indication that one or more Chicago Cub baseball players had been corrupted. This investigation has now been concluded. There is no indication that any Chicago Cub player was corrupted or that any player performed under his abilities, at least intentionally. The investigation is now completed and the case closed. There will be no future announcements. The investigation has been closed and no further action will be taken."

Under ordinary circumstances no such announcement of a closed case would have been made. In this case, however, the press was aware of the investigation and an announcement seemed necessary.

Richards had one more problem. He contacted George Mandich, an ex-FBI agent, and asked Mandich to arrange to get a message to Fay Vincent, the baseball commissioner.

"Basically," he told Mandich, "what we had here was an approach to Sammy Watson by some people who worked for the Chicago family of La Cosa Nostra and who propositioned Watson to throw games. Watson refused. As far as our investigation could determine Watson did not do anything illegal, as least not under the terms of the Sports Bribery Statute. In failing to inform the officials of his team of the approach he may have violated team and league guidelines but that is your province, not ours. I want the commissioner to know that Watson cooperated completely with our investigation and has given us a full statement which I believe is complete and accurate. He did so in full faith without any representations being made to him and he was forthright from the moment we contacted him. Also, I want the commissioner to know that no other Chicago Cub was involved, and certainly not Ricky Robustelli who was completely unaware that any mobster had made such an approach to his teammate. This would have happened in any event whether Robustelli was on the team or not. He had nothing to do with it and had no knowledge of the situation, nor did any other Cub player as far as we know."

Richards was confident that his message would be delivered completely to Vincent.

Richards knew that the FBI announcement to the press had made no mention of Ricky Robustelli. Richards understood why the official announcement couldn't mention that, but he wanted to make very clear to the press and public that Ricky had never been involved. Quick telephone calls to his usual media contacts made it clear to them that he would appreciate it if they spotlighted the part of the FBI announcement stipulating that no other Cub player was involved. Once again, "inside sources within the FBI" could be quoted as saying that Ricky Robustelli was in no way connected with the original allegation or with any part of the investigation based on the initial information. The media was glad to comply with Richards' request. It was the only clarification or enlargement of the announcement that they had received. The opposite side of the coin was soon the media focus. Television commentator Walter Jacobson did a program stressing how unfair the fans had been to Ric-K. The *Sun Times* ran a column on the new aspect of the situation.

A groundswell of public warmth for Ricky Robustelli developed. The huge sign with the blue letter reappeared at the top of the bleachers. When he next took the mound and recorded his first strikeout, the big sign "K" went up in the front row of the right field grandstand and nine more were added as he mowed down the opposition with a total of ten strikeouts. Rick not only had been exonerated, but had found his way back into the fans' hearts.

Bill Richards had a smile on his face again.

There was one guy who was not smiling, however.

"The Man" was upset.

What a way to run a fucking business! Accardo thought. He would have to look into this.

CHAPTER FORTY SEVEN

A Command Performance.

Ricky and Rocky Robustelli met again at Ciel Bleu shortly after the FBI announcement that RIC-K had been cleared of any suspicion of dumping Cubs games.

Rick brought it up immediately upon his father's arrival.

"I'm glad all that fuss about a fix of our games is over."

"Kid," Rocky responded, "let that be a lesson to you. What some guys will do when they get hot for a broad. A no-good one in this case, as I understand it."

"What are you talking about?"

Rocky practically burst at the seams. Finally, he could tell his son a story that his so-called friend, Bill Richards, hadn't been able to. Sammy Watson's sordid affair and its possible implications were soon made clear to Rick—minus any mob involvement, of course.

Rick was devastated. Sammy had been his roommate for a time.

"I'm sure sorry about Sammy. I've heard rumors about his being traded soon. He's a nice guy. It's a shame he had to get mixed up like he did. I feel very bad for him."

Rick considered his father for a moment.

"Dad, did your people have any part in this?" Rick asked.

Rocco fixed his gaze on his son for a moment. "Rick, let me just say this to you. As soon as I found out about this, I put a stop to it. Right away. You got me to thank for putting an end to it."

"You and Bill Richards," Rick replied. "He was the one who got it out that I wasn't involved, that I had nothing to do with this and that I was never part of the FBI investigation."

His explanation didn't sit well with Rocco—not at all.

"Kid, every time something good happens you give all the credit to him. Anytime anything bad happens, I get the blame."

"Well. I'm sorry, Dad."

"You should be," Rocco shot back. "Listen, I told you I put a stop to it as soon as it came to me. You got me to thank that Richards found out it was the catcher, not you. Believe me. I ain't gonna say no more, but that's the facts."

"I believe you, Dad, if you say so," Rick said. "But don't think that Bill hasn't been very good to your family, especially me, for years. You guys hate each other, especially you, but look at all he's done for me."

"What?"

"Well, first of all he coached me on a half dozen teams. Taught me the game really, gave me a lot of chances to show what I can do. He and Jeannie looked after Linda and I a lot. He took me under his wing and Jeannie took Linda under hers. You weren't around much, and we had no mom. A lot of people knew who you were then and would have made it tough on Linda and I if the Richards hadn't been so close to us."

Rock didn't seem much impressed.

Ricky was wound up. "Then that situation with the box seats. I know that is a sore subject with you, but I was right, Dad. If you had taken that season box and been there a lot it would have put the spotlight on you and that would have fouled me up at the time. I could handle that now. It's kinda become part of Chicago lore, I guess. It's accepted. But when I was trying to get my feet on the ground, find out whether I had what it takes, that would have put a lot of pressure on me, put the focus on the wrong part of what I am. I don't know how he did it, but what Bill did then, that was a big thing."

"Big fuckin' deal!" Robust didn't seem convinced.

"Then another thing," Rick continued. "You know the major league baseball had me on some kind of blacklist. They were going to keep me from being drafted at any time. I never could have played baseball after college. Never played pro ball. But Bill went to New York and talked to Peter Uberroth, the commissioner of baseball for me. Got me off that list. If it wasn't for him, I wouldn't be pitching for the Cubs today."

Rick let this soak in, although he was aware his father was already aware of it.

"And, Dad, for all his trouble, for all he's done for me and Linda, I have reason to believe you either tried to kill him or you had him injured. I can never understand that, Dad."

"All right already. Enough. You look at this guy through your rose colored glasses. I look at him through another set of glasses, let me tell you that, sonny. You see one side of him, I see another."

"That's exactly what I'm trying to get across to you, Dad," Rick shot back. "There is another side of him. A good side. Sure, he's got a job to do and he does it."

Rocco was angered at this point. "What you're telling me is that you're on his side, is that what this is all about, Kid?"

"No, not really, not on his side against you. You're my father and I love you. But I like Bill too. Maybe I love him too. I wish there was some way you could get together."

Rocco grunted, "No fuckin' way, Rick. Just get any fuckin' thoughts you might have about that out of your mind. No fuckin' way!"

The pair finished their meal without much more to say to each other. Later, Robust reflected on the evening.

First Connie, now Rick. Can't they see there is no fuckin' way?

The next day Rocco Robustelli got a call. It was Butch Blasi.

"Meet J.B. at Meo's noon tomorrow." It was an order.

There was only one man in the whole world who had the power to give Rocco an order.

Robust arrived at Meo's as ordered. Joe Batters got right down to business. He was never one for niceties.

"Rocco, I got word you're fucking around with several million dollars. They tell me you put personal affairs ahead of our business. Explain that to me."

Robust didn't have to guess what Batters was talking about.

"Joe, you're a family man. I have always admired you because you don't fuck around. Clarise and the kids always come first with you. Why not with me? Can't I protect my family? My kid was gettin' a bad rap. He didn't deserve that."

Accardo looked Robust straight in the eye. It was a tough thing for Rocco to return his gaze.

"Rocco, you got two families you got to look out for. Your personal family and the family of 'our thing.' I'm sorry if you believe that I would put my personal family above La Cosa Nostra. But I never had to. But you did. You got hundreds of soldiers dependin' on you. You let them all down. Besides that there are guys, big guys, who have lost some confidence in you over this. You have lost respect, Rocco. I'm disappointed in you. 'Our thing' ain't as strong as it used to be. Several million dollars ten years ago wouldn't mean much. But it sure as hell does today. That takes the wrinkles out of the bellies of some of our soldiers. You disappoint me, Rocco."

"Joe, first of all it was my kid. He means a lot to me. Second, if I though we was gonna lose millions I would have given it a lot more thought. Do you follow baseball? Do you know when these fuckin' Cubs last won a pennant? 1945! You think they're gonna become big winners all of a sudden this year. We don't need no fix to keep that from happening. If I thought we did, it would be different."

"Rocco," Joe Batters said, "in this business we don't take no chances. Not with several million. Especially today. You made a bad decision, a mistake. It's gonna cost you. In respect. Even if the Cubs don't win it. Not only that, Rocco. I don't like it when a man under you comes to me and complains about you. You're my boss. You're supposed to be runnin' things here. Now I got a top man under you comes to me and finks on you. You think I like that?"

"I'd like to know who that is," Rocco said, quietly. He knew he was not about to find out. Not from the old Capone shooter.

"I'll say this to you. The man didn't do it easy. He talked to the rest of the capos first. He came to me representing them, Rocco. That's my point. You have lost a lot of respect. That's hard to make up. Let me tell you something, Rocco. I've got a decision to make here. Maybe I made a mistake. Maybe you're not the man for this spot."

Rocco flushed. This was serious.

"Another thing," Accardo continued. "I'm the consiglieri. I'm the guy makes the big moves. You got a thing big as this, several million down the drain, your job is to come counsel with me. That's understood. Do you come to me on this? No. The first I hear about it is when a man under you comes to me as a representato of the capos and complains to me about his boss. Then I sit here wondering what he is talking about. Does my boss come to me? No. This is a major mistake, Rocco. First, you don't come to me to get my approval and, then, you take a big chance that we lose several million. You lose the respect of your people, your capos. That gives me a real headache, Rocco. A real problem. I'm tellin' you today, I got to give this a lot of thought. OK, I'm finished. You can go."

Finished? He can go? Rocco had never been talked to like that before—like some schoolboy called to the principal's office. Rocco realized he was in a tight spot. He had a pretty good idea who blew the whistle on him.

Dirty fuckin' rat. Ferriola. His underboss, his number one man. It had to be Ferriola.

Rocco realized he was on probation. And when the Chicago Outfit rid itself of one of its own, it wasn't by demoting him.

CHAPTER FORTY EIGHT

Crisis!

The mother of all indictments! RICO.

Robust. Gotti. Ferriola. Accardo. Alex. The rest of the Black Forest visitors from the National Commission of the La Cosa Nostra. The rest of the upper echelon of the Chicago mob. Pignazio. Connie. Walsh. Tocco. Solano.

The implications were staggering!

Fred Foreman, Jeff Johnson, Bill Richards and a host of other FBI agents and Assistant United States Attorneys had crafted the evidence and presented it to a federal grand jury. It returned a true bill and the indictments followed.

Agents all over the country fanned out to make arrests based on the indictments. Arrests were consummated in Chicago, New York, Lake Tahoe, Philadelphia, Miami, Buffalo, Boston, Las Vegas, Detroit, Cleveland, Pittsburgh and Newark.

Richards and Johnny Bassett handled Rocco personally. They appeared at Rocco's door at Outer Drive East at six in the morning and banged on the door.

"Who the fuck is that?" Rocco shouted.

"It's me, Rocco. Bill Richards. Open up. We have a warrant for your arrest."

There was no reply. Richards added, "We give you thirty seconds, Robust. Thirty seconds and the door comes down!"

Other doors on the floor were popping open. Heads appeared. Some of the condo owners knew who their neighbor was. Others did not.

Thirty seconds elapsed. Just as Richards and Bassett were about to crash their shoulders into the door, it opened. Rocco was in his pale blue pajamas.

Richards and Bassett stepped through the door. "Rocco Robustelli, I hereby place you under arrest. The charge is RICO."

Bassett stepped forward with the handcuffs. He was to play the hard cop today, Richards the good guy. Richards stopped him. "John, let's give Rock a chance to shave, get into some clothes, then we'll cuff him."

Rocco looked at Richards. "Boy, I bet you're getting your rocks off this morning, aren't you?"

Richards smiled. "It's been a long time coming, Rocco. I won't try to kid you, yeah."

Richards and Bassett escorted Rocco into his master bedroom.

"Rocco," Richards said, "we have the legal right to search incidental to the arrest. Ordinarily we'd have somebody stay with you to guard you while we do that. But if you want to shave, take a crap, get dressed, take your time."

"How about I got a right to call my lawyer?" Rocco demanded.

"You have a right, but not until you get down to our office and we mug you and fingerprint you, then you have a right to an attorney. But, go ahead, call your attorney and he can get you set up on your bond so you will have just a minimum of time downtown."

Robust looked at Richards.

"Thanks," he said, dryly.

"One thing though, if your attorney is Constance Constable, don't bother. She's also being arrested."

Robust lost the color in his face. "What! What for?"

Richards didn't make a big thing about it. "It's all one big RICO case, Rocco. I don't have to tell you more than that, but I will. She's being arrested because you used her to courier skim from the Summit in Lake Tahoe to you here in Chicago."

"Bull shit. That's bull shit," Rocco shouted. He was shocked that Connie would be going down on this indictment. Even if acquitted, it would be the end of her career in the law.

"Rocco, I shouldn't be talking to you about this. We should surprise you with this, but I followed her myself. From the Midland

Hotel where she picked the skim up from Pignazio to you at Gentlemen's Attire."

"You can't prove she gave anything to me, not alone skim from some place called the Summit." Rock had his chin up.

Richards leaned forward and lowered his voice.

"Rock, we had a mike in your office there for months."

Just to make sure Robust understood, Richards went a step further. "A Title III, Rocco. That means everything you said in there for many months can be used against you in a court of law. Which reminds me, before you say anything to us now or later you don't have to. Anything you say can be used against you if you do decide to answer anything we ask. You have a right to an attorney, and, if you can't afford to retain one, the court will appoint one to defend you. You understand that?"

Rocco knew he was under arrest; it went with the territory. Rocco knew the fate of his predecessors and had realized it could happen to him. Now that the time had come, he could cope with it. What worried him, however, was the knowledge that he had allowed Gentlemen's Attire to be bugged. He immediately realized how the FBI had learned about Lake Titisee.

Rocco, the toughest son of a bitch in the valley, sat down on his bed.

Richards had waited decades for this. It was his moment of glory, his greatest career victory. He didn't make a big thing of it, however. While Bassett conducted the search of Rocco's suite, Bill Richards sat with Rocco Robust. By his demeanor, he made it clear he was a gracious winner and that he would not twist the knife.

Maybe this Richards guy wasn't the "fuckin' asshole" Rocco had always thought him to be. He was his enemy, sure, but maybe there was a side of Richards that Ricky and Linda had seen and he had not.

Richards let Robust make his call from his condo before they started for the federal building. Pat Tuite was able to get the wheels in motion so that Rocco would not spend several hours in the Marshall's lockup. The rest of the arrestees would bristle in the lockup until mid afternoon.

Rocco was given other favorable treatment. Richards suggested to Bassett, in front of Rocco, that he not be handcuffed.

"No need all these nosy neighbors look at this as some kind of exhibition," he said.

Richards knew Robust was not going to break and run or resist the arrest. Why not make the accommodation? He had won. Although he knew if the tables were reversed he would not get the same treatment, why rub it in Rocco's face? Rocco Robustelli was handled very gently by his long time adversary, the guy he had tried to cripple years ago and the guy he had exchanged blows with outside the Swamp Fox on Cape Cod.

That evening Rocco Robust received another command from Tony Accardo. If Rocco thought he had been given a bad time the previous week, it was nothing compared to this. At the same moment Rocco was taken in his condo, Tony Accardo was arrested at the guest house of his daughter in Barrington Hills. FBI agents were not as open with him, however, as Richards was with Robustelli.

Tony Accardo was making it a point to find out why Rocco had been given such nice treatment. He did not know yet that much of the evidence had been garnered at Gentlemen's Attire, and that it was all admissible in federal court. Only Rocco knew it now, thanks to Bill Richards. And Rocco wasn't telling. He knew he was on thin ice with his consiglieri, "The Man," and he wasn't about to break through it until he had to.

Accardo's primary concern was Connie.

"How tough is your broad, Rocco? And what can she say about you and the rest of us? What does she know about me, for instance? And Joe Ferriola? And John Gotti and the rest of the wise guys from the east? I understand you had her over in Europe with you when you went to the Commission sit down. What does she know about this? What does she know about the connection guys, Gussie and Pat Marcy and John D'Arco when they were running her for Congress? You been fuckin' this bitch for a long time, Rocco. What kind of pillow talk have you two had?"

Rocco blanched. Was Accardo trying to plant a seed in Rocco's mind that Connie should be hit? That she should be put away to keep her from talking about all of them? Rocco didn't have to look back far in Chicago mob history to find dozens of such people who were slain in gangland fashion to prevent similar action.

When Gino Martini drove Rocco back downtown, he didn't seem to have the same deference he had before. He had also been indicted. When he delivered Rock to Outer Drive East, he didn't seem to want to leave him. All in all, Gino was acting a little strange.

Robust decided he was getting paranoid. "What the hell, I'm the fuckin' boss in Chicago, who's gonna give the order to hit me?" He knew the answer to that, however. It wouldn't be a first for the consiglieri.

When Rocco met Connie for dinner as usual that evening, she was white and shaken. Her composure was shot. She quickly downed a double instead of her usual sip of Chardonnay. Rocco was dismayed. Had he dragged her down to this? Why had he ever decided to use her as the skim courier from Lake Tahoe? What a mistake that was!

Rocco realized that Connie was in great danger, not only of going to prison, but of being killed by the Chicago mob. He had to do something.

"Babe, we got to get away from Chicago. It might not be the best or safest place to go at the moment, but we love Lake Tahoe. Let's go. Right now."

Connie was ready. Her life in Chicago was in shambles. She was a disgrace to herself and her peers.

Without ordering, Rocco and Connie ducked out the other entrance to Tiffs Too, sped through the elevator area, bypassing the lobby, and exited through the office building adjacent to the west of the Sheraton Plaza. Rocco directed a taxi to O'Hare.

The pair arrived late that night at the Summit. Rocco realized that it was not the safest place for Connie at the moment. When they were found missing in Chicago, the mob might suspect that they had fled to The Summit. But Rocco felt that they had a day or two cushion to decide something.

The couple slept into the afternoon the next day. Connie was exhausted emotionally. That afternoon they remained in the penthouse suite.

When "Mountain" Dew reported for work that evening, Sam Scafidi sidled up to him.

"Keep your eye out for Robust and his broad. Chicago wants to know where they are. If you see them around, let me know. We think they might be in their penthouse, but the door is locked from the inside and even security can't get in there."

Shortly thereafter, "Mountain" Dew excused himself to go the men's room telephone. He called the number he had for Chuck Thomas.

"Something's up with Robust and Constable. The Chicago mob is looking for them here. You might want to call Richards."

Richards was on the next flight to Reno.

In the meantime, Rocco and Connie were having a long, serious discussion. Rocco didn't let on to Connie that he had concerns for her personal safety. He could not see any light at the end of Connie's black tunnel. Even the bright blue lake looked dark and dank this afternoon.

Rocco also knew only too well that Tony Accardo's thoughts weren't directed only at Connie Constable. A few of them must concern Rocco Robustelli.

Rocco contemplated that not only was he the source of most of the charges in the indictment, but that it had been his carelessness that allowed Gentlemen's Attire to be miked by the FBI. That would be reason enough to be brought down. Thanks to Richards, only Rocco knew that at this point. When Accardo, Gotti and the rest found it out on discovery, Rocco would have major problems. There was a lot for Rocco Robustelli to think about at the moment.

A loud knock on the door brought both Rocco and Connie back to reality.

"Rocco! I know you're in there. Bill Richards. Want to talk to you!"

Richards had arrived at Lake Tahoe early that evening. He had a quick chat with "Mountain" Dew in the men's room, from one stall to the next, and had then hustled up to the penthouse suite.

Connie had been thinking about Tom Foran's suggestion months ago. He had indicated that Richards was a guy who could be trusted. When she saw that Rocco was not going to admit Richards to the suite, she brushed by him to the door. Rocco caught her there. He wrestled with her. She became hysterical.

"Rocco, Rocco, he is the one person who can help us!" she screamed.

Rocco realized he had a tigress by the tail. There was no way he could stop her.

"OK,OK, calm down, Connie. Let's see what he wants." He opened the door. Richards was alone.

"I'd like to come in and talk to both of you," he said, very quietly and very forcefully.

To Connie Constable, in the depths of despair, Bill Richards was a savior. He was a figure of authority, somebody who might make some sense of what she was going through.

"What do you want?" Rocco demanded.

"Rocco, behave yourself. Mr. Richards wants to help us," Connie pleaded.

Rocco erupted. "Help us! Sure as fuck he wants to help us! He's the fuckin' guy who got us both into this. Don't you realize who this is and what he's done to you! This is fuckin' Adolph Hitler! Come to help us? Bull shit!"

Richards was the only calm one in the room.

"Rocco, she's right. I want to help you. Maybe her most, but both of you because you're bound up together in this now. Tight."

Rocco strode into the master bedroom shouting over his shoulder, "I want no part of this!"

When Rocco was gone, Connie Constable assumed an air of calmness.

"Sit down, please," she said to Richards, gesturing to the sofa.

Richards sat. Connie sat down on the other end of the long davenport.

Connie spoke first. "We have a mutual friend. Tom Foran."

"Tom is the best. He and I go back a long way. But you and

I have a lot of mutual friends, Connie." Richards named six or seven attorneys.

"Oh, I didn't know you were an attorney," Connie said.

"Yes, but I've never practiced. My brothers are attorneys, three of them. I intended to join them, but never have."

Connie and Richards had developed a common bond.

"I wish I had enough sense to join the FBI. I wouldn't be sitting here now," Connie smiled.

"Well, there are worse places than the penthouse of a major hotel on Lake Tahoe," Richards responded.

"You know that's not what I mean," Connie came back.

"Well, I think I might have a solution for you, but it would take both of you. I'd have to clear it with people over me in the FBI and with the Justice Department now that you are indicted." Bill advised.

"I'm sure I know what you mean. But I could never do that without Rocco." Connie seemed adamant.

"I admire you for that, I guess. Have you discussed this with him?"

"No, not really, although we have skirted around it. I tried to bring it up a couple months ago and again this afternoon, but he isn't ready to think about anything like that." Connie seemed sure of that.

"But you would if he would, is that what you're saying?" Richards asked.

"I think my position right now is that I'd like to have a discussion with you and Rocco as to what we're talking about, what we would have to do and what you would do." Connie stated.

"It's very simple. You would tell us everything you know about Rocco and everything he's involved in, including the people he is involved with. Then we would help you go someplace where you are safe. We would recommend to the judge that, in return for your testimony, you be given a very lenient sentence. That sentence would depend on the people who are convicted based on your testimony. To be very up front with you, you may or may not have to spend some time in confinement. Then we'd put you someplace where you would be relatively safe. Presumably money would be no problem to Rocco, I'm sure he got a stash someplace, probably in Switzerland. Maybe you'd want to live there. I'll be honest with you, the mobs, all of them, will never quit looking for you if you ever decided this in the way you want to go. But look at the alternative. You'll go away for 10–12 years. When you come out you won't be able to practice law, that's for sure. You'll be mid-forties, starting all over. No pension, not much hope of much, with a record, an ex-con. That's the alternative."

Neither said anything for five minutes. Connie explored her options. Either one left her chilled.

Finally, she turned to Richards and said, "Let me get Rocco out here."

Connie entered the master bedroom suite of the penthouse. She was gone for twenty minutes. When she returned, Rocco was with her.

"Connie has been tellin' me all the bullshit you been givin' her," Rocco announced.

"Rocco, I wouldn't call it that. I've been trying to level with her as I will with you. I've been explaining what alternatives you have, or, more to the point, don't have. There is no point bullshitting either one of you, Rocco. I want you to know exactly what it is you have to live with—and that's the point—what you have to live with. I don't think I have to tell you, Rocco, your people are thinking." Richards put it to Rocco squarely.

"More bullshit," Rocco snapped.

At that point there was knock on the door. Rocco went to the peephole. It was Gino. Rocco put his finger to his lips. He wanted quiet. The knocking continued.

Rocco's peephole gave him a wide view of the corridor outside his suite. Gino was not alone. He was flanked on each side by others. They seemed to be carrying something. It didn't seem to be flowers.

Rocco stepped away from the door and motioned Connie to stand clear. If shots were fired through that door he didn't want her in the line of fire.

Minutes went by. Rocco dared not return to the door. The door was securely fastened with two double locks and a sturdy chain. Quietly, he motioned Connie and Richards into the master bedroom suite.

"It's Gino. He's got no reason to be here. I ran off on him in Chicago." Rocco looked solemn.

"Your driver? What would he be doing here? Is that off base?" Richards wanted to know.

"Yeah, he's off the fuckin' base, that's for damn sure," Rocco replied. Although Rocco had not mentioned the others, they were foremost in his mind. Crossing to his dresser, he took out a Magnum and quietly went back to the peephole.

The trio had obviously decided that Rocco was in the penthouse, but was not going to acknowledge them and open up.

Rocco's manner had changed. The last ten minutes had changed his perspective. The mob had obviously made a decision.

"Richards, let's talk. What are you offering?" Rocco obviously was a different man. He now had no alternatives. Ten minutes ago, he had been a tough, strong mobster. Now, he was a frightened human being. He knew it would take more than courage to leave his penthouse. It would take recklessness, stupidity. Who knew where Gino and his pals had taken up their posts? He was sure the mob would not give up just because he had failed to respond to their knock. He had worked this side of the street himself.

Rocco had always been aware of the perils of his position in the mob. One day you're up. The next day, perhaps through no fault of your own, you're down. Robust turned to Richards.

"You packin'?"

Richards nodded. Robust was relieved. He realized he could not fight this battle himself. If it came to that, he had the top fuckin' G man at his side! What a change of direction his life had taken in ten fuckin' minutes!

Richards left it up to Rocco, but it was now quite obvious. Robust was in the hands, like it or not, of the FBI. He was painted into a corner.

Rocco looked at Richards. It was if he was saying, "OK, you

win." Richards couldn't do what he would be able to do, however, without exacting an agreement. He hammered it out, quickly, concisely. There was no ambiguous "do you understand?"

Connie and Rocco Robustelli would agree to plead guilty to the charges against them. They would be able to negotiate for a red ction of some of the counts in the indictment depending on the discretion of the Justice Department. Richards could not promise exactly how that would come down. Both would testify to the extent of their knowledge about the mobs. That would include the skim of the Summit, the murders, the intimidations, the labor racketeering, the gambling, the loan sharking, the chop shopping, the street tax, the involvement in legitimate businesses, and, by all means, the identities of those public officials, police officers, labor leaders, judges and anybody else "on the pad."

When Rocco agreed to all that, Richards hunted up a piece of paper. He wrote, "I, Rocco Robustelli, hereby agree to testify fully for the United States government against Tony Accardo, John Gotti, Gus Alex and Joe Ferriola among dozens of others in return for leniency on my RICO indictment." Richards was not going to move an inch further without Rocco's signature, witnessed by Connie Constable. He had Rocco right where he wanted him—although he would be glad when he had Rocco someplace else. He wasn't going to make the effort to do what he must do now to extract Rocco from the Summit without an agreement.

Rocco resisted. Connie screamed at him. Finally, Rocco signed.

They weren't over the hump yet. They had to get to safe ground. Richards picked up the phone. It was dead.

Richards checked his .38.

"Here's what I'm going to do," he told Rocco and Connie. "I've got a pal downstairs on the floor. He's an undercover FBI agent. You will recognize him when you see him. I'm going to send him right up. Watch the peephole and, if he's clear, let him in. Then I'm going to round up a crew of agents, but they have to come all the way from Reno. That'll take an hour or so. So I'll make my call and then I'll be right back up here. I'll fight my way in if I have to. Hold the fort here and we'll do our very best to get you out, safe and sound, as soon and as best we can."

Richards then checked the corridor from the peephole. There didn't seem to be anybody around. He quickly exited, slamming the door behind him. He dashed down the corridor towards the elevator. As he rounded the corner, he recognized Gino Martini immediately. He didn't know the other two. He had not drawn his snubby.

"Martini, get the hell out of the way unless you want to go down for assaulting a federal officer!"

Martini recognized him at once. Richards moved right into him, not around him. He pushed towards the elevators and punched the down button.

The bluff worked. When the elevator arrived, Richards boarded it as he glared at Gino. The doors closed and he was home free! At least for the time being.

Richards hustled to the floor of the casino, looking for "Mountain" Dew. Spotting him, he motioned to him, fiercely. "Cappy" Capitano left the pit and hustled towards Richards. He realized something was up. Richards told him what he had in mind.

"Mountain" Dew hurried to the elevator, express to the penthouse. When he reached the penthouse level, he stepped off. Gino Martini recognized him immediately as "that South Philly good fella."

Without a word, "Mountain" Dew hustled to Robust's penthouse suite and banged on the door. Gino and his partners watched in bewilderment. Robust recognized Dew from his vantage point behind the peephole and opened the door. "Mountain" Dew wasn't armed, but Rocco had a spare in his bedroom. Connie sat in a corner of the bedroom, feet tucked under her, trying to make herself as small as possible. Now, all they could do was wait.

In a little over an hour, a sextet of FBI agents entered the Summit. It looked like a raid. Led by Richards, they hustled to the express elevator to the penthouse level. When they arrived, the hit trio was still in place. They were quickly apprehended and disarmed.

"Open up, Rocco. It's me! It's all clear," Richards shouted. He pushed the unarmed Gino and the other two gunmen into the suite ahead of him.

"OK, do it as quick as you can, but pack what you'll need, don't leave anything you want. Then we'll get out of here."

In twenty minutes, they did. The FBI agents surrounded Connie and Rocco and marched them to the elevator, down onto the casino floor, and out to the Bureau cars. They were soon in a safe house. They had left Gino and his partners in the suite. Richards would deal with Gino later; he was unimportant at the moment.

Although Connie seemed to be comfortable with all that has happened, Rocco realized that he had no options. Once the mob had come after him, he had no alternative but to put himself in the hands of his long time enemy. He was now something he had despised all his life—a stool pigeon. Not only would be spend the rest of his life finking on his former associates, but he would now be the hunted, not the hunter.

Robust was despondent. Connie's life and his own were inexorably entwined. Bill Richards, his nemesis, would also become his jailer, debriefing him of his vast knowledge of the mobs. Rocco would not be easy to live with. It wasn't a particularly comforting thought for Connie or Richards either.

Rocco Robustelli, aka Rocky Robust, had come to the end of his reign. His former enemies had become his allies and his former allies had become his enemies. Bill Richards had become his confederate and Tony Accardo had become his foe. Richards would now attempt to protect him, Accardo would now attempt to have him killed.

Robust would spend the rest of his life forced to look over his shoulders, wondering if and when and how and where death would come. The irony was that he would now be forced to depend on the one person he had hated all his life—Bill Richards.

Epilogue

It was no easy battle for Bill Richards to convince his supervisors in the FBI and the attorneys in the Justice Department that it was wise to grant Rocco Robust leniency in return for his testimony against his old associates. The usual process is for a little fish to catch the sharks. But, in this case, Rocco was the shark. The Justice Department felt that it would be freeing the shark to catch minnows. Richards argument was that Tony Accardo and Gus Alex were not minnows. Richards pointed out that Accardo had been a killer for Al Capone and that Gussie Alex had been one of the first visitors to Capone after he had been released from Alcatraz.

"You can't be more major than those two guys," Richards stated. "When you add in John Gotti and all the top bosses of the eastern families, look at the bag you've got. Not to mention all the politicians, public officials, policemen, judges, labor leaders, and anybody else on the pad of the Chicago mob. Look at all the basic intelligence he can give us: how the mob operates in all its aspects. We have never had an absolute boss come over before. Never before have we had a member of the Commission turn. It would be a major mistake to give all that up for just his conviction."

In the back of most minds was Richards' regard for Robust's children. Could he be making his recommendation because of his compassion for them?

Approval was finally given to the tentative deal Richards had worked out with Robust and Connie Constable at the Tahoe Summit.

Since both Robust and Connie wanted the freedom to move

and act as they pleased, they were not placed in the Witness Protection Program, especially since they did not need the monetary support it provided. Although Robust would not admit it, fearful of the IRS, he had plenty stashed away in the vaults of the Liechtensteinische Landesbank in Vaduz. Enough to enable him and Connie to live most comfortably the rest of their lives.

When the pair discussed their hideaway location with Richards, they told him they had decided on San Francisco. Richards protested that it was too close to a location where Robust was well known, Lake Tahoe, and that the mob could easily locate them there. The three finally decided on Cupertino, a town about an hour's drive from Nob Hill and Union Square.

Cupertino gave Rocco and Connie the ability to drive into San Francisco just about as often as they wanted, stay at the St. Francis or the Fairmount or any of the other fine hotels for just a night or so and then return to their safe haven. They found that they enjoyed such San Francisco delights as the Carnelian Room on top of the Bank of America Building, Victor's on the top of the St. Francis, the Top of the Mark at the Mark Hopkins, Alfreds where Rocco enjoyed their specialty, the veal picatta, and the Compass Rose, the lounge at the St. Francis.

Bill advised them to avoid Ernie's, the only five star restaurant in California, due to the extreme popularity of the place, thereby increasing the chances Rocco or Connie would be recognized. However, the pair often disregarded his advise. The temptation was too great. The genial general manager and host, Terry Fischer, didn't recognize them, but Beverly DeLaney, the hostess, began to get the feeling that there was something that didn't quite add up when "Mr. Pierre" called to make a reservation for two. "Pierre" just didn't seem to fit. However, Rocco and Connie were able to enjoy the brocade Victorian ambiance of the famous eatery without being identified. They were lucky, however, as one night they dined at Ernie's just two nights after Tony and Clarice Accardo had entertained Gus and "Schatzie" Alex.

Both, however, took Richards' advise to stay away from the North Beach restaurants and Jack's, which served their favorite dishes. North Beach was favored by many of Rocco's former associates and Jack's by visiting attorneys who would have recognized Connie.

Rocco and Connie took their time to explore San Francisco, since neither had ever been there before, and did all the things visitors do there. They saw the Embarcadero, where Rocco discovered Gabbiano's behind the big clock and the Ferry Building, Ghiradelli Square and Fisherman's Wharf, Golden Gate Park, Sausalito over the Golden Gate Bridge, Market Street—where Connie was able to find the books she wanted at Stacey's Bookstore near the newly renovated Sheraton Palace—Tiburon, The Presidio, Chinatown, The Coit Tower, the Transamerica Building, Union Square—where Connie shopped for hours at Saks, the May Co. and Macy's—Oakland, the Napa and Sonoma Valleys, where they enjoyed the tram ride up to the top of a mountain where the Sterling winery is located. Connie even got Rocco to make a visit to Grace Cathedral on Nob Hill across the park from the Fairmount and the Mark Hopkins. He seemed to be praying. One day, he even surprised her by suggesting they walk down Nob Hill from the Stanford Court, where they stayed one night, to Old St. Mary's Catholic Church in Chinatown, where it was obvious he did pray. Connie began to realized that the old tiger was changing his stripes. Slowly but surely.

Actually, Rocco was asking a God he finally had come to recognize to support him in his impending ordeal when he would testify in open court, right in the face of his old partners in crime. That would take courage.

Although Rocco is still on call by the government, he has now moved, with Connie, to Europe. He finally took her to the spot where he had hoped that she could have accompanied him the last time he was over there. They found a villa behind Lake Titisee in the depths of the Black Forest where they will live four or five months a year. The rest of the time they travel, never to Chicago or New York or Philadelphia, but occasionally back to San Francisco where Rocco has found a warm spot in his heart for Old St. Mary's. They also travel a great deal around Europe, retracing their odyssey to Vienna, Innsbruck, Salzburg, Zurich, Lucern and Geneva. They have also discovered Grindelwald, up in the Jungfrau, near the Eiger, and love it there.

Rocco did what he had promised to do. As a result, Richards was vindicated for recommending that he be granted leniency in return for his testimony.

Rocco and Connie would each spend time in prison in consonance with their guilty pleas to the pending indictments against them, but that time was minimal.

Meanwhile, Ricky continued to prove himself with the Cubs. He didn't get 200 K's in his first full season, but came close with 192. Many people don't remember Branch Rickey, the long time general manager of the Brooklyn Dodgers, but he had what came to be known as one of the best yardsticks for measuring the success or lack thereof of a pitcher—matching hits allowed against innings pitched and walks against k's—The Rickey Factor. Ric-K led the league in this regard. Rick didn't win 20 games in his rookie year, but he got 18.

Tony Accardo should not have worried about the Cubs. Even though Sammy Watson continued to do his very best, before his trade, it was not enough. The Chicago mob won its millions even without the fix. They became so relaxed about the whole thing as June turned into July and the Cubs were 12 1/2 games out, in fifth place, that they didn't even bother Sammy. Charley Bones left him alone. Unfortunately, so did Galaxy Jones. The mob quit giving her a stipend to romance Sammy and, when they did, she had no further interest. She moved from her apartment off Stony Island, not a nice neighborhood anyway, and moved onto the Gold Coast, onto Diversey. She became a big hit in the singles bars there, especially at Butch McGuire's, and Sammy was unable to find her any longer, not on Stony Island and not at the Blue Note. Galaxy had rocketed to another space, from the south side to the north side—from down under to up yonder. Sammy was sad for some time, but he eventually got over it. His game improved and he had a fine season as it turned out, although not enough to help the Cubs overcome their traditional trials and tribulations. They haven't won a pennant since 1945. Fifty years! If the Cubs figure to win on their fiftieth anniversary in 1995, they will have to rely on Ricky Robustelli.

Sammy Watson was eventually traded. He went to the Toronto Blue Jays, a long way from 63rd Street and Galaxy Jones. He still showed the ability he demonstrated with the Cubs when he was an All-Star. He would run into Galaxy Jones one last time, but wouldn't know it. He was walking down Michigan Avenue when a beat up, bag of bones approached him. Her light skin was now translucent. Although it was Christmas time and the avenue was very well lit, Sammy didn't recognize the skeleton. Her hair was long shorn of its lights, her clothes were sloppy and she had no coat.

Through dimmed eyes, however, Galaxy recognized her old lover. She called him "Baby" and "Honey," but he didn't recognize the scratchy voice and pushed her away.

Just another worn out old whore, he thought to himself. He strode briskly down the street, oblivious to her cries as she fell to her knees.

"Call 911" a passerby shouted to a cabbie.

Galaxy would never bump into Sammy again. She expired of AIDS at Cook County Hospital.

Linda Robustelli is an executive producer for a major national television show. She continues to use her real name rather than the name Linda Roberts, which had been suggested to her by her agent. The mob has never bothered her or her brother. She and Ricky see their father only on rare occasions.

Jeannie Richards remains close to both of her "families." She is proud of all her "children."

"Mountain" Dew, aka Cappy Capitano, has returned to field agent status in the FBI. He is no longer undercover and is assigned to the "O.C." Squad of the New York office.

Gino Martini returned to working in the Blue Island area of Chicago, since Joe Batters felt he bungled the hit on Rocco and deserved no consideration. On Rocco's testimony, however, he would soon be sent to prison for life for his participation in the murder of Jimmy "The Bomber."

The Tahoe Summit was sold to Pogo Yashudo, the wealthy Japanese industrialist, and is now known by another name.

The Safari in Laughlin never got off the ground. Plans for its construction were aborted when Robust disappeared and the Chicago mob was put into disarray.

Bill Richards continues his fight against the mob. However, he spends a great deal of his time these days at Wrigley Field with his pal, Jack Brickhouse, the Hall of Fame broadcaster, formerly the voice of the Cubs. Richards is most often there on the days when Ricky Robustelli is pitching. Ric-K is all the more ingrained in the hearts of the Cub fans these days, still a "celebrity," for more reasons then just his fine hurling. Bill Richards also spends considerable time in Tucson these days where his son is a sportscaster and where Linda Robustelli keeps a permanent home. She and young Bill are still good friends, but not romantically. He also spends a lot of time in Scottsdale, where his three grandchildren are following in their father's footsteps as star student-athletes. Bill also catches up with Rocco Robust and Connie Constable, most often in Cupertino and San Francisco, but also at Lake Titisee in the Black Forest as he debriefs them and prepares them for their continued revelations on Joe Batters and his Chicago La Cosa Nostra.

REAL LIFE

Bob Richards today is Marketing Director for the Colonial Life and Accident Insurance Company for the state of Arizona. He lives in Scottsdale with his wife Earlene and their three boys, Chris, Matt and Tim. He coaches the Little League team on which all three play.

Bill Richards III continues to be involved in broadcasting in Tucson, Arizona, where he is also involved as a private investigator. After years of bachelor hood, he finally married the right girl, Kelly Freeman.

Al Tocco, never a particular friend of Robust, is serving a 200 year sentence in a federal prison — without chance of parole.

Joe Ferriola died of kidney failure.

The long reign of Tony Accardo, the tough Joe Batters, finally came to a conclusion. He was taken into the intensive care unit of St. Mary's of Nazareth Hospital on the west side of Chicago on May 15, 1992. On May 20th, his family decided to withdraw the life supports and he died on May 27th. It was the end of an era. Accardo was the only living link between Al Capone and his successors in the Chicago mob. No one in mob history could match his tenure or success. He was "The Man" in Chicago since the mid-forties. For almost half a century, Accardo had the first and last vote when it came to decisions affection major policy of the Chicago family of La Cosa Nostra. He enforced the code of *omerta* to its letter. Under Accardo, the Chicago family was one of the few to refrain from anything to do with narcotics. As Rocco Infelice said on the hidden wire, it was "either jail or the cemetery" for a "made" member to be caught dirty with drugs. In addition, it wasn't until May 17, 1992 — as Accardo lay in the intensive care unit — that the mob bombed a car used by Sharon Patrick, whose father, Lenny,

had agreed to testify against Gussie Alex in his upcoming trial.
Never before had the Chicago mob threatened the *family* of a
defector. This was a tenet covered by *omerta* and would never
had been tried under Accardo's regime. He would be missed — not
only by his old comrades — but also by the law-abiding citizens of
Chicago .

John Bassett, George Benigni, George Mandich and Chuck
Thomas have all retired from the FBI. Thomas is currently the
security representative for the National Football League in Las
Vegas and assistant to the chief of the corporate security at Caesar's
Palace. George Mandich continues to be the security representative of the NFL in Chicago. He also works as a private
investigator.

Jim Mansfield and Warren Donovan died of natural causes after
retiring from the FBI. God bless them.

Eli's Place for Steaks on Chicago Avenue continues to be Bill
Richards' favorite restaurant, although Harry Carey's rivals it.

Gino Lazzari has retired from the FBI and from the Pennsylvania
Crime Commission. Andy Sloan and John Osborne have also retired
from the FBI and are living in the Philadelphia area.

The Chicago Crime Commission continues to rank as the most
respected crime commission in the country, although rivaled by the
Crime Commission of New Orleans.

Herb "Speedy" Newman continues to be Las Vegas' prime
"sports investor."

Joe Yablonsky has retired from the FBI and is now a consultant
on security for John Marrell and Company with his offices in
Cincinnati. He is working on his memoirs.

Jim Mulroy is retired from the Bureau and is operating James T. Mulroy and Associates, a private investigative firm, in Dumont, New Jersey.

Frank Gerrity is retired from the FBI.

Jack Danahy is retired from the Bureau and is operating Danahy Associates in West Nyack, New York.

Tommy Toland has retired from the FBI and is now the president of Intercon Special Services, a private investigative firm, in Jackson Heights, Queens, New York.

Former Congressman Roland Libonati died in April 1991 at the age of 90.

Bob Long, Bob Walsh, Gerry Buten and Burt Jensen continue to serve as FBI agents in Chicago.

As for the "lovable losers," the Chicago Cubs, it turned out to be a typical season. Even with the change in managers from Don Zimmer to Jim Essian, the Cubs continued on their losing ways. The mob, as it turned out, had nothing to worry about. The Cubs played worse under Essian than they did under Zimmer. When the season ended, they were a long way behind the division champs, Pittsburgh, 20 games out, in 4th place.

The luck of Gus Alex ran out at the age of 75. In 1991, he was indicted on racketeering and extortion charges and was confined for the first time in his life. However, he was to spend only two nights in the Metropolitan Correction Center when his attorney, Carl Walsh, pleaded the "bleak, unnecessary and sad" conditions—and his heavy ulcers—made him unable to eat the food there. Before releasing him, United States Magistrate Joan Gottschall ordered him to wear an electronic monitor at all times, remain in his Lake Shore Drive condo except to visit his doctor, surrender his passport, post $25,000 cash bond and allow unannounced visits from the FBI at any time. She also warned him not to intimidate witnesses or associate with known felons. In 1992, Alex's co-defendant, Lenny Partick, pleaded guilty and agreed to testify against him and another co-defendant, Mario Rainone He co-operated with the government by wearing a wire. Alex's attorney later announced that Alex was suffering from Alzheimer's disease and asked that the case be dismissed. However, Gussie was convicted in late 1992 and may well be confined for the rest of his life. He was also ordered to pay restitution of some two million dollars and to pay the expenese for each day of his incarcerations.

In a voters' referendum approved on March 17, 1992, the First Ward lost much of its political muscle when the Loop area was redistricted into the 42nd Ward. Although it was certified on March 24th, several suits by interested parties have been filed to block it. Meanwhile, John D'Arco, Jr., the Illinois State Senator from District 10, was convicted in early 1992 for taking bribes to pass legislation. The prime witness against him was Robert Cooley, an FBI mole who carried a wire, a body recorder, for the FBI for three years as part of operation GAMBAT (Gambling Attorney, Cooley). Initial phases of that operation resulted in convictions of Wilson Moy, the unofficial mayor of Chinatown (in the First Ward); David Shields, the second most powerful local judge in Chicago and Pat DeLeo, the son-in-law of D'Arco, Sr., for bribery.

Dominick "Toots" Palermo was convicted of extorting protection money and sentenced to 32 years in prison on March 26, 1992. Palermo became the boss of "The Heights" in the late 1980's, succeeding Frankie La Porte, Al Pilotto and Al "Caesar" Tocco. The Evidence included tapes from a FBI bug at the Taste of Italy restaurant and testimony of Tony Leone, a former soldier who turned against his mob mentor.

Peter Ueberroth resigned as baseball commissioner, but his career took a different turn when the mayor of Los Angeles appointed him to head "Rebuild L.A." a task force appointed to reconstruct the areas of Los Angeles devastated by rioting immediately following the decision in the Rodney King trial. Ueberroth would use some of the methods that made his direction of the 1984 Los Angeles Olympics so successful.

In early 1993 Pat Marcy, the First Ward power broker, and Fred Roti, the alderman, went on trial for racketeering, conspiracy to racketeer, bribery and extortion. Macry was accused of fixing a 1977 murder trial of mob hitman Harry Aleman and 1986 trial of Michael Colella, accused if beating a woman police sergeant. Also of soliciting money to obtain a judgeship for a client. Roti was convicted. However Marcy suffered a heart attack during the trial. He later died.

Rockey Infelice and his underboss, Solly DeLaurentis, were convicted on 20 charges on March 10, 1992 following a four month trial that exposed the day-to-day machinations of the Chicago outfit. The chief witness against the Infelice crew, including Lou Marino and Robert Bellavia, was "B.J." Jahoda, one of Infelice's top subordinates, who cooperated with IRS agent Tom Mariarity by "carrying a wire" and recording conversations between Infelice and top Chicago mobsters.

John "No Nose" Difronzo, Sam "Wings" Carlisi, Donald "The Wizard of Odds" Angelini and seven others were indicted in San Diego charged with bribery, extortion and conspiracy in an attempts to skim a gambling operation on the Rincon Indian Reservation near San Diego and for foreible attempts to collect money allegedly owed to the late Tony Spilotro, the Chicago mob boss in Las Vegas who was slain in gangland fashion in the summer of 1986. DiFronzo and Angelini were convicted and sentenced to 37 months in prison. Carlisi was not convicted but he has now been indicted in Chicago and is currently being held in the Metropolitan Correctional Center there awaiting trial in the fall of 1993.

John Gotti, the boss of the New York Gambino family, was convicted in the United States District Court of New York on June 23, 1992. He was sentenced to life in prison without chance of parole for 13 counts of RICO: murder, conspiracy to murder, loan-sharking, illegal gambling, obstruction of justice, bribery of a public official and tax fraud. Five of the counts were for the murder of mob rivals, including Paulie Castellano, who preceded Gotti as boss of the Gambino family.

An important element of Gotti's conviction was the planting of a "bug" in his headquarters, the Ravenite Social Club, by the FBI.

In 1987, the investigation of John Gotti was assigned to New York FBI Special Agent George Gabriel of the "Gambino Squad." After conferring with supervisor Bruce Mouw, Gabriel and the other 14 agents on the squad, having previously determined that Gotti's headquarters was the Ravenite Social Club on Mulberry Street, utilized a building two blocks away to observe scores of highly placed Gambino family members arriving to meet with Gotti and his two top men, Sammy "The Bull" Gravano and Frank Locascio. Armed with information from a highly placed informant within the Gambino family, Gabriel prepared an affidavit and obtained a Title III, allowing a Special Operations Branch to plant a "bug."

For some time, the mike produced, then was silent for a period of nine months. It soon became obvious that Gotti and his men were suspicious and were not using the main room for their conversations. Gabriel prepared affidavits for, and obtained, Title III's on three locations: a hallway in the rear of the club, a vacant apartment on the second floor, and the sidewalk outside the club.

There, from November 1989 on, Gotti talked freely with his associates for almost a year, while Gabriel and his associates recorded the conversations. Finally, Gabriel, Mouw, Frank Storey, the Deputy Assistant Director In Charge of Organized Crime Investigations, and Jim Fox, the ADIC, were convinced they had enough to convict Gotti, Gravano, Locascio and other Gambino good fellas. The case was taken to United States Attorney Andrew Maloney and they were indicted.

Gabriel got a real break when Gravano decided to plead guilty and agreed to testify against Gotti and the rest, preferring to spend the rest of his life in the Witness Protection Program than in prison. The jury took thirteen hours of deliberation before reaching its decision.

Gotti, at 51, will spend the rest of his life in prison, but there are several capable capos, including his own son, willing and anxious to take his place. It is likely that he may even be able to call the big shots from his prison cell.

In the same week Gotti was sentenced, eleven members of the New England family and of the New Jersey waterfront Genovese family, as well as Vic Orena, the boss of the Colombo family in New York, were all indicted. On June 15th, Vittorio "Vic" Amuso, the boss of the Lucchese family, was found guilty of a 54-count RICO indictment.

Many battles have been won and the tide has been stemmed. But it still rolls on.

The mob is a tough opponent. They can well come back. Unless the same resources are continuously poured into the fight, the war could still be lost.